The McGraw-Hill
36-Hour
Negotiating
Course

Other Books in The McGraw-Hill 36-Hour Course Series

The McGraw-Hill
36-Hour Negotiating Course

Mark K. Schoenfield
Partner in Torshen, Schoenfield & Spreyer, Chicago
Member of the Illinois Bar

Rick M. Schoenfield
Partner in Ettinger & Schoenfield, Ltd., Chicago
Instructor, Chicago-Kent College of Law
Member of the Illinois Bar

McGraw-Hill, Inc.

New York St. Louis San Francisco Auckland Bogotá
Caracas Hamburg Lisbon London Madrid
Mexico Milan Montreal New Delhi Paris
San Juan São Paulo Singapore
Sydney Tokyo Toronto

Library of Congress Cataloging-in-Publication Data

Schoenfield, Mark K.
    The McGraw-Hill 36-hour negotiating course / Mark K. Schoenfield,
Rick M. Schoenfield.
    p.   cm.
    Includes index.
    ISBN 0-07-055518-4 (cloth) :   — ISBN 0-07-055517-6 (paper) :
    1. Negotiation in business.   I. Schoenfield, Rick M.   II. Title.
III. Title: McGraw-Hill thirty-six-hour negotiating course.
HD58.6.S35   1991
658.4—dc20   91-16527
                                                                  CIP

1 2 3 4 5 6 7 8 9 0   DOC/DOC   9 7 6 5 4 3 2 1

ISBN   0-07-055518-4 {HC}
ISBN   0-07-055517-6 {PBK}

*The sponsoring editor for this book was James H. Bessent, Jr., the editing
supervisor was Alfred J. Bernardi, and the production supervisor was Suzanne
W. Babeuf. It was composed in Baskerville by McGraw-Hill's Professional Book
Group composition unit.*

Printed and bound by R. R. Donnelley & Sons Company.

*All entities and persons used in the examples, negotiating scenarios, and cases in
point in this book are fictitious, and do not depict any living or deceased persons, or
any entity.*

To Barbara, Laura, and Jeffrey, for their
fairness in negotiating and, most of all, for their love.

—MKS

To Bobbi.
          —RMS

And to our parents.
          —MKS & RMS

Contents

3. The Strategic Underpinnings of a Successful Negotiation   34

4. Tactical Control of the Information Exchange Process   81

5. Situational Tactics—Part 1   112

6. Situational Tactics—Part 2   136

7. Situational Tactics—Part 3   168

8. Tactics Involving More Than Two Negotiators   197

12. Systematic Planning: Negotiation Stages   **299**

Answer Key to Comprehension Checkups   **331**

**Final Examination: The McGraw-Hill 36-Hour Negotiating
Course** (following Index)   **1**

Acknowledgments

Mark K. Schoenfield acknowledges the influence of the following persons on his thoughts about negotiation: Jerry Torshen, Jim Seckinger, Lou Cohn, Melissa Nelken, Rick Green, Jack Heinz, Andy Gordon, Jon Waltz, the late Bob Childress, and those lawyers, business professionals, and executives who have been teaching team members and participants at the many negotiation programs taught by him.

Rick M. Schoenfield acknowledges learning from working with Joe Ettinger, and from the following present and past members of Northwestern's clinical teaching program: Tom Geraghty, Diane Geraghty, Steve Lubet, and Mark Schoenfield.

The authors also acknowledge the excellent assistance of their editors: Jim Bessent, Fred Bernardi, and Arthur Pomponio.

Introduction

The McGraw-Hill 36-Hour Negotiation Course is designed as a self-study seminar. Its structure is based on programs taught by Mark K. Schoenfield to management executives, attorneys, and other business professionals. By completing this self-study seminar, you will improve your negotiating knowledge and skills. For those with busy schedules, this approach provides a flexible-time course which otherwise could require attending a program for four to five working days.

The materials are presented as a series of building blocks, with each chapter building on knowledge acquired in earlier chapters. Each chapter is structured for easy assimilation of the material. Key terms and concepts are listed at the start of every chapter that will alert you to the important points to look for as you read. In addition, within the substantive portions of each chapter, the key concepts also are highlighted within boxes, so that you can consider them within an appropriate negotiating context. At the end of each chapter, a short objective test allows you to check your understanding of the material presented in that chapter. In addition, you should review again each key concept to ensure that you understand it. You should not expect to memorize the material. Your study should be aimed at learning the key terms and concepts and digesting the discussion.

There are 12 chapters. Please consider the following guidelines with regard to methods for self-study. To complete the course in 36 hours, it is suggested that you devote an average of 3 hours to each chapter, though this will vary with the length of the chapter. A general framework for the study of each chapter is suggested below.

- Ten minutes to review key concepts and read key terms at the start of each chapter.

- Two hours and 20 minutes to read the substantive portions of a long chapter, and 2 hours for a shorter chapter.

- Thirty minutes to complete the test at the end of each chapter, check your answers, and review any portions of the chapter related to incorrectly answered questions.

These guidelines, of course, are simply general suggestions. No one can rush through the materials and really learn all of the facets and subtleties of negotiating. Also, many people either read at a slower pace, or take somewhat more time to absorb written information. Therefore, do not be discouraged if you need more time than suggested. The important goal is to learn how to negotiate more effectively.

Learning will be easier and faster if there is continuity to your self-study. You should try to schedule blocks of time of at least 2 hours for study. Try to work in a quiet place and without interruptions. However, it also is important to allow your mind to really absorb the information before proceeding to something new. Therefore, you should take *short* study breaks every 1 to 2 hours, and not study more than approximately 6 hours a day. If you have to stop before finishing a chapter, try to finish it later in the same day or on the next day. Finally, to create the concentrated study needed for maximum learning, you should schedule yourself to complete the course over a period of no more than 3 weeks.

Chapter 1 presents an introduction to the optimal approach to negotiating. After identifying some of the basic problems of negotiation, the chapter suggests the fundamental concepts involved in managing them.

Chapter 2 concerns goals. Since goals form the basis of a negotiation, they are the natural starting point. Chapter 2 will address ways to classify basic negotiating goals in a form that is conducive to decisions about fundamental negotiating behavior. The classification of goals leads directly to the analysis of potential strategies to achieve them. Chapter 3 presents concepts and techniques to analyze negotiation strategies.

The discussion of strategy is followed by five chapters (4–8) that define and describe tactics. While strategy concerns broad decisions, tactics are the various maneuvers through which the negotiator implements the strategy of choice. A wide and varied range of tactics is presented, because each works well in some negotiations or parts of negotiations, and poorly at other times. While most negotiators are aware of a few strategies and tactics to use during negotiations, the most effective negotiators tend to employ the complete spectrum of strategies and tactics.

Chapter 9 presents various legal considerations when negotiating, including dealing with attorneys, formal agreements, the use of other documents that can be evidence of an agreement, and alternative dispute resolution.

Chapter 10 presents the communication skills necessary for negotiating optimal results. The chapter also integrates communications skills with issues surrounding the negotiating environment. Finally, it offers some tips on using certain communications technology.

Chapters 11 and 12 concern planning the negotiation. Together, they present a 14-step planning methodology that is appropriate to help organize and execute any negotiation. Planning encompasses a blending together of the analysis of goals, strategies, and tactics. Communications skills are essential in negotiating optimal results. After the discussion on planning, Chapter 12 will explore the skills involved in both the disclosure of information and the receiving of information.

These methods, techniques, and insights can improve one's negotiating arsenal by providing more ways to control and affect the negotiating process. The technical, multilayered nature of the material is deliberate. Simplistic views of negotiating, even if correct on occasion, can have only limited effectiveness. Given the wide range of situations, needs, interests, goals, and possibilities that are faced by negotiators who want a professional approach, such simplistic views often will be ineffective. Truly enhanced negotiating performance flows from understanding the complexities that can arise and the various means to deal with them.

One important final point regards the optional final examination. If, at the end of your studies, you want to receive a certificate for successfully completing the course, you may take the final examination and mail it to McGraw-Hill. It will be graded and, assuming a passing grade, you will receive a handsome certificate of completion that is suitable for framing or for presenting to an employer to demonstrate your continuing educational training.

1
The Optimal Approach to Negotiating

Key Concepts

1. Uncertainty and lack of control create much of the difficulty in negotiating, but both can be reduced by improving your skills.

2. Negotiating is an informational process and not just a series of offers and counteroffers.

3. Critical information when negotiating includes the positions, needs, interests, and goals of the parties and negotiators.

4. Negotiating is a dynamic process.

5. Identifying critical personal skills can help you know how to improve your negotiating.

6. The client makes the ultimate decision about the minimally acceptable terms for an agreement. As the client's representative, the negotiator often counsels the client, and thereby might influence the terms. The client and the negotiator are a team.

7. The negotiator generally decides strategy and tactics.

8. Effective negotiators neither avoid conflict (conflict-averse) nor seek it out (conflict-happy). Rather, they *manage* conflict.

9. The optimal approach to negotiation requires structure, flexibility, planning, and a thorough understanding of goals, strategies, and tactics.

The Language of Negotiating

To make full use of the key concepts, you must understand the following key terms:

Informational process	Ultimate decision (bottom line)
Dynamic process	Conflict-averse
Interpersonal process	Conflict-happy
Team approach	Optimal approach

Introduction

Most business professionals recognize the importance of negotiations in their lives. They spend substantial portions of their professional time negotiating. In addition, like everyone else, they also negotiate in their personal lives. Their effectiveness as professionals is strongly influenced by the degree of their negotiating ability. Their negotiating skill, or the lack of it, also influence how employers, coworkers, business associates, other professionals, and clients perceive their business effectiveness. Although much of their time and energy is expended in negotiating, few professionals fully understand the art and science of negotiation. Therefore, what many business professionals need is an optimal approach for planning and executing their negotiations. This chapter presents the basics for understanding the optimal approach to negotiation.

Before commencing your study, note that the term "client" frequently appears in the materials. Some business entrepreneurs negotiate strictly for themselves. However, most business entrepreneurs, executives, or professionals negotiate for a company, partnership, corporation, or some interest beyond their own. That is true even if they have an ownership interest but less than sole ownership. For convenience, negotiating for anyone other than oneself is called negotiating for a client. Client will be used as a generic term for the party represented by the negotiator, unless otherwise indicated. As you will see, this distinction between the negotiator and the client is important in analyzing interests, setting goals, obtaining authority, and determining who should be present at the negotiating sessions.

Another term often used is "decision maker." When the negotiator is employed by an entity (corporation, partnership, association, and so forth), often another person makes the ultimate decision regarding the acceptability of terms and conditions. This person is called the decision maker. Very often, the decision maker is someone other than the negotiator. Also, whenever a negotiator is not strictly negotiating for himself or herself, but for another person or an entity, the negotiator's personal goals are likely to be different. For example, the negotiator may want to look good to a superior, while the organization may be seeking a low price. While these goals are related, they are not the same. The distinction and its use in negotiating will be explained throughout the book.

Basic Problems of Negotiation

Key Concept 1

Uncertainty and lack of control create much of the difficulty in negotiating, but both can be reduced by improving your skills.

Virtually everyone recognizes the uncertainty present in negotiating. Uncertainty and lack of control are the two key factors that can make negotiating a difficult, frustrating, anxiety-filled, and stressful endeavor. The negotiator may be uncertain about such factors as:

1. What his or her superior, principal, constituency, and so on, really wants to achieve.
2. What is realistically possible to achieve.
3. What the other party really wants.
4. What the other negotiator is really seeking.
5. The best means of influencing the other party and its negotiator.

Uncertainty and lack of control are compounded by the many factors that can lead to failed negotiations. These include:

1. Lack of a sufficient understanding of the negotiating process.
2. Inadequate prenegotiation information gathering.
3. Improper analysis and planning.
4. Ineffective communication.
5. Lack of knowledge about and ability to use a broad range of strategies and tactics.
6. Becoming lost if a lack of movement or a deadlock occurs.

7. Inadvertently being placed in a position (or placing another in a position) where compromise is impossible without loss of face.

8. Allowing emotions to govern decisions (sometimes the result of a failure to counsel properly).

9. Difference of opinion by the parties, due to a difference in the information each possesses — a disadvantage for everyone.

10. Unrealistic expectations by one's superior, principal, constituency, or some other party to the negotiation.

11. Habitually negotiating with only one style where trade-offs cannot readily be made between them.

12. Linking multiple matters together.

13. Bottom-line positions which, because of miscalculation of benefits, detriments, and risks, have little or no overlap for an area of potential agreement.

The aim of this book is to help negotiators improve their skills, and thereby:

1. Reduce their levels of uncertainty, stress, and anxiety.

2. Increase their degree of control and efficiency.

3. Improve and maximize their negotiating results.

The basic problems of uncertainty and lack of control can be effectively managed through a negotiating approach that improves the negotiator's perceptions, analytical skills, and communication abilities. The approach also includes a flexible system for choosing appropriate strategies and tactics to help achieve negotiating goals. These strategies and tactics encompass a wide variety of techniques and methods, including the use of power, competitiveness, persuasion, bargaining, cooperation, problem solving, or combinations of these. These strategies and techniques can help negotiators adapt to any situation and achieve optimal results in realizing goals. This approach will benefit anyone who negotiates serious matters.

Of course, all of the problems in negotiations cannot be completely eliminated. However, they can be significantly minimized (and the negotiator's performance can be markedly improved) through an increased awareness of the negotiating process. Improved understanding is a basic premise for optimal negotiating. The starting point for this increased understanding is the consideration of the very process of negotiation.

Negotiation as a Process

Key Concept 2

Negotiating is an informational process and not just a series of offers and counteroffers.

Negotiating is a process through which parties determine whether an acceptable agreement can be reached. It is far more than just a series of offers and counteroffers. It is not merely a choice between being competitive or cooperative. Rather, negotiating is an **informational process** through which information is exchanged, evaluated, and used as the basis for decision making.

Key Concept 3

Critical information when negotiating includes the positions, needs, interests, and goals of the parties and negotiators.

Effective negotiating entails the controlled gathering and exchange of a wide variety of information in order to assess the situation of each party and the potential for agreement. This information includes the parties' positions, needs, interests, and goals. To the extent that a negotiator's personal position can influence the process, the information also includes the position, needs, interests, and goals of the negotiator.

Information must be obtained effectively and efficiently as well as disclosed selectively and persuasively. By doing so, the negotiator's effect on the process is maximized. Disclosures may be verbal or nonverbal, that is, by word or by action. Strategically or tactically, information can be gathered or conveyed to indicate facts, arguments, offers, and positions. By systematically planning and analyzing information to understand the needs, interests, and goals of the parties and their negotiators, one can determine the best means to advise one's own negotiator or client, and to motivate the other party to move in the desired direction. With authorization from the decision maker after proper counseling, the negotiator chooses from a wide range of strategies and tactics to fit the situation, thereby maximizing the odds of achieving optimal results. Strategies and tactics are covered fully in Chapter 3.

Negotiation as a Dynamic Process

Key Concept 4

Negotiating is a dynamic process.

Negotiation is a highly **dynamic process,** rather than a static one. This means that from start to finish, the process is subject to constant assessment and change. Even before interacting, the parties and their negotiators begin the process by separately assessing their needs, interests, and goals in order to determine their positions. Typically, during their interaction in negotiating, those assessments are subject to change. New information is received which must be evaluated and categorized. First offers and tentative conclusions are confirmed or contradicted. Perhaps a series of offers and counteroffers is made. Decisions are made to remain with or alter positions and plans. Messages are conveyed through oral and written communications. Some unknowns always are present, although astute negotiators have techniques to minimize their effect. Finally, there is either acceptance or rejection, in which case the process might recommence. In addition, negotiations involve not only the substantive matters being sought but also the ways in which the process of the negotiation itself will be conducted. It is this dynamic, shifting nature of negotiation that in large part makes it difficult and complex.

By viewing negotiation as a dynamic process of controlled information exchange, a negotiator can become more effective. Any risk from failing to gather, disclose, withhold, or fully consider information will thus be minimized. Also, the negotiator will focus on seizing every opportunity to achieve better results.

Negotiation as Interpersonal Process

Key Concept 5

Identifying critical personal skills can help you know how to improve your negotiating.

Negotiation is necessarily an **interpersonal process**, that is, one that involves the participation of more than one person. The most effective negotiators tend to have certain types of abilities in dealing with themselves and others that help them to achieve optimal results. These abilities are listed below in the order in which they often emerge during the process of negotiating:

1. Being in control of oneself.

2. The ability to elicit the needs, interests, and goals of those on whose behalf the negotiator is acting.

3. The ability to properly counsel those persons regarding the realities of the situation.

4. Obtaining clear authority from the appropriate decision maker.

5. Understanding and being able to utilize the full range of effective strategies and tactics.

6. Planning efficiently.

7. Being credible.

8. Perceptively analyzing the other party and its negotiator.

9. Being able to tolerate conflict and ambiguity.

10. Knowing or learning the relevant market factors.

11. Disclosing information selectively and persuasively.

12. Obtaining necessary information.

13. Listening to and perceiving the real information being conveyed.

14. Making changes in strategy and tactics, or counseling those for whom the negotiator is acting regarding terms, as appropriate during the negotiation.

15. Being both patient and tireless.

16. Knowing when and how to either close the negotiation with an agreement or to terminate it because a desirable agreement cannot be reached.

Methods to achieve or enhance these abilities for effective negotiation are explored in the sections that follow.

The Role of the Client and the Role of the Negotiator

Key Concept 6

The client makes the ultimate decision about the minimally acceptable terms for an agreement. As the client's representative, the negotiator often counsels the client, and thereby might influence the terms. The client and the negotiator are a team.

Most often, the negotiator represents a client, such as an employer, company, partnership, or other principal or constituency. That being the case, the negotiator and the decision maker of the party represented should form a team and use a **team approach;** that is, the negotiator and decision maker work together cooperatively, dividing the responsibility for different types of decisions. The client makes the **ultimate decision** about the minimal terms for an agreement. The ultimate decision, or **bottom line,** reflects the terms which the negotiator *must* achieve, as well as the outer limits of his or her negotiating authority. These limits must be clearly understood by both the negotiator and the decision maker regardless of whether that decision maker is the negotiator's superior (employer) or part of an outside entity. Also, if the negotiator has special knowledge or particular insights, he or she should advise the decision maker to help determine the appropriate bottom-line position.

Sometimes the client or decision maker will give discretion to the negotiator to decide on terms, subject to previously established general concepts or acceptable guidelines. Even so, the negotiator's personal needs, interests, and goals must be subordinate to those of the party being represented. The final decision must be for the client's benefit.

Key Concept 7

The negotiator generally decides strategy and tactics.

In general, the choice of strategy and tactics is left to the negotiator. Assuming his or her professional-level standards and direct involvement in the negotiation, the negotiator generally is the most knowledgeable about the negotiating situation. There are, however, certain exceptions in which the client should either influence or actually make the strategic or tactical decisions. These exceptions occur whenever:

1. The choice of a strategy or tactic may itself have a direct impact on the business or personal life of the client, apart from the ultimate resolution of the negotiation.

2. The client is a sophisticated negotiator in his or her own right and is directly involved in the negotiation process.

Given these exceptions, by taking a team approach, the negotiator can utilize his or her training and skills while respecting the client's role in determining the strategic or tactical decisions of the negotiation. The client's role will be examined further in the chapters on goals and planning (Chapters 2, 11, and 12).

Conflict: Negotiators Who Love It or Hate It Too Much

> ### Key Concept 8
>
> *Effective negotiators neither avoid conflict (conflict-averse) nor seek out (conflict-happy). Rather, they* manage *conflict.*

Negotiations inevitably involve a degree of conflict. The degree of conflict is determined by a combination of:

The extent of the differences between the parties' positions.

The personalities and the personal styles of the negotiators.

Conflict-Aversion. Of all the flaws a negotiator can have, the single most devastating is to be **conflict-averse.** This means that a person would rather concede just to avoid facing conflict than strive to prevail. While conflict, by nature, is not pleasant for anyone, conflict-averse negotiators are so deeply affected by conflict that it clouds their judgment and seriously lowers their level of performance.

Those who are conflict-averse become uncomfortable with and, consciously or unconsciously, fearful of negotiations. People who fear negotiation identify it with strife, conflict, anxiety, losing, pressure, or being dominated or coerced. In other words, they identify it with negative possibilities. By contrast, the ideal negotiator focuses on the positive possibilities of negotiating, without unrealistically ignoring its undesirable aspects. There are three steps to help overcome an aversion to conflict:

Step 1: Self-realization and acknowledgment. One must recognize one's aversion to negotiation.

Step 2: An improved understanding of the negotiation process and the tools a negotiator uses to deal with conflict. These tools are planning, strategy, tactics, and communication skills.

Step 3: A determined application of this increased awareness. With increased knowledge and experience, a conflict-averse negotiator gains confidence and ability in facing difficult or unpleasant situations.

Conflict-Happy. A different flaw is presented by those who are **conflict-happy.** These people seem to have a psychological need to seek out or create conflict. Conflict-happy negotiators can unwittingly undermine their own efforts, since creating unnecessary conflict can be seriously counterproductive.

Negotiators who are conflict-happy should strive to modify their behavior by limiting their desire for conflict to those situations in which it is required or appropriate. Conflict-happy negotiators can follow their preferences when tactics like intimidation or the exercise of power are the best way to achieve the ultimate goals of the negotiation. To moderate their conflict-happy tendencies, these negotiators should follow the same three steps as those recommended for persons who are conflict-averse.

The Optimal Approach

Key Concept 9

The optimal approach to negotiation requires structure, flexibility, planning, and a thorough understanding of goals, strategies, and tactics.

Effective negotiators are neither conflict-averse nor conflict-happy. Rather, by taking the **optimal approach** to negotiation, they avoid, create, minimize, or maximize conflict, as the situation demands. For them, conflict decisions are based solely on the short-term and long-term effects these decisions will have on the ultimate goal of the negotiation. Taking the optimal approach to negotiating requires both structure and flexibility. The chapters that follow provide a step-by-step procedure for learning the optimal approach to negotiating.

Comprehension Checkup

The answers to these questions appear on page 331.

1. Negotiation is simply a series of offers and counteroffers.   T   F

2. Good negotiators neither create nor avoid conflict.   T   F

3. Unless the situation is one in which the negotiator represents only himself or herself, it is the client who ultimately determines the minimal terms for an agreement.   T   F

4. The negotiator always decides the strategy and tactics to be used.   T   F

5. The needs, interests, and goals of a party and of its negotiator are always the same.   T   F

2

Goals in the Negotiating Process

Key Concepts

10. The goals of negotiations are determined by the client party.

11. Negotiation goals must be concrete.

12. Goals can be points essential to the deal, or merely points desired.

13. The goals of negotiations influence strategies and tactics.

14. To negotiate effectively, the negotiator must know the goal(s) of the negotiation.

15. It is the negotiator's job to ensure that complete information is considered for an informed judgment.

16. Aggressive goals seek to damage an opponent.

17. A competitive goal means getting more than the other party.

18. With cooperative goals, agreement leads to mutual gain.

19. Self-centered goals seek a particular result regardless of what the other side receives.

20. Defensive goals seek to avoid a particular result.

21. Each negotiation usually has multiple goals.

22. Priorities must be set when there are conflicting goals.

23. Time, information, and events can alter goals; therefore, goals should be periodically reevaluated.

The Language of Negotiating

To make full use of the key concepts, you must understand the following terms:

Decision maker	Zero-sum game
Essential goals	Cooperative goals
Desired goals	Win-win negotiating
Aggressive goals	Expanded pie
Competitive goals	Self-centered goals
Limited pie	Defensive goals

Introduction

Key Concept 10

The goals of negotiations are determined by the client party.

Negotiation goals are determined by a **decision maker,** who may or may not be the negotiator. The decision maker can be an owner of a business, some other superior in an organization, a client, or a person negotiating on behalf of his or her own business.

Key Concept 11

Negotiation goals must be concrete.

Determining the nature of negotiation goals is essential in determining a bottom-line position. Also, the nature of goals helps determine the negotiator's authority when the negotiator is not the decision maker. The negotiation goals also affect the choice of strategy and tactics.

Before determining a bottom-line position (as well as strategy and tactics), the negotiation goals must be examined as guideposts in negotiating. Goals can be general or specific. However, the goals must be translated into concrete points which can be:

1. Offered or accepted in a negotiation with specific detail.

2. Incorporated into specific terms within an agreement.

3. Legally enforced (unless all that is desired or possible is a statement of principle or intent which is not or may not be enforceable in court due to its generality).

If the goals cannot be used for these purposes, they must be clarified.

The negotiator performs his or her job more efficiently and effectively by understanding the impact of negotiation goals on the negotiating process and by understanding the specific goals of one's own side and those of the other. When the negotiator is not the decision maker, it is necessary both to understand the decision maker's goals and to provide advice when necessary. This advice may require continuous questioning and reevaluation of information.

Key Concept 12

Goals can be points essential to the deal, or merely points desired.

The two primary categories of negotiation goals are essential goals and desired goals. **Essential goals** are those tangibles or intangibles which must be achieved. **Desired goals** are those which, although not essential, also are sought. It is important to separate negotiation goals into these categories, since essential goals are "deal killers" unless they are achieved, while desired goals determine how good a deal is, as well as, at times, which party's offer should be accepted.

Key Concept 13

The goals of negotiations influence strategies and tactics.

The nature of a negotiation goal can influence the choice of strategy and tactics, since some strategies and tactics are more appropriate and useful for certain goals than for others. Therefore, before selecting the strategy and tactics to be used in the negotiation, the nature of the negotiation goal or, more usually, goals, must be analyzed. This chapter will explore various methods to identify, analyze, and classify negotiation goals. In the next chapter, various strategies and their relationship to negotiation goals will be explained. Chapters 4, 5, 6, 7, and 8 then will discuss tactics, including the relationship of tactics to the various strategies dictated by the negotiation goals.

Starting to Define the Negotiator's Role

Key Concepts 14 and 15

To negotiate effectively, the negotiator must know the goal(s) of the negotiation.

It is the negotiator's job to ensure that complete information is considered for an informed judgment.

When the negotiator is not the decision maker, it becomes necessary to elicit the decision maker's goals. If the negotiator regularly works for the decision maker, or has handled similar matters for that decision maker, he or she may already be familiar with certain aspects of the decision maker's goals. Even so, the negotiator should confirm any such assumption to ensure that the goals have not changed. An informal conversation with decision makers who are well known should be sufficient to confirm goals. If the decision maker is less well known, a more specific confirmation, generally in writing, is useful to guard against misinterpretation.

An exception to the rule that the decision maker's goals be reconfirmed each time can be a series of related negotiations that occur at approximately the same time, even though different parties may be involved. Even so, the best practice is to explicitly ask the decision maker if the same goals apply to each related transaction or matter.

Comparing Objective and Subjective Goals

There may be instances when the negotiator perceives differences between reasonable, usual goals that one would expect and the specific goals announced by the decision maker for a new negotiation. The usual goals might, at least provisionally, be considered the *objective goals* of the situation. In this context, an objective goal is one which most people on the same side of the negotiation usually consider valuable; they are the goals which people on that side would ordinarily strive to achieve.

Sometimes the objective goals are disregarded, adjusted, or abandoned. In a given situation, a decision maker might announce goals that supersede the objective goals. Since the new goals originate from idiosyncratic views of one person — the decision maker — they can be considered *subjective goals*. Subjective goals are based on the decision maker's personal values, needs, feelings, or experiences. The negotiator should analyze any differences between objective and subjective goals. By asking the decision maker pertinent questions, or by providing the decision maker with advice, the negotiator can be sure of the appropriateness of subjective goals. It is important for the negotiator to be alert to possible emotional issues which might be inappropriately influencing the decision maker's goal setting. By comparing objective with subjective goals, the negotiator can help ensure that the right goals are chosen.

The Six Categories of Negotiation Goals

Negotiation goals encompass a wide range of both tangible and intangible desires. Although some negotiation goals have certain similarities, important distinctions exist between categories of goals which in turn affect the negotiator's choice of strategy and tactics. The categories are:

1. Aggressive goals
2. Competitive goals
3. Cooperative goals
4. Self-centered goals
5. Defensive goals
6. Combinations of goals

Aggressive Goals

Key Concept 16

Aggressive goals seek to damage an opponent.

Aggressive goals are those which seek to undermine, deprive, damage, or otherwise injure a rival or opponent. The focus is *not* on one's own result but on the effect on the targeted party. Aggressive negotiation goals may even result in an economic loss for the party espousing them, at least in the short-run. In such instances, however, the damage to the opposition provides the desired gain. The motivation may be revenge for past deeds (including prior negotiations) or may reflect what the decision maker perceives as long-term interests.

Examples of Aggressive Goals.   The following list presents examples of aggressive goals:

- Taking a customer or supplier away from a competitor in order to hurt the competitor.

- Causing someone else to lose the respect of others, resulting in a business loss, personal unhappiness, or both.

- Precipitating unfavorable publicity for another, leading to a loss of customers for a business or votes for a candidate.

- Punishing an opponent, such as bringing suit to teach the other party that adverse actions will result in costly and time-consuming consequences.

Dealing With Emotionally Charged Situations.   Aggressive goals may be logical in a business or economic context. However, they are likely to elicit strong, and perhaps unpleasant emotional responses. For example, the participants in a divorce case might express deep anger or even hatred or revenge. Business disputes sometimes lead to similar, deeply hostile feelings. Provided that the aggressive goal is made as a fully informed choice, a negotiator who is not the decision maker should respect an economically unwise but emotionally satisfying goal. However, advice from the negotiator may be necessary to ensure that the decision maker's choice is indeed an informed one.

The decision maker should be counseled to focus on whether it might be wise to control strong emotions in order to achieve an attractive economic settlement. If the decision is an intensely emotional one, the decision maker may not be able or willing to discuss the true reasons for the decision, especially if it is relatively soon after the event that motivated the emotional goal; the emotional factor still may be too high and intense. When the judgment of a decision maker is distracted by intense feelings, he or she might try to rationalize goals which are actually self-defeating for the sake of emotional satisfaction. In these instances, the decision maker is unlikely to really hear and absorb any advice offered.

Over time, emotional decision makers may become more willing to recognize and discuss real motives and to listen to sensible advice. As the anger or hurt pass, so may the decision maker's commitment to pursue the matter in an aggressive or counterproductive fashion. Thus, it is important for negotiators to occasionally check with decision makers to determine whether their willingness to discuss their motivation, or their ability to discuss alternative solutions, has changed.

In the end, unless the course to be taken is illegal or unethical, the informed decision of the decision maker governs, regardless of whether he or she continues to favor the emotionally based decision. After all, ultimate responsibility belongs to the decision maker. Also, it is important for negotiators to be sensitive to emotional influences on all types of goals, not just those which are aggressive. Emotions can often interfere with effective goal setting.

Competitive Goals

Key Concept 17

A competitive goal means getting more than the other party.

A **competitive goal** is one in which one side seeks to gain more from the negotiation than the other side. In fact, the negotiator hopes to obtain as large a comparative advantage as possible. Thus, there is an inverse correlation between the competitive goals of opposing sides. More to one side means less to the other, and each side seeks to attain as much as possible.

Examples of Competitive Goals. The following list presents examples of competitive goals:

- Receiving the highest possible price.
- Paying the lowest possible price.
- Getting a better public image than another person or entity.

A competitive goal almost always results when one side is to pay money to another. From the payer's perspective, paying less is better, since each dollar paid is a loss to the payor if the item could have been obtained for a lower sum. The payee, of course, has the opposite point of view. More dollars received means a better bargain.

Such situations involve what may be described as a **limited pie.** A limited pie situation is one in which the value of the negotiated item is

fixed. For example, suppose that the sale of a diamond is being negotiated. The buyer is willing to pay up to $60,000 for it. There is a set
amount of money potentially involved. Neither side's actions will
change the total of the outer limit. Figure 2-1 illustrates the concept of
a limited pie.

Figure 2-1

The limited pie consists of $60,000. If the diamond can be purchased
for $40,000 instead of $60,000, the buyer is at a competitive advantage:
each dollar more to one side means one less dollar to the other side.
Bargaining under these circumstances is sometimes depicted linearly,
with each side trying to move the other toward its end (see Figure 2-2).

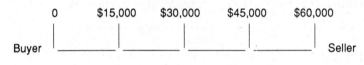

Figure 2-2

In terms of game theory, which is a mathematical view of maximizing
gains and minimizing losses, this limited pie situation, wherein one side
wins something and the other loses, is referred to as a **zero-sum game**.
In a zero-sum game, a gain to one party creates a direct and propor-
tional loss to the other. By its very nature, the situation is a competitive
one.

Fundamental approaches to competitive goals include:

1. Pushing hard to press the other side as close as possible to its bottom
   line, such as by using extreme positions and very small concessions.

2. Persuading the other side that the best resolution that it can achieve
   is less favorable than it anticipated, but that an agreement still can be
   at or above its bottom line.

3. Persuading the other side to alter its bottom line by influencing its
   objective or subjective valuation of the items at issue or of the costs of
   those items.

4. Considering reevaluation and shifting one's own bottom line if the other side's bottom line would otherwise preclude an agreement.

Negotiators may define a goal as competitive in another way. The magnitude of the differences between the parties in and of itself can lead to the conclusion that the negotiation is a competitive one. Studies of bargaining behavior have found that the greater the conflict that the sides perceive, the more likely negotiators are to act competitively. That is, they react to large differences between each side's positions as necessarily arising because of limited pie, or zero-sum, factors. This reaction to such large differences may or may not be correct. Careful analysis is essential to determine whether the negotiation really involves a competitive goal, an aggressive goal, one of the other three discussed below, or some combination of goals.

Cooperative Goals

Key Concept 18

With cooperative goals, agreement leads to mutual gain.

Cooperative goals are achieved through an agreement that leads to mutual gain for all negotiators and their respective sides. The essential factor for a cooperative goal is being able to achieve your goal with an absence of a corresponding cost or loss for the other side. In this way, both sides gain. For example, a cooperative goal would recognize a positive correlation between each party's achievement of its goals. This achievement is also referred to as **win-win negotiating.** The success of one's cooperative goals, then, depends on the goals of the other party; a cooperative goal must be shared in order to be feasible.

Examples of Cooperative Goals. The following list presents examples of cooperative goals:

- Forming a joint venture, partnership, or corporation to engage in business opportunities to achieve a mutual profit.
- Acquiring tax advantages by structuring a transaction or settlement so that both parties gain. Perhaps the parties will split the tax benefit, or one will receive a cash payment and the other a direct tax benefit.
- Establishing a payment plan under which the payor gains the right to

pay less at the present moment in exchange for which the payee later receives more money in the form of interest.

- Achieving increased respect from others through the blending of both parties' strengths into a unified entity or program.

Two important aspects in forming cooperative goals are the size of the pie and the nature of the parties' relationship. In the example of negotiating the purchase of a diamond, the price could reach $60,000. The pie was assumed to be a limited one (capped at $60,000), in which the dollars gained or saved by one party resulted in a directly corresponding loss or cost to the other party. By contrast, negotiating cooperative goals uses an **expanded pie** approach (see Figure 2-3). An expanded pie refers to a situation in which the value of the negotiated item can increase. Within the context of a cooperative goal, the increased value is shared by all parties. Assume, for example, that the parties could structure the diamond purchase so that both parties would achieve a tax advantage of $5000 regardless of the negotiated price of the diamond. A cooperative goal then emerges: that of achieving a tax advantage for both the seller and the purchaser. Thus, the value of the pie has been increased from $60,000 to $70,000 without additional cost to either party.

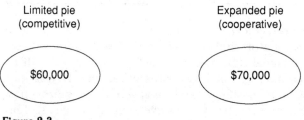

Limited pie (competitive) $60,000   Expanded pie (cooperative) $70,000

Figure 2-3

Note that $10,000 of the pie is not subject to negotiation. Each party can achieve only a $5000 tax gain. Neither party can obtain any tax gain without the cooperation of the other party in structuring the transaction. Neither party gains its tax benefit if the other fails to also obtain a tax benefit. It is therefore advantageous to both parties to cooperate and expand the pie.

Short-Term Versus Long-Term Considerations.   Cooperative goals can apply to either the short- or long-run. For example, the sale of an item with tax advantages to both parties involves a cooperative goal. To achieve the advantages probably requires only a single interaction between the parties (the sale of the item). That type of cooperative goal is a short-term one. By contrast, a joint venture to engage in a business together, and to achieve mutual profits, involves a continuing interaction between the parties. This type of cooperative goal has a long-term purpose.

Long-term cooperative goals, such as a joint venture or partnership, may require the negotiator to demonstrate a greater willingness to reach an agreement. This commitment (or gesture of good faith) can prove to the other party that the deal itself is viable. One's willingness to act cooperatively should favorably impress the other side and enhance the likelihood that the long-term roles and benefits will in fact occur. With a long-term cooperative goal, the demonstration of a cooperative spirit may be as important in making the proposed deal seem attractive as the defined roles and tangible benefits.

Self-Centered Goals

Key Concept 19

Self-centered goals seek a particular result regardless of what the other side receives.

Self-centered goals are those that depend solely on what one's own side achieves. Thus, this type of goal is neither inherently antagonistic nor helpful to the other party. With a truly self-centered goal, the results for the other party are simply a neutral by-product of attaining one's own goal. This type of goal does not necessarily require any particular cooperation from the other party beyond the creation of the agreement itself.

Negotiating Scenario_____

Two large accounting firms merge. The tremendous size of the new firm raises a self-centered goal to find sufficient prestigious space in a single location. The goal is reached when the new firm negotiates a lease for 15 floors in a major midtown New York office building.

Examples of Self-Centered Goals.   The following list provides examples of self-centered goals:

- Obtaining a particular property.
- Selling a specific property.
- Improving a business or personal relationship.
- Gaining respect from others.
- Developing a relationship with a new customer or supplier.
- Gaining vindication.
- Obtaining financing.
- Receiving favorable publicity.
- Receiving tax benefits without cost to the other party.
- Obtaining a position within an organization that can lead to important contacts that may be personally beneficial in the future.
- Resolving a dispute.
- Making a loan.

Of course, depending on circumstances, many of these examples could also involve competitive, cooperative, aggressive, or defensive goals, or a combination of goals.

Defensive Goals

Key Concept 20

Defensive goals seek to avoid a particular result.

Defensive goals are those in which one seeks to avoid a particular outcome. It is this avoidance aspect that distinguishes defensive goals from self-centered ones. In the latter case, the negotiator focuses on attaining something.

Examples of Defensive Goals.   The following list provides examples of defensive goals:

- Avoiding a loss of respect.
- Preventing a strike.
- Avoiding the loss of a good customer or supplier.
- Restructuring financing to prevent an imminent foreclosure.

- Maintaining a business or personal relationship.

Defensive goals sustain survival or prevent damage to one's side. Since negative consequences can be as powerfully motivating as positive ones, it is essential to recognize each side's defensive goals. By focusing on the other side's defensive goals, you may find power, win-win, trade-off, and other negotiating possibilities.

Combinations of Negotiation Goals

Key Concept 21

Each negotiation usually has multiple goals.

In some instances, there will be a single goal. A property owner's sole self-centered goal could be to sell a property regardless of price. Of course, a prospective buyer could have the single, corresponding self-centered goal of purchasing regardless of price. More often, however, each side will have more than one goal for the negotiation. In the example, the property owner and the purchaser probably both have competitive price goals as well as self-centered goals. As Case in Point 2-1 demonstrates, it is usually simplistic to think that in real life there is only a single type of goal in a negotiation. In almost all instances, there will be several goals.

Case in Point 2-1_____

In a collective bargaining negotiation, a transportation firm seeks to have its employees make prompt deliveries in order to maintain its business volume. This is a self-centered goal. A defensive goal is suggested if the maintenance of volume is intended to avoid a loss of customers. The goal is also aggressive to the extent that the same activity lures new customers away from competitors, a result which is likely to weaken the latter.

Collective bargaining negotiations can also involve conflicts between different types of goals. For example, a company's first priority might be to cut labor's wages. This is an example of *distributive bargaining*, since wages represent a benefit which is distributed from the company to labor. Labor's first priority, however, might be to secure new equipment which operates more safely than what is presently available. Although the new equipment is costly, labor officials have shown that it will help reduce the number of injuries and the corresponding health and disability payments that management must make. Since both sides would seem to gain, the negotiation is an example of *integrative bargaining*. This situation reveals two sets of problems and goals: the company's desire for reduced wages (a competitive goal) and labor's desire for new equipment (a cooperative goal). Before either set can be addressed, however, the difference in goals and priorities must be faced.

Reconciling Conflicting Goals

It is easy to see how the goals of opposing parties can conflict. Sometimes, however, one's own goals may also conflict with each other. If one's own goals initially seem to conflict, the negotiator must evaluate to determine whether the conflict can be eliminated. The negotiator must learn whether the conflict is real or merely due to confusion, a lack of clarification, or misinformation.

Key Concept 22

Priorities must be set when there are conflicting goals.

When personal goals genuinely conflict, they must be balanced and prioritized in order to determine the least favorable result that the decision maker finds acceptable as opposed to not reaching an agreement at all. That will constitute the bottom-line position.

By prioritizing goals, conflicts can often be avoided. Case in Point 2-2 demonstrates many of the negotiation goals that can come into play, and how a conflict between them can be resolved.

Case in Point 2-2

A property to be sold is a business that includes an industrial building. In this transaction, the owner desires to sell the business in order to:

Be rid of the building (self-centered).

Have increased liquid assets (self-centered).

Avoid further losses since the business was operating at a deficit (defensive).

Maximize the sale price and thereby maximize net profits (competitive).

Structure the sale itself to minimize taxes without cost to the purchaser (self-centered).

Distribute profit-sharing benefits to minimize the taxes of the employees and the owner (both self-centered and cooperative with respect to the employees and self-centered with respect to the owner).

Obtain promises of continued employment for long-time and valued employees with whom personal relationships have developed, thereby maintaining the quality of the relationships (self-centered), avoiding a loss of respect (defensive), and eliminating the need for severance pay (self-centered).

A cooperative goal also exists since certain of the goals can only be accomplished with the support and agreement of the purchaser who will receive the corresponding benefit of valuable and experienced employees. Also, if the seller were forced to negotiate severance pay with the long-term employees, he or she might also have either a competitive goal to minimize that pay, or a self-centered goal of keeping that expense below the level which the owner felt comfortable paying.

The competitive goal of minimizing severance pay conflicts with both the self-centered goal of maintaining good personal relationships with the employees and the defensive goal of avoiding a loss of respect. The owner must reexamine all of his or her goals. In this case, the conflict is avoided because the owner decides that the cooperative negotiation for continued employment by the purchaser of the business is the most important goal. Since the employees can keep their jobs, the issue of severance pay becomes moot.

Conflicts can often be avoided by successfully prioritizing goals. In Case in Point 2-2, the owner of property has the typical competitive goal of maximizing the sale price. However, the owner also may have the self-centered goal of just wanting to be rid of the property because it no longer meets her needs for size, prestige, or income. Those two goals can conflict. The owner then must determine at what point the sale price is sufficient, although not necessarily maximized, to sell the property which no longer fulfills her other needs. In other words, conflicting goals must be prioritized.

Conflicting goals can also arise when the party is not monolithic, but instead experiences internal conflicts and bargaining confrontations. In such instances, the negotiator may hear different goals expressed by different members of the group or entity. The negotiator may also hear shifting goals expressed due to internal negotiations. In such cases, active counseling with the ultimate decision maker is essential to avoid misunderstanding and misdirected effort. This counseling may reconcile different goals or lead to agreed priorities among goals.

Key Concept 23

Time, information, and events can alter goals; therefore, goals should be periodically reevaluated.

Goals often change as a negotiation progresses. The negotiation itself may influence one's goals. New facts can emerge. Resistance by the other party can lead to reevaluation of one's position. External factors, such as outside economic conditions, may also affect one's goals. Financial considerations may shift, policies may be altered, or alternative opportunities may be presented.

Conflicting negotiation goals can also be generated by situations that involve strong, antagonistic feelings toward the other party; examples include the enforcement of covenants not to compete, antagonistic disagreements between joint venturers during a project, and partnership breakups. In a negotiation, one side may seek to maximize the monetary recovery, and at the same time either gain vindication, punish the other party, or increase the other party's respect or fear without regard to legal or other costs. At least, this can be the initial posture. Obviously, the goal which seeks maximum monetary recovery conflicts with the goals that disregard costs. This conflict not only affects the determination of a bottom line and the choices of strategies and tactics, but it also affects the timing of serious negotiations because the priority between the conflicting goals can change over time. A party may reprioritize its goals to favor monetary goals once fighting with the other party releases enough emotion to satisfy the earlier goals of vindication, punishment, respect, or fear. It is clear, then, that goals and priorities can shift. New information, changed feelings, different outside circumstances, and a variety of other factors may influence goal setting.

Case in Point 2-3_____

While in the process of selling their home, the Brons purchase a replacement home. They now have the defensive goal of avoiding the dual expenses of paying for and maintaining both properties. The achievement of the defensive goal by selling the first property conflicts with the original goal of maximizing the sale price. The offers they receive are for lesser amounts than they expected. This situation requires that the Brons either prioritize or compromise the differences between the two goals. That is, either they decide to maintain both properties until they can sell the first for the price they want, or they lower the price in order to be rid of the property. Lowering the price represents a compromise.

Case in Point 2-4_____

During the course of a negotiation to sell raw materials, the seller becomes overstocked because a large order was canceled. A defensive goal arises: to avoid staying overstocked. The new defensive goal assumes the highest priority, leading the seller to lower the price offered to a manufacturer. This decision reflects a change in the competitive goal of obtaining a high price.

Goals Should Be Periodically Reevaluated

Due to the potential for goals to change, the negotiator may need to check periodically to ascertain whether the goals have remained the same. The negotiator may need the counsel of the decision maker if new information or different circumstances seem to warrant a reprioritization of goals. The precise identification and categorization of goals is essential for the negotiator to properly choose among potential strategies and tactics. It also is important to prioritize multiple goals, especially those that conflict. Negotiators should be prepared to abandon a nonessential goal in order to achieve another, more important one. The decision maker, after appropriate advice, must determine the priorities for the goals. The process of reviewing new information or circumstances is ongoing.

Learn the Other Side's Goals

Negotiation goals are especially important with respect to the tactics of obtaining and disclosing information. At times, discovering the true nature of the other party's goals can provide a significant advantage for the negotiator. Also, the selective disclosure of your true goals can sometimes be essential to move the other party forward toward agreement.

Adopting the Proper Attitude
to Achieve Desired Goals

Negotiation goals define the purpose of the negotiation. That purpose, as perceived by each negotiator, may affect not only the choice of strategies and tactics, but also the attitude and behavior of the negotiators. A cooperative negotiation requires a cooperative attitude, while an aggressive one may require a professionally adversarial, although not necessarily unpleasant, tone. The successful negotiator can adjust personal attitudes and behaviors to achieve goals.

Comprehension Checkup

The answers to these questions appear on page 331.

1. Negotiation goals can be _____.
   a. tangible   d. a, b, and c
   b. intangible   e. a and c
   c. subjective

2. There are _____ categories of negotiation goals.
   a. 2   d. 6
   b. 4   e. 10
   c. 5

3. In negotiating terms, "competitive" and "cooperative" describe _____.
   a. attitudes   d. tone
   b. goals   e. a, b, c, and d
   c. strategies

4. The negotiator seeks a deal to block a rival from using a supplier. The negotiation goal is _____.
   a. aggressive   d. self-centered
   b. competitive   e. none of these
   c. defensive

5. The seller wants a price of $100 per unit, but the buyer only wants to pay $70 per unit. Each has a(n) _____ negotiation goal.
   a. aggressive   d. cooperative
   b. defensive   e. a and d
   c. competitive

6. Aggressive negotiation goals can be _____.
   a. cost-effective   d. variable
   b. emotionally based   e. all of these
   c. logical

7. Neither party can qualify to bid for a project except by combining their resources. The negotiation goal is _____.
   a. defensive   d. aggressive
   b. cooperative   e. none of these
   c. competitive

8. The limited pie to be divided among potential partners is $800,000 per year in profits. The negotiation goal is _____.
   a. defensive   d. aggressive
   b. cooperative   e. none of these
   c. competitive

9. By restructuring the terms of the proposed transaction without changing the value of what each party already will receive, a significant tax savings will result. The negotiation goal is _____.
   a. cooperative   d. competitive
   b. self-centered   e. defensive
   c. aggressive

10. During a negotiation, goals _____.
    a. always remain the same   c. always change
    b. sometimes change

11. Mr. Jones is negotiating with several banks to obtain financing at the lowest rate. The goal is _____.
    a. self-centered   d. competitive
    b. cooperative   e. aggressive
    c. defensive

12. L.J. Company wants to prevent its major competitor, P&J, from entering into a new product portion of the market. L.J. and P&J each seeks to negotiate a joint venture with M.R. Laboratory, a small research and development firm which has the most advanced technology. L.J.'s negotiation goals are:
    a. self-centered and cooperative   d. cooperative and competitive
    b. aggressive and defensive   e. aggressive and cooperative
    c. competitive and self-centered

13. Due to increases in its overhead, a company needs to increase sales by charging lower prices. In the short-run, however, immediate cashflow is required. Over the long-run, a price increase is essential because of a limited potential market for sales. The negotiation goals now must be:
    a. ignored   d. unchanged
    b. aggressive   e. cooperative
    c. prioritized

3
The Strategic Underpinnings of a Successful Negotiation

Key Concepts

24. Strategy is the overall approach for conducting the negotiation.
25. Tactics are particular actions used to implement a strategy.
26. A variety of factors determine the best strategy for a negotiating situation.
27. Personal credibility is critical to the negotiation; it cannot be taken for granted.
28. Negotiators can often gain credibility by getting other parties to identify with them (and vice versa).
29. A no-concessions strategy is tough and dangerous, since concessions usually are expected.
30. A no-further-concessions strategy is possible when the other party can be forced to make the final concession, or when the situation has changed.
31. A strategy of making only deadlock-breaking concessions is okay when the risk of nonagreement is acceptable.

32. The most generally useful negotiating strategy is high realistic expectations with small systematic concessions (HRESSC).

33. Conceding first is a viable strategy if you do not concede too much and if it will create momentum, enabling you to later demand a reciprocal concession without appearing weak.

34. Problem solving is a strategy for creating a procedural agreement to solve a common problem that has been identified.

35. Reaching agreement is not necessarily the end purpose of all negotiating goals and strategies.

36. The move-for-closure strategy consists of acting to close the deal by creating a firm agreement.

37. Using different strategies at different stages of the negotiation or for different issues is usually the most effective method of negotiating.

The Language of Negotiating

To make full use of the key concepts, you must understand the following terms:

Strategy	Optimal settlement
Tactics	Problem solving
Personal credibility	Delay
Gamesmanship	Influence
Identification	Third parties
Concessions	Closure
Deadlock	Sequential changes
High realistic expectations with small systematic concessions (HRESSC)	Issue-oriented changes

Selecting Your Strategy

Key Concepts 24 and 25

Strategy is the overall approach for conducting the negotiation.

Tactics are particular actions used to implement a strategy.

Strategy is the overall concept chosen by the negotiator for conducting the negotiation.

The choice of strategy is approved by the decision maker before it is executed by the negotiator if the strategy itself may impact the client's personal or business interests. For example, a business may not want a no-concessions strategy to be used in a particular negotiation because of a concern about unhappy third parties, such as lenders or the public, which will occur if no agreement is reached. This may involve making concessions, trading concessions, refusing to make concessions, or other methods of negotiating. The most common and useful strategies will be outlined in this chapter.

Before describing and explaining the various strategies available, it is useful to distinguish between strategy and tactics. Whereas a strategy provides the overall approach used throughout the negotiation, a **tactic** is a particular action used at a specific time during the negotiation to serve a more limited role or purpose.

Key Concept 26

A variety of factors determine the best strategy for a negotiating situation.

Strategies are chosen for use in a particular negotiation in order to achieve your side's goals. The nature of those goals will affect the choice of strategy or strategies, as shown in the following sections. The choice of strategy also may be affected by the answers to a number of questions, such as:

Does the negotiation involve a transaction or a dispute?

Is there more than one issue involved?

Can new issues be introduced into the negotiation?

Are the parties' interests short-term or long-term?

Are the parties' relationships long-term, limited to one negotiation, or somewhere in between?

Is the negotiators' relationship long-term, limited to one negotiation, or somewhere in between?

Are the parties' interests economic, noneconomic, or both?

Do the parties value the negotiable items in the same way?

Are the parties negotiating voluntarily or not?

Are the negotiations being conducted privately or publicly?

Are the negotiations the subject of publicity?

Is the client an individual, a group of individuals, a company, a union, or some other type of organization?

Does what is at stake have great or little value to the parties?

Who stands to gain or to lose the most?

Is the negotiation a routine matter or is it unusual?

Are the parties equally or unequally powerful in terms of needs, facts, the law, economic resources, morality, and so on?

Is the negotiation being conducted face to face, by phone, in writing, or through a combination of these means?

Are there viable alternatives (such as a refusal to sell) available? If so, to what degree are they acceptable?

In addition, the choice of strategy is affected by the negotiating approach, personal characteristics, and the psychological orientation of the other negotiator.

Establishing Personal Credibility

Key Concept 27

Personal credibility is critical to the negotiation; it cannot be taken for granted.

Before focusing on specific strategies, the issue of personal credibility must be examined. **Personal credibility** refers to having the trust and confidence of those participants in the negotiation who are essential to reaching agreement. That there is no substitute for integrity has been commonly remarked over the years by students and practitioners of the art of negotiating. Even in large metropolitan areas, reputations tend to develop and become known. A lack of credibility can be a devastating handicap. The worst type of credibility problem is a reputation for dishonesty. Maintaining credibility can be even more complicated when negotiating with people from other cultures. For instance, the Japanese traditionally are often very concerned with integrity and trust for long-term relationships. Personal credibility is without question one of the most important qualities of a successful negotiation.

Case in Point 3-1

Imagine a negotiation in which one negotiator did not believe anything said by the other negotiator — not the demands, professed reasons, promises, threats, or anything else. Obviously one would neither want to, nor be able to, reach an agreement if the other negotiator was not credible. Negotiations in cases such as this might sound like the following:

"I will not make any concessions."

"Oh yes you will."

"Here is a guaranteed appraisal for $45,000."

"It is not genuine."

Or, they might sound like this:

"Let's exchange financial statements to decide on a fair percentage division of the profits for a partnership combining our two businesses."

"Your financial statement is so highly exaggerated that it's a fraud."

These examples are intentionally exaggerated to help illustrate a fundamental point about strategy: No matter which strategy is chosen, it cannot effectively influence the other negotiator's behavior and decisions unless it is believed to be credible by both sides. Otherwise, the strategy will be disregarded by the other negotiator. A crucial component for creating a believable strategy is the personal credibility of the negotiator. That credibility must be established and maintained.

Common Attributes of a Credible Negotiator

Confidence. Personal credibility tends to be attributed to negotiators who exhibit certain characteristics. A credible negotiator tends to be comfortable and confident, without being brash or arrogant. These qualities demonstrate a genuine sense of strength without being offensive. They also show that the negotiator has a realistic sense of what the negotiation can accomplish.

Preparedness and Organization. A credible negotiator also tends to be prepared, organized, and businesslike without being stuffy. Candor needs to be projected and, at times, so does a willingness to proceed without conceding. This tends to force the other negotiator to respect the positions that one takes and to act in a serious manner, rather than engaging in **gamesmanship,** the attempt to win through questionable expedients rather than good faith efforts. It also tends to make the other negotiator more forthright. Having the authority to take positions and acknowledging that fact also are helpful, although not essential factors.

Knowledgeableness. Part of being prepared, of course, is being knowledgeable about the matter being negotiated. Negotiations have little chance of success if the negotiator is unfamiliar with the relevant issues. Knowledge of the specific context in which the negotiation occurs is also important. For example, negotiators of union contracts should know about the specific business involved and the laws surrounding union negotiations. Of course, no negotiator can be expected always to know everything, but he or she should seek to know as much as possible through diligent preparation. Within these limits, however, it will not diminish, and may even enhance, one's credibility to candidly admit when something is not known. Credibility can be enhanced simply by inquiring about relevant information.

Honesty. It is most important for the negotiator to behave honestly. One cannot be believable unless one is *perceived* as honest. This requirement does not mean unilaterally disclosing information, except, of course, when such disclosure is appropriate. It does mean, however, that one not engage in lying. As negotiations usually cannot involve total openness and candor, lies must be distinguished from accepted practices, such as concealing one's bottom line from the other party.

Firmness. One important method to establish credibility is to always follow through on one's word, whether it is a promise or a threat. When actions which were forecast do in fact occur, the other negotiator learns to listen carefully to you and to respect your words. One must always be concerned with his or her reputation, especially in repeated negotiations with the same negotiator or party. It is important to be known as a person who will do or act as she or he says.

Creating and Preserving Trust

Both negotiators and the parties to negotiation tend to trust the other side when the other side is perceived as:

1. Being similar to them.
2. Having a positive attitude toward them.
3. Being dependent on them.
4. Showing cooperation and trust.
5. Willing to make concessions or work toward a joint solution of the issues.
6. Being cooperative, open, and nonthreatening.

Being Alert to Multiple Parties. Since the "other side" frequently consists not only of the other negotiator but also a client party, the perception of one of them can overcome or negate the perception of the other. The situation becomes even more complex when the party, the negotiator, or both, consists of multiple individuals or entities, each of which can influence efforts to create or maintain a sense of trust.

Keeping the Negotiation Free of Personal Issues. Statements of requirements may have to be cushioned so as to avoid making trust a personal issue between the negotiators. Consider the following model statements:

> "Given the past problems between our clients on whether someone agreed to something or not, we need to have the offer in writing with all of the terms clearly spelled out. This has nothing to do with you personally. But, we will all be better off by avoiding any misunderstanding."

> "I am certainly willing to accept your word. But, in order to prevent issues of trust from coming up during negotiations, I always insist that agreements be put in writing. This also avoids any questions if later on either of us were to be hit by a car, or some similar event were to happen."

Countering Tips for the "Trust Me" Approach. Some negotiators use a "trust me" approach as a tactic to foreclose demands for specific information or agreements. Unless one believes that such trust is completely warranted under the circumstances, the "trust me" approach should be rejected and countered, although care should be exercised that this is not insulting or unnecessarily antagonistic. Countermeasures to the "trust me" approach include:

1. Reference to the need for a complete written agreement without separate oral portions, regardless of the source.

2. Citing a need to probe the source of the other negotiator's information (not their personal truthfulness).

3. Pointing out that if one or both negotiators are unavailable at a later time, confusion or disagreement may result.

4. Citing custom and practice, with the corresponding need to require certain measures.

5. Citing your client's suspicions or requirements while denying that you are either suspicious or somehow unsatisfied.

Using Actions to Support Your Words.   At times, a negotiator has to devise actions in order to create a sense of trust.

Case in Point 3-2

A condominium association sued a contractor who had damaged the condominium while making repairs to the adjoining building. A second dispute arose when the contractor failed to sufficiently secure large plastic sheets that were being used as drop cloths while painting the adjoining building. At night, these plastic sheets blew noisily around in the wind and disrupted the sleep of the condominium residents.

Both to prevent the problem from recurring and to create a sense of trust and goodwill, the contractor quickly offered to remove the plastic sheets at the end of each working day. The trust and goodwill that were created later benefited the contractor when negotiating the more complex and significant issue of damage to the condominium. Of course, once the parties agreed that the plastic would be removed each afternoon before the workers left, the contractor then had to ensure that this was done. Otherwise, trust would be destroyed; also, he would have to negotiate the more important damage problem from a much more difficult position.

Building a Sense of Identification

Key Concept 28

Negotiators can often gain credibility by getting other parties to identify with them (and vice versa).

Negotiators can increase their credibility by getting the other party to identify with them. **Identification, in this sense, means orienting one's** behavior in accordance with the behaviors and precepts of another individual or group. Sometimes, identification can be elicited simply by behaving in a reasonable, professional manner. However, since professional behavior is expected, additional behaviors, such as empathy and understanding, may be even more important to achieve identification.

A negotiator can foster identification by means of empathy through:

1. Focusing on the parties' real interests rather than the position they are taking.

2. Considering those interests in terms of some objective criteria of value or fairness, such as comparable prices or wages.

3. Avoiding making the people on the other side personally part of the problem to be resolved (whenever practical).

Losing Credibility Through Negative Identification

Identification also can operate in reverse, thereby causing a loss of personal credibility. For instance, a negotiator may display a total lack of concern for the legitimate needs of the other party. That lack of concern can be perceived by the other side as a lack of basic fairness. If so, there will be a negative identification and a loss of personal credibility, since someone who is not fair is less likely to be believed.

Cultivating Allies to Enhance Credibility

Allies can be useful in creating trust. A third party who is respected by the other party, or its negotiator, can serve as a reference to establish credibility.

A method of enhancing credibility related to the cultivation of allies involves the fascination many people have with celebrities. People often want to meet such personalities. The negotiator might try to be identified with the celebrity. For most negotiators who are not insiders or celebrities in their own right, personal acquaintance with powerful or celebrity figures can give the negotiator a status comparable to the celebrity's. This identification may create the perception that the negotiator is more interesting to deal with than someone without such status.

On the other hand, if talk of relationships with powerful persons, celebrities, or insiders is seen as mere boasting or as an unsuccessful attempt to intimidate, the results will likely backfire. Indeed, it may even unintentionally introduce an unwelcome power struggle into the negotiation. The person without celebrity status might seek to prove that he or she is neither impressed nor intimidated by famous people.

Credibility in the Company You Keep

In establishing or maintaining credibility, it may be necessary to separate oneself from people who are not credible to the other party or its negotiator. Two approaches are possible if your client or associates are not trusted by the other side. First (and preferably), the other side can be persuaded that its perception is unjustified. That, however, may be a difficult or an impossible task. Second (as either an alternative or a fallback position), one can acknowledge the other side's perception without agreeing with it. At the same time, one must then establish or maintain one's own credibility, clearly delineating one's own reputation as separate from those who are distrusted.

When to Establish Credibility

Just as other work and preparation occurs before the actual negotiation, so does establishing one's personal credibility. Often there is contact between the negotiators before the formal negotiation. Early meetings or discussions might be more informal and pleasant. This is the time to begin building trust and establishing credibility. Trust can be gained in the ways described in the previous sections. Note that the need for personal credibility continues throughout the negotiating process.

Strategy 1: No Concessions

Key Concept 29

A no-concessions strategy is tough and dangerous, since concessions usually are expected.

The first negotiating strategy to be examined is one of making no concessions at all. This strategy is often the toughest to take because compromises are almost always expected by the other side. With a no-concessions strategy, the negotiation becomes a unilateral process. Once the position is announced, the only possible agreement is the one defined by the initiating party. The negotiation might still involve discussion about whether there should be agreement on the terms, and perhaps a test of whether there will truly be no concessions. However, if this strategy really is being used, no other terms will be considered by the initiating side unless they involve only some restructuring, without granting any fundamental concessions.

When to Use the No-Concessions Strategy

When the Balance of Power Is Strongly in Your Favor. Concessions are simply those positions that are given up, or conceded, during a negotiation. A no-concessions strategy is most useful when the party employing it has so much more power than the other party that it can dictate the terms. The strategy generally succeeds because the powerful party is able to threaten to inflict some kind of damage on the other side. It might also succeed due to the weaker party's extreme need for whatever the powerful party has to offer. Regardless of the source of power, the key to implementation is to have so much more power than the other side that it is forced to accept the terms offered.

An Historical Aside

The no-concessions strategy is sometimes called *Bulwareism,* from General Bulware, a former chief operating officer of General Electric. During Bulware's administration, the labor movement was extremely weak in comparison to G.E.'s management. Labor's weakness resulted in an inability to mount an effective strike. Bulwareism refers to management's demand that employees agree to certain terms and conditions without any discussion of potential concessions by the company.

This "take-it-or-leave-it" strategy was successful for a number of years during which the disparity of power between G.E. and the unions forced the employees to accede to what, from their point of view, were extremely poor terms. The employees yielded to the company because otherwise they would have been discharged, with new workers hired to take their place. Employees also feared that they would not be able to find other employment, or at least employment with comparable wages.

The no-concessions strategy worked well for G.E. for approximately 20 years. Ultimately, however, it led to a very costly strike. Nevertheless, its 20-year effectiveness would seem to qualify it as a successful strategy.

When You Are in a Disproportionately Weak Position. Oddly, a no-concessions strategy can sometimes be successfully employed by an apparently weak party. The seemingly weak party threatens some drastic action which is actually capable of inflicting harm on a stronger party. For example, a weak party can implement the strategy by threatening bankruptcy. A credible threat of bankruptcy can transform an apparently weak party into a very powerful party because of the adverse consequences it can create. In the case of bankruptcy, the assumption of power occurs when two conditions are met:

1. The choice of bankruptcy is more advantageous to the weak party than the terms unilaterally set by the strong party.

2. The strong party receives far less from a bankruptcy proceeding than what the offered terms provide.

When Another Party Is Waiting in the Wings. Another circumstance in which the no-concessions strategy can be highly effective is when the party employing it has a high level of confidence that a third party will accept their terms, even if the other party rejects them. When such confidence exists, the response of the other party in the negotiation becomes almost irrelevant. If the other party accepts the offer, one's goal has been attained. If it rejects the offer, it doesn't really matter since the same benefits can be obtained through an agreement with someone else.

When the Dollar Amount Is Too Low or Time Is Too Short. Available money and time also can be factors leading to a no-concessions strategy. This can occur in two ways:

1. *Cost-efficiency.* The dollar amount involved may be too small to justify expending much time negotiating.

2. *Available time.* The amount of time available may be too limited for an elaborate negotiation.

In either of these circumstances, a strategy of no concessions should be considered. However, other strategies should not be dismissed.

When the Same Terms Must Be Available to Everyone. A different circumstance leading to the choice of the no-concessions strategy arises when the same terms must be available to everyone. In this situation, the party employing the no-concessions strategy must be consistent with various other parties. Consistency is needed to avoid setting a precedent that will cause either:

1. An abandonment of its no-concessions policy.
2. Hostility from others who were told that the terms were not negotiable, or that they were receiving terms as favorable as anyone else would receive.
3. A lawsuit where equal terms are legally required.

The most common example of this type of situation is a price which is set so that it is "competitive" in the marketplace, but which is not negotiable. Nonnegotiable terms may encompass an entire transaction, or be limited to a specific portion of it. In the latter case, the total negotiation includes both negotiable and nonnegotiable terms.

When Bids or Written Proposals Are Sought.   A different form of the no-concessions strategy entails the use of bids or written proposals as the start and end points for the negotiation. In effect, the party establishing the bidding procedure says, "Give me your best offer on a take-it-or-leave-it basis; then your offer will be compared to your competitors' best offers. The most attractive offer wins." A variation of this procedure involves some negotiation with the best bidder, either by design or by necessity, because certain terms were not covered by the bid.

Choosing a bid procedure forces the other party to make the first and, usually, the only offer. It normally forces the bidder to make a reasonable offer because of competition in the bidding. However, the integrity of the bid process depends on the existence of viable competitors, fairly drawn requirements, and specifications that do not favor one competitor over another, and the absence of illegal horizontal price fixing.

Bear in mind that a bidding procedure can eliminate the flexibility that is often needed in negotiations. Also, its use may be limited by custom or rule in a trade, industry, or profession.

Drawbacks of the No-Concessions Strategy

The danger of a no-concessions strategy is that it might preclude an agreement the terms of which, although less favorable, are still acceptable. People generally expect a negotiation to involve some give and take. They may be offended by a no-concessions strategy, interpreting it as an attempt at coercion. Or they may simply not believe it. Under these conditions, the negotiation may become stalled until the negotiator either exercises sufficient power to force an agreement, or switches strategies and makes concessions. A strategy shift away from no concessions might be read as a failed attempt at bluffing, a position to be avoided.

Negotiators should carefully avoid inadvertent bluffs by rashly miscalculating the use of the no-concessions strategy. To avoid embarrassment, if the other party refuses to acquiesce to a no-concessions strategy, a negotiator must be prepared to either:

1. Terminate the negotiation.

2. Extricate himself or herself from the situation through some face-saving maneuver.

To minimize the risk of a negative result to the no-concessions strategy, an especially sensitive and careful evaluation must precede its use. One must determine in advance whether it is likely to work, or if it is too risky in view of its potential risks.

To further reduce the risk of a negative reaction to the no-concessions strategy, it may be important to act in a nonaggressive manner, without appearing either apologetic or defensive. It may also be helpful to accompany the demand with reasons why your side is not in a position to offer anything else, and to explain how the demand is fair. A nonaggressive demeanor and a reasonable explanation of your no-concessions position may reduce potential antagonism and can allow the other side to respond affirmatively without losing face.

While the no-concessions strategy is often thought of as harsh or one-sided, it need not be. For example, an offer under the no-concessions strategy could be structured using the win-win tactic, so that the offer presented is very positive and appealing to the other side.

Countering Tips for the No-Concessions Strategy

The following countermeasures can be used if you find yourself on the receiving end of a no-concessions strategy:

1. Appeal to a higher level of authority in an attempt to change the party's position.

2. Ignore it and proceed as if concessions are possible.

3. Present cost-saving or win-win measures that justify a concession.

4. As a seller, offer less (such as fewer services), thereby effectively increasing the price.

5. As a buyer, demand more, thereby, in effect, reducing the price.

6. Terminate the negotiating session.

Restructured proposals or new information also can be used as countermeasures, thereby changing the negotiating situation which the no-concessions strategy originally addressed. The most useful tactics in this regard are:

1. Disclosing new information

2. Creating facts

3. Proposing win-win situations

4. Inserting new issues

5. Creating deadlock

6. Creating surprise

7. Engaging in litigation

Goals Compatibility

With respect to negotiation goals, the no-concessions strategy should be considered for goals that are aggressive, competitive, or self-centered, provided that the other conditions conducive to an effective no-concessions approach are present. These goals involve neither the interaction of cooperative goals nor the strong need to reach an agreement often found with defensive goals. Thus, the no-concessions approach is inappropriate for defensive goals and rarely, if ever, useful for cooperative goals. By comparison, if the goal is the aggressive demonstration of power to establish precedents for future situations (and the party actually possesses sufficient power), then the no-concessions strategy will be the best approach to achieve that goal.

Strategy 2: No Further Concessions

Key Concept 30

A no-further-concessions strategy is possible when the other party can be forced to make the final concession, or when the situation has changed.

While the no-concessions strategy is implemented at the outset of the negotiation, the no-further-concessions strategy is implemented after some concessions have been made. Sometimes, if parties are close to reaching an overall agreement or resolving an issue, one party may be able to achieve an agreement on its terms by switching to a strategy of no further concessions. The other party is then forced to make the last concession. Similarly, the negotiating situation may change so that a no-concessions strategy can now be used. The negotiator must judge whether such a shift in strategy will succeed or jeopardize the entire matter.

In discussing this strategy, it is assumed that the party choosing it is doing so not because it has reached its bottom-line limit of authority, but because it believes that it can force the other side to accept its terms. That is entirely different from a party which has reached its bottom line by refusing to yield anything further because it believes that no agreement would be preferable to more concessions.

Except for the distinction concerning the timing of the strategy, the considerations discussed with respect to the no-concessions strategy also apply to the no-further-concessions strategy.

Countering Tips for the No-Further-Concessions Strategy

The countermeasures to this strategy are the same as those for its parent, the no-concessions strategy. These countermeasures include appealing to a higher level of authority to change the party's position; ignoring the strategy and proceeding as if concessions are possible; presenting cost-saving measures that justify a concession; offering less or demanding more to effectively alter the price; terminating the negotiating session; disclosing new information; creating facts; creating win-win proposals; inserting new issues; creating deadlock or surprise; and entering into litigation.

Strategy 3: Making Only Deadlock-Breaking Concessions

Key Concept 31

A strategy of making only deadlock-breaking concessions is okay when the risk of nonagreement is acceptable.

A **deadlock** is an impasse or standstill, a state of inaction resulting from the opposition of equally powerful uncompromising parties. The strategy of making a concession only to break a deadlock is the next toughest strategy after the no-concessions strategy. This strategy constitutes a form of brinksmanship. Issues are pushed to the point of deadlock, which occurs when the other party is actually or virtually ready to cease negotiating.

This strategy generates an atmosphere of tension and difficulty. In response to it, the other party may cease negotiating for a number of reasons. For instance, it may come to believe that a satisfactory agreement cannot be reached due to the opponent's intransigent attitude. The other party may also become too tired or too offended by the strategy to proceed further. Under these conditions, the other party may not even respond to last-minute concessions aimed at reviving the negotiation.

Therefore, the decision to use the deadlock-breaking concessions strategy should be made with the same high degree of caution used to decide on the no-concessions strategies. This strategy may necessitate employing the same sensitive methods described for making the no-concessions strategies more palatable to the other side.

Goals Compatibility

A strategy of compromising only to break a deadlock is potentially viable for aggressive, competitive, or self-centered goals. In contrast, cooperative goals require a more open, less tense process aimed at obtaining a mutually beneficial outcome. Also, this strategy generally is inappropriate for defensive goals because of the high need to reach an agreement that defensive goals usually involve.

Strategy 4: High Realistic Expectations With Small Systematic Concessions (HRESSC)

Key Concept 32

The most generally useful negotiating strategy is high realistic expectations with small systematic concessions (HRESSC).

Successful strategy generally involves making initial offers that are well distanced from one's bottom line, and in keeping concessions few, small, and reciprocal. Concessions should also be rationalized or justified on some basis other than the mere pursuit of agreement.

HRESSC refers to the strategy of combining high, realistic expectations with small, systematic concessions. Thus, the strategy entails a planned approach both to the objectives of the negotiation and to the compromises that may be employed to reach those objectives. As a general rule, it is the strategy which achieves the best results. That does *not* mean that HRESSC is always the best strategy (that depends on the situation); however, it is generally the most useful strategy.

The HRESSC strategy requires assessing the objective value of the matters at hand in the negotiation. This is necessary to properly formulate high, but realistic expectations. The assessment is of whatever is at stake in the negotiation, for example, the value of the assets that are available in a transaction.

The Expectations Component of HRESSC

How High Is High? How Realistic Is Realistic?   High realistic expectations mean that the negotiator has neither undervalued his or her own side's position, thereby losing a feasible opportunity, nor overvalued it so unrealistically so as to block any chance for an acceptable, but unspectacular agreement. By avoiding those pitfalls, the opening position is established sufficiently high that it allows for a real opportunity to make a highly favorable settlement. However, the opening position is not set so high that the other negotiator feels that an agreement is impossible. If the opening position is miscalculated so that it reflects a high but unrealistic expectation, the negotiator may be placed in the unfortunate position of having to make a large concession, thereby essentially restarting the HRESSC strategy. Choosing and executing the right opening position is examined in further detail in Chapters 11 and 12.

The Concessions Component of HRESSC

With respect to possible concessions, the HRESSC strategy has three components. These are:

1. The size of the concessions

2. The use of apparent concessions which actually involve no cost to the negotiator's side

3. The advance planning of concessions

How Small Is Small?   As its name indicates, the strategy involves making small compromises. A small concession is a relative concept. A $500 negotiation may involve $25 to $50 concessions. For a $10,000 negotiation, $250 to $500 concessions are relatively small. In contrast, for a $10 million negotiation, a $500 concession would be laughable.

What is relatively small depends on two factors. First, it must be considered in light of the range of value of that which is being negotiated (say, dollars) at the time when the negotiation begins. Second, this relativity must be evaluated in terms of the aggregate amount involved in the negotiation itself. That aspect of the evaluation normally involves both objective and subjective considerations of what the matter is worth. This strategy can be utilized for monetary or nonmonetary negotiations. When money is not directly involved, often the subjective evaluation of the relative size of the concession becomes increasingly important because adequate objective measurements either do not exist or are more open to question and disagreement.

Why Keeping Concessions Small Is Important.   Small concessions are important because they tend to prevent missed opportunities to reach an optimal settlement. An **optimal settlement** is the most favorable point at which an agreement with the other side can be formulated. If large concessions are made, it is difficult to know whether the agreement could have been reached at some point between the last rejected offer and the large concession which finally led to resolution. With small concessions, relatively little has been relinquished in that last concession before the agreement was reached.

Giving a large last concession creates the distinct possibility that a great deal more was given away than was necessary. Similarly, multiple concessions should not be made so rapidly that collectively they in fact become a large concession. Speed is also a relative term. If the negotiator receives desired reciprocal concessions, then speed is less significant since the goal has been reached. However, when small concessions are made in rapid succession without receiving desired concessions in return, they can, once again, amount to a large concession. Small concessions also may reduce the other party's expectations. They may create or reinforce an impression that the negotiator is not willing to agree to substantial concessions.

Often, negotiators only make small concessions as they near the boundaries of their authority, perhaps after having already made very large ones. Although this can be appropriate, it is a mistake to just follow a pattern of reducing the size of concessions as one nears the limits of one's authority. To do so makes the negotiation far too predictable.

Small concessions are an integral part of the HRESSC strategy. With other strategies, larger concessions can be used where small concessions are inappropriate or clearly useless. Note, however, that the use of small concessions can also be a tactic for other strategies. Whenever possible the negotiator using the HRESSC strategy (with its systematic concessions) seeks to make concessions which apparently concede something, but, in fact, relinquish nothing or little of value. Like small concessions, systematic no- or low-cost concessions are used to avoid missing opportunities for an optimal settlement.

Why Keeping Concessions Systematic Is Important.   The term "systematic" describes the procedure of systematically exhausting a series of concessions of the same cost level before moving to concessions of the next greater cost level. The alternative concessions at the same cost level constitute the system:

Cost level	Cost to own side	Concession	Concession	Concession
1	$10,000	A	B	C
2	$20,000	D	E	F

To make systematic concessions, the negotiator first plans alternative concessions at the same cost level. (Concessions A, B, and C at Level 1 and D, E, and F at Level 2.) In this negotiation, concession A is offered first. If rejected, then alternative concession B is tried, followed by C. Only after trying and failing with alternative concessions A, B, and C at Level 1 does the negotiator begin offering any concessions at Level 2. Level 2 concessions (D, E, and F) are systematically explored to determine whether any one of them will bring about an agreement before the negotiator offers concessions from a next higher cost level.

Case in Point 3-3_____

A buyer first offers to pay $25,000 to the seller. Several concessions and 45 minutes later, the buyer increases the offer to $42,000. The seller rejects that offer and makes a counterproposal of $50,000. The buyer reasonably estimates that she can use the

$42,000 previously offered to generate payments totaling $50,000 if the payments are made over a 2-year payment period. Accordingly, the buyer concedes and accepts the $50,000 price on the condition that the payments can be spread out over 2 years. Assuming that the price concession with payments over time still has greater value to the seller than the immediate payment of $42,000, the buyer has proposed a concession at no immediate cost to herself, which has enough value to the other party to obtain a satisfactory agreement. The buyer negotiated systematically in that after trying a series of offers, all of which the seller rejected, the buyer was able to negotiate for a second-level offer without having to agree to pay the full $50,000.

Advance Planning of Concessions

The other part of the concept of systematic concessions is that, prior to the negotiation, the negotiator plans the compromises that might be offered at different points in the negotiation. Both the concessions themselves and the timing or circumstances under which they will be offered are anticipated. While this approach is not independent of the other party's actions, neither does it merely react to those actions. Rather, it provides flexibility to take the initiative or react depending on what actually occurs during the negotiation. Advance planning is likely to help maximize one's results and minimize the pressure to merely respond to the other negotiator's actions. This approach helps a negotiator to move in the direction he or she prefers.

Countering Tips for the HRESSC Strategy

Countermeasures include using one's own HRESSC strategy against that of the other party. Other countermeasures include the no-concessions, no-further-concessions, deadlock-breaking-only concessions, and problem-solving strategies.

Goals Compatibility

The HRESSC strategy is very useful for competitive, aggressive, self-centered, or defensive goals. It also can be used when the major goal is a cooperative one, to the extent that some competitive elements are also part of that cooperative goal. Its basic usefulness is as a means of probing and testing the other party's reactions to determine an optimal settlement point.

Strategy 5: Concede First

> ## Key Concept 33
>
> *Conceding first is a viable strategy if you do not concede too much and if it will create momentum, enabling you to later demand a reciprocal concession without appearing weak.*

As the name implies, the concede-first strategy consists of making the first concession. Making the first concession may disarm the other party, reduce tension, create goodwill, and generate an atmosphere of movement and compromise. In addition, making the first concession allows one to later demand a reciprocal concession in the spirit of fair play. It is the making of the concession without a simultaneous or as soon as possible demand of something in return that distinguishes this tactic from other concession-based tactics, such as bargaining.

The following model statement shows how a negotiator, after making the first concession, can later use the initiative to try to gain reciprocation:

> "You know, you really cannot expect us to concede anything else. We made an important concession at the outset of this meeting and you still have not given us anything significant in return. At this point, you are ahead; and it isn't fair to expect more from us. We are willing to be flexible, but only if you demonstrate flexibility as well."

The name "concede first" might be construed to imply that this strategy is limited to the opening stages of the negotiation. However, this strategy also can be effectively used at the opening stage of negotiating a particular issue within the overall negotiation. Due to its inherently limited nature, though, it must be used in conjunction with one or more other strategies.

Anticipating and Overcoming Problems That Could Arise When Conceding First

If the concede-first strategy is adopted, the concession must have some value to the party that is receiving it. From the perspective of the party making the initial concession, it must not have so much value that it seriously undermines that party's subsequent bargaining position. Although the initial concession must cause the other party to feel as though it has received something worthwhile, it must not be so large as to remove important bargaining chips from the giver's arsenal. Too large a concession adversely affects the giver's ability to maneuver during the remainder of the negotiation. Negotiators never want to be in the position of having to withdraw an offer in order to continue negotiating.

It can be difficult and sometimes impossible to successfully withdraw a concession without sabotaging the entire negotiation. To many negotiators, once concessions are given, they can not be altered. Therefore, this first concession must be planned and structured so that it will not be necessary to attempt to withdraw it later, even if the other side subsequently refuses to make a reciprocal concession.

Furthermore, the concede-first strategy, particularly if the first concession is too large, can have seriously detrimental, unintended effects for the conceding party. The recipient may perceive this first concession as a sign of weakness. Such a perception can lead the other party to raise its expectations of what it can obtain, and to consequently harden its position. Therefore, caution should be exercised before deciding to implement a concede-first strategy.

The danger of backfiring can be tempered by the mode of presentation. Not only the timing and the size of the initial concession, but also the manner in which it is made can affect how the other party perceives and reacts to it. Certainly, the party giving the concession should appear confident and avoid the appearance of weakness. Giving an explicit explanation for the concession is an additional method of minimizing the possibility that the concession will be misunderstood.

When and When Not to Use the Concede-First Strategy

A corollary to the principle of avoiding the perception of being weak is that the concede-first strategy should not be chosen if one actually is operating from a position of weakness. Doing so might only increase the other side's knowledge or perception of that weakness. Furthermore, the strategy relinquishes a bargaining chip that a weak party cannot afford to give away without obtaining a specific, agreed, reciprocal concession in return.

The concede-first strategy also can be used in those rare circumstances when any real negotiation may lead the other party to discover information that will harm the negotiator's client. In this case, it might be more important to keep the information confidential than to secure a concession.

Case in Point 3-4_____

An opportunity exists to negotiate an issue of tax liability with the I.R.S. There is a significant danger, however, that to do so will lead the I.R.S. to discover information that will be even more costly for the client. Accordingly, the decision is made to concede first, seeking a quick resolution before the other issues are uncovered.

The key questions in deciding on this strategy are whether, in the specific negotiating situation and given the particular other negotiator and other party, the concede-first strategy will:

1. Reduce tension, create an atmosphere conducive to reaching an agreement, and allow one to demand a reciprocal concession.

2. Cause the other party to infer that it is in a position to increase or harden its demands or its aspirations. (Regardless of whether or not this inference is correct, it is, of course, totally counterproductive for the party making the concession. Once made, the inference becomes the reality for the other party and can be extremely difficult to change.)

It is necessary to focus closely on the other party and its negotiator because the effect of the concede-first strategy is so dependent on their perception of it. If they are taking a hard, competitive approach, then the concession is likely to be seen as weakness. Early signs of this perception from the other side include their taking an extreme initial position or the use of high-pressure, emotional tactics, such as acting outraged. Those behaviors should be viewed as warning signs not to employ the concede-first strategy.

Countering Tips for the Concede-First Strategy

A danger of the concede-first strategy is that the concession will be accepted by one who refuses to acknowledge that reciprocity is appropriate or required. Accordingly, a refusal to reciprocate is a countermeasure to the concede-first strategy when it can be done without adversely affecting the ultimate outcome of the negotiation. No countermeasure should be employed when the concede-first strategy allows the other party to create movement in their desired direction. Then, the concede-first strategy should not be resisted by the other party, but rather used to pursue its own ends.

Goals Compatibility

The concede-first strategy is used far less often than the HRESSC or problem-solving strategies. It can be used effectively to achieve competitive, cooperative, self-centered, or defensive goals, depending on the specific context of the negotiation. Rarely, if ever, can it be utilized for aggressive client goals where the other party is a target to be injured by the aggression. If, however, the target of the aggressive goal is a third party and the other party in the negotiation is the means to achieve that goal, then the strategy can be useful.

Case in Point 3-5

A condominium association has been negotiating with unit owners who have altered their units without the required approval. One of these alterations involved the placement of security shutters on outer windows. Knowing how important and emotional the issue of security can be, especially among those who have been victims of crime, the association decides to use this issue to establish trust and good relations with the owners. In this way, it hopes to be able to later demand reciprocal concessions on the remaining issues with the concede-first strategy.

Strategy 6: Problem Solving

Key Concept 34

Problem solving is a strategy for creating a procedural agreement to solve a common problem that has been identified.

Generally speaking, problem solving is the second most useful strategy after HRESSC. It is conceptually quite different from the concession-based strategies which center on either relinquishing or refusing to relinquish something of value.

The Four-Step Problem-Solving Process

Unlike concession-based strategies, **problem solving** focuses on creating a procedural agreement that the negotiators will work together to discover and identify problems that are preventing agreement, and to determine whether any common interests can be used to resolve those problems. Common interests are those which both parties have apart from their individual needs. The parties' separate needs often are disclosed in the process of establishing the boundaries of the common interests.

After agreeing to work together and identifying negotiation problems, the negotiators discuss the matter further to determine common interests. The negotiators then proceed to the last, and most crucial step in the problem-solving process: the discovery of fair, mutually beneficial solutions to problems. When problem solving is successful, both sides feel that they have won. To summarize, the operative steps are:

1. A procedural agreement to use problem solving.

2. Identification of the problems preventing agreement.

3. Determination of any common interests and limiting separate needs.

4. Discussion to discover fair, mutually beneficial solutions.

Problem solving is described in game-theory terminology as a win-win strategy. For purposes here, however, the phrase "win-win" will be used to denote a *tactic* employed as a unilateral endeavor by a single negotiator. In contrast, the phrase "problem solving" is used to denote a *strategy* that is a joint endeavor of the negotiators.

Case in Point 3-6_____

A manufacturer and a dealer were engaged in a dispute about a service. They agreed, in effect, to problem solve, and discussed that the service was covered by their contract in only general terms and thus subject to varying interpretations. The two parties agreed that it would be to their respective advantages to clarify the general terms of the contract. Indeed, both sides agreed that the generality of the language was the very problem that had interfered with their ability, from time to time, to agree on an appropriate business arrangement. Each outlined certain needs. In discussing their common problem, the parties then agreed that the manufacturer could terminate the dealer if certain specific acts occurred (which they then clearly listed in the contract). The manufacturer also retained the right to terminate under other provisions of the agreement that were already established. They agreed as well to treat past disputes as moot misunderstandings.

Laying the Essential Foundations for
the Problem-Solving Strategy

In order for problem solving to be a useful strategy, certain conditions must exist:

1. There must be an agreement by the parties and negotiators to work together to identify the problems preventing agreement, and to formulate a mutually advantageous solution.

2. To ensure good faith, the parties must have a mutual interest in solving the particular problems in the same way.

3. The negotiators must identify the same problems and agree on how to define them.

4. Parties and negotiators must realize that a win-win solution is possible and that problems will not be solved simply by one side yielding to the other. Instead, the participants will strive to create a previously unconsidered, mutually beneficial solution.

The first three conditions may exist at the start of a particular negotiation situation, or they may require development through reasoning, persuasion, negotiation, or sensitivity to the other party's real needs. Sensitivity to others is probably the most important aspect of this problem-solving strategy since it can be successful only when the other party's real needs are satisfied. Of course, one's own needs must also be satisfied by the same agreement.

Achieving a Clear Distinction
Between Objectives and Needs

Needs, or interests, provide the motivation for a party to seek something in the negotiation. Objectives are those goals which the party says it desires in order to meet its needs or interests. Since objectives are not needs or interests, parties engaged in problem solving must move beyond stated objectives to discuss real needs and interests. In this way, the negotiators seek to identify both their common interests and nonconflicting separate interests, without losing sight of the conflicting interests that need to be addressed. Thus, problem solving focuses more on interests and needs than on negotiating positions.

The negotiator must recognize that the decision makers on both sides may place different values on the matters that can be conceded, so that the possibility of an agreement is increased by trading concessions across issues. By determining these different values, the problem-solving strategy helps identify both sides' needs. In this sense, problem solving begins by jointly attempting to determine the actual needs of each side.

Maintaining Attitudes of Empathy and Cooperativeness

In adopting a problem-solving strategy, negotiators should appear cooperative and empathetic to help build the trust needed to solve problems in good faith. A cooperative or empathetic attitude may also help defuse an initially competitive, emotional, or antagonistic attitude on the part of the other party or negotiator. Attitudinal problems with the people involved in the negotiation must not be confused with the substantive problems at issue. They must be handled separately. A cooperative and empathetic demeanor may also help negotiations when the other party's psychological needs include the manner in which the negotiation is conducted.

One method for engaging the other negotiator in a problem-solving effort is to raise the problem in the form of a question or a request for suggestions. The question or request may be either direct or implicit. The following model statement suggests one way to engage another negotiator in problem solving.

> "I noticed a hole in our proposal at this point regarding how to cover your purchaser's ability to pay in the future, especially if there are changes in her practice. I really don't know how to cover this. We could have an escrow, but that may not be a good idea. Do you have any suggestions?"

The Related Roles of Creativity and Patience in Problem Solving

Problem solving often requires a degree of creativity with respect to both the way in which the problem is perceived and in the way mutually beneficial solutions are created. Often, the negotiation must be reexamined to find the issue that is causing the impasse, rather than to continue discussing the issues as they have been previously articulated. Patience and perseverance may be needed, since the problem-solving process may be slow.

Properly Defining the Problems.   The definition of the problem is important. It should be as simple and direct as possible to facilitate focusing on a specific direction for seeking solutions. To the extent possible, the definition also should depersonalize the problem. This can alleviate the danger that the negotiators or the parties will be too judgmental, or take matters too personally. Once the problem is defined, unless an acceptable solution can be presented in the initial discussion that follows, a solution may be uncovered by identifying each obstacle impeding settlement as exactly as possible.

Keeping the Focus on Mutual Interests. Avoid focusing on adverse or potentially undesirable outside forces. Instead, concentrate attention on areas of mutual interest. Outside forces to avoid include:

1. Government action.

2. A jury or a judge deciding the facts at trial so that one side wins totally while the other side loses totally.

3. A competitor gaining an advantage.

4. The expiration of a financing commitment.

Broadening the Pie and Trading Concessions Across Issues. Problem solving can involve devising some means to broaden the pie so that it is no longer the same fixed amount which must be divided. In this way, a zero-sum, win-lose game is converted to a win-win or positive-sum game. Unlike concession-oriented strategies, the problem-solving strategy allows a solution which may involve trading concessions. Typically, however, this would consist of exchanging concessions on issues that have differing value to the parties so that both sides feel they are gaining something. This type of exchange is greatly facilitated whenever one or both of the concessions can be given at no cost to the party providing it. At other times, however, a competitive element within an issue will necessitate some competitive bargaining.

Both to expand the pie and to find concessions that the parties value differently and are willing to exchange, it may be useful to consider the distribution of resources in terms of:

What will be distributed

When it will be distributed

By whom it will be distributed

How it will be distributed

How much will be distributed

Case in Point 3-7_____

The local hockey team and figure skating associations are negotiating with each other over the use of the community ice rink. Each feels that its current ice time is inadequate. They consider the resource distribution questions:

What: ice time

When: year round

By whom: the rink director

How: the same, current equal hours unless the associations agree otherwise

How much: 17 hours a day; 50 hours a week

The associations discover that hockey needs far less ice time in the spring and summer, but that the figure skaters' needs do not decrease as much. The hockey associations trade to get more winter hours but less total hours, when its unmet needs are greatest. The figure skaters wind up with more hours overall, allowing them to expand their program.

Generating an Array of Options

Attempts at problem solving may benefit from generating a variety of options before reaching a decision on a course of action. Participants are encouraged to raise suggestions, not to fix solutions. Suggestions are made with an acknowledgment by all parties that someone else may later devise a better suggestion.

Brainstorming.   Of course, consistent with the strategy's philosophy, these suggested options should be devised with a view toward mutual gain. Either brainstorming, perhaps with the other side, or obtaining different perspectives from different experts or other sources, may be helpful. Brainstorming for problem solving is a process which requires that the participants:

1. Speak spontaneously or think out loud (as long as it is relevant and constructive).
2. Refrain from evaluating or criticizing the statements of others until after all initial ideas are elicited.
3. Be willing to repeat one's ideas if others want to hear them again.
4. Build on the suggestions of others by adding to or modifying them.
5. Persist in the effort even if there is a prolonged silence.

Additional Practices Which Aid Problem Solving

Seeking to focus on principles which can then provide a guide for the specifics of an agreement also may be beneficial. It is not easy to agree that a specific, concrete resolution is fair. Useful principles to determine fairness are needed; however, these can be difficult to derive. Principles need to constitute objective criteria for evaluating a resolution of the issues. When the solution to the problem involves agreement on a standard or a formula that ultimately will be used to resolve the issue, the standard or formula should entail criteria as specific as possible. This specificity helps to avert future disagreement in determining the resolution.

In seeking solutions, one can look to precedent and community practice. However, the problem-solving negotiator should be wary of allowing precedent or community practice to repress creativity and innovation. This is particularly true where precedent and community practice were themselves the product of a prior negotiation, the results of which neither fully solve the problem in question nor totally satisfy the goals for this negotiation. Thus, depending on the particular circumstances, precedent and common practices should not be automatically accepted, but instead should be treated as starting points for thought.

Creative-Solution Scenarios: Three Successes

The following series of examples illustrate productive problem-solving efforts. They also demonstrate the necessity of a cooperative atmosphere.

Scenario 1: Ending a New Venture Without Undervaluing Shares. Two businessmen plan to launch a new venture as equal owners. The two are quite enthusiastic about this apparently lucrative opportunity. After having agreed on what they had considered the major issues, they stall on how to value their respective interests should a future disagreement prompt one to buy out the other. However, they do agree that they are firmly committed to proceeding with the deal, and that it is essential that they determine a way to value their shares in case of a buyout. One then suggests that, if they cannot agree on the value of their respective shares at the time of a management deadlock, each party should have the right to offer the entire business for sale to an outsider. The party which procures an acceptable offer from an outsider would then have to allow the other party an opportunity to "match" the outsider's offer by paying an amount equal to one-half of it for the first party's one-half interest. If the offer was not so matched, the business would be sold to the outsider and the proceeds would be split equally between the two owners. They agree that this method avoids the undervaluing that could arise from trying to sell one-half of a potential deadlock, or from a statutorily forced dissolution sale.

Scenario 2: Building Trust by Volunteering to Be Penalized on Failure to Uphold a Deal. The seller and the purchaser of a piece of commercial real estate property have agreed on the price of the property and on other economic terms. The seller occupies a portion of the location, and will be moving out. The purchaser needs to have its own store in the property by a certain date, so it is extremely important that the seller vacate the premises on time. The seller assures the purchaser that it will move out on time and explains the economic reasons which strongly motivate it to do so. The seller also explains the circumstances which constrain any earlier move. The buyer remains quite concerned about the timing of the move and is reluctant to proceed. The seller then offers to add a Draconian penalty clause for any late move, except due to acts of God. The seller is confident that the penalty clause will never need to be invoked. The purchaser now is satisfied and signs the contract. This method of assuaging the buyer's fears does not involve any time or expense to the seller.

Scenario 3: Creative Use of the "Most-Favored" Technique. A purchaser of goods is unwilling to enter into a long-term agreement without significantly higher discounts than those currently available. The requested discounts far exceed those which the seller is willing to consider. The parties argue back and forth about the general advantages and disadvantages of a long-term contract, as well as about the price trends each of them foresees over the long-run. Unable to find a common figure or a mathematical formula, an impasse develops. They decide to try to explore both their feelings about the discount and the methods they should use to determine it. During the ensuing discussion, the seller learns that the buyer's real concern is that she does not want to have some competitor later receive a lower price through a more favorable discount. This is not a meaningful concern for the seller in light of the other advantages provided by a long-term contract. Thus, the seller does not object to adjusting the discount in the future should such a situation arise. Accordingly, the seller solves the problem by offering the purchaser a "most-favored nation" clause, under which the buyer is entitled to receive discount terms as favorable as those given to any other buyer in the future during the term of the contract.

In each of the foregoing illustrations, the four necessary conditions for the use of the problem-solving strategy were present (see page 59).

If the appropriate conditions do not exist, negotiators cannot productively engage in problem solving. The following scenarios demonstrate
some of the problems that can arise when the appropriate negotiation
conditions are not satisfied. Each scenario is followed by an analysis of
the situation to discover what the problems are, and how they might be
solved.

Abortive Problem-Solving Scenarios

Scenario 4: Finding No Common Ground.   A manufacturer (M) and a
vending company (V) have a contractual dispute.

> v: "We basically agree that you violated the contract, but we can't seem to
> agree on an amount to settle. That's the problem."
> m: "That *is* the problem. You want too much to settle this."
> v: "Oh, no. You just aren't willing to pay enough."

Analysis. This is *not* an example of a problem-solving strategy. The
negotiators agree on a defined "problem" all right, but there is no attempt to identify common interests or to work together to formulate a
mutually beneficial solution. An approach under which both parties
"win" by having their vital interests protected could lead directly to an
agreed settlement figure, or to a formula or method through which an
agreeable settlement could be determined. Instead, there is a fight over
the monetary amount of the settlement, so that only one party will benefit (that is, win) at the expense of the other party.

Scenario 5: Facing Dangers in Problem-Solving Negotiations.   The
CEO of a company calls in two of his department managers. He informs
them that cuts are being made in the company and that their departments have overlapping functions. The CEO then directs that each determine how to eliminate the overlap between their departments and
how to implement a personnel reduction of at least 20 percent. The two
managers negotiate with the CEO in a cooperative, problem-solving way
regarding the required reduction. The CEO relents to the extent that
the minimum reduction in force will be 15 percent. The two managers
then agree to cooperate with each other and to meet again with the
CEO in two weeks.

Two weeks pass. At the meeting, one of the managers presents a plan
for his department that follows the original, cooperative, problem-
solving approach. He proposes eliminating 17 percent of his department's employees. The other manager, however, views the situation differently. She sees it as a competitive one in which her power and
responsibility are threatened. From her perspective, this is an issue of

protecting her turf. She devises quite a different proposal. Her recommendation is accompanied by a detailed cost-benefit analysis. She proposed that, because of economic efficiencies, her department only be cut 5 percent while the other department be cut by 30 percent.

Analysis. This illustrates the dangers and the problems that can arise when needs and interests clash rather than coincide during problem-solving negotiations. It also reflects the potential danger of being the one to rely on problem solving if the other party will not participate in good faith. In this situation, one of the managers is motivated by her own aggressive, competitive, self-centered, and defensive goals. The other manager and the CEO will have to adjust their strategies in accordance. The situation has become quite different than it was at the outset.

Settling for the Middle Ground
Scenario 6: Seeking Any Kind of Common Ground

v: "You won't pay as much as this is worth, given our losses as we documented them to you."

m: "We've narrowed the difference a great deal. We both will benefit by saving considerable expense if we can resolve this without a lawsuit."

v: "I can agree with that."

m: "As I see it, we each have a really strong opinion on the value of the case, and the problem is that we can't find a way to resolve the difference that remains."

v: "I'll agree with that as well. Where are you headed since you obviously have something in mind?"

m: "If that's the problem and we agree that both of us would benefit from a prompt resolution without further expense, could we consider either of two solutions? First, do we agree that we have an honest difference of opinion based on each of our experiences with these matters?"

v: "That's fair."

m: "Then we should split the difference, since, while either of us may be right, it's equally likely that the right number lies in between each of our figures."

v: "Before I consider that, what is your other proposal?"

m: "We could do an abbreviated form of alternative dispute resolution just on the remaining difference. I suggest a short binding arbitration. Each of our two present positions would form the outer parameters for any decision. That way any decision will resolve this at your figure, my figure, or somewhere in between."

Analysis. Here, both parties had the defensive goal of wanting to avoid substantial and perhaps unnecessary litigation expenses. Their attitude was partially cooperative, rather than strictly competitive. Another way that the discussion in the breach of contract case could proceed is shown in Scenario 7.

Scenario 7: Avoiding the Pitfall of Linear Thinking

V: "You won't pay as much as this is worth. Let's get serious, settle this, and give us a check."

M: "That's out of the question at the numbers you're talking about."

V: "What's the real problem? Do we disagree that much on the amount?"

M: "It's less a disagreement on the amount than the economic realities. The numbers that you're talking about present a serious, if not impossible, cashflow issue. The amount is somewhat too high as well, but cashflow is the major problem."

V: "I can work with you on that. Of course, if we accommodate you with some sort of reasonable time payment plan, there will have to be an interest factor."

Analysis. Here, again, there was a consideration of more than just the narrow issue of the amount of money to be paid. Linear thinking about the amount was expanded to allow for new possibilities. Furthermore, a degree of cooperation was present. Needs and interests were disclosed by introducing the cashflow problem and the payment plan issue. The parties' goals, although still competitive, also became self-centered and cooperative. Each side began to see a way to maximize its own results without having to be entirely competitive since, at least in part, the disclosed needs and interests did not conflict.

Scenario 8: Using Problem Solving for Aggressive Goals. Problem solving also can play a role in aggressive goals, at least if the aggression is directed toward a third party, not toward the other party in the negotiation.

V: "You won't pay as much as this case is worth."

M: "We think that your figure is too high."

V: "Perhaps there is another way that would allow me to settle for a smaller amount."

M: "What do you have in mind?"

V: "Well, your contract for raw materials with our competitor, X Corporation, is about to expire. If you contracted with our subsidiary instead of with them—on the right terms, of course—we could come down significantly on a settlement figure in this case."

M: "Let's discuss some specifics."

Analysis. Here, one party saw an opportunity to achieve an aggressive goal, cutting into the business of a competitor. At the same time, the other party had an opportunity to save money on the settlement by a contract that might not be costlier than one it would enter anyway.

Countering Tips for the Problem-Solving Strategy

The primary countermeasures to problem solving are:

1. Refusing to engage in it.
2. Secretly maintaining win-lose solutions, while articulating them with credible rationales that make them appear to be mutually beneficial, win-win resolutions.

Goals Compatibility

The problem-solving strategy is most often associated with cooperative goals, since both involve situations in which resolving the problem creates a mutually beneficial, win-win outcome. Similarly, just as cooperative goals are associated with long-term, trusting, and mutually beneficial relationships, so is the use of problem solving.

To the extent that only a strictly competitive goal is at issue, problem solving often does not provide a useful approach, since a competitive goal seeks to take as much as possible from the other party and does not seek a win-win outcome. This assumes, though, that the negotiation is truly a zero-sum game with only competitive issues. Typically in such instances, the issue is the payment of money, which the parties value in a similar way.

A competitive goal, however, can have problem-solving aspects. While acquisitions and mergers generally involve competitive goals, problem solving sometimes can be necessary because of uncertainty about the future of the newly structured entity. The negotiation may require sharing otherwise confidential information or accepting payments based on contingencies.

Aggressive, self-centered, or defensive goals may allow for the use of the problem-solving strategy. However, a cooperative element must also be present. Thus, problem solving could be appropriate for the same breach of contract case in Scenario 4 if the parties and their negotiators were willing to work together to achieve common goals as well as their competitive goal of wanting the most favorable (highest or lowest) settlement.

Strategy 7: Goals Other Than to Reach Agreement

Key Concept 35

Reaching agreement is not necessarily the end purpose of all negotiating goals and strategies.

Normally, parties negotiate in a genuine attempt to reach an agreement. They want to make a contract, resolve a dispute, create a partnership, and so on. At times, however, a party may negotiate with a purpose in mind other than reaching an agreement. Negotiations that are not directed toward final agreements might well be disingenuous, distorted, or an exercise in gamesmanship. This type of engagement may occur either initially or at any other time during the negotiation.

This strategy can be used to achieve any type of goal. If used with a cooperative goal, however, great care must be taken to avoid poisoning the relationship between the parties. If one is discovered negotiating for purposes other than to reach agreement, especially in an otherwise cooperative negotiation, the party using this strategy may be perceived as disingenuous, manipulative, or in some other highly unfavorable way. This perception could make further negotiations either extremely difficult or impossible.

A Strategy of Delay

One possible reason to negotiate without seeking an agreement is to **delay.** A delay through negotiation occurs when participants intentionally stall during the proceeding in order to gain some kind of advantage. Delay may be necessary to allow other events to develop, or to avoid the consequences that will follow a breakdown in the negotiation. With these possibilities in mind, one party may try to cause a delay by negotiating without any intention of moving forward or of making a good faith effort.

Case in Point 3-8: Allowing Other Events to Develop

An investor was negotiating the formation of a limited partnership. In reality, however, the investor wanted to stall any decision concerning whether to proceed with a new partnership until reports arrived regarding an alternative investment opportunity. The investor knew that he was financially incapable of investing in both opportunities. By appearing to negotiate, the investor hoped to prevent the potential partner from seeking to replace him with other investors until he could decide which opportunity was preferable.

Case in Point 3-9: Avoiding the Consequences of a Breakdown in the Negotiation

A management negotiating team believed that the union would strike rather than accept the company's best offer. The team also believed that after several weeks of a strike, the union would soften its position. The company's business was such that it experienced significant seasonal sales fluctuations. In addition, management feared that certain extremists in the union would engage in sabotage if the company attempted to speed up production to stockpile goods in anticipation of a strike. Weighing these factors, the management negotiating team adopted a strategy of delay. Accordingly, it proceeded to negotiate in a manner which confused and prolonged the process until a slower sales period.

Delay can create costs. For instance, environmentalists may discourage a developer through protracted litigation. If the developer cannot build on its property, not only is it losing money from paying to maintain it, but also from receiving return on its investment. In time, the developer may decide to abandon the project because it has become too expensive. Through delay, the environmentalists could convince the developer to turn the property into a park, which will be purchased by the city. The delay gives the environmentalists a stronger position from which to continue the negotiations. As the developer loses money, it becomes more willing to listen to alternative ideas.

Negotiating as an Exercise in Information Gathering

Another use of the delay strategy is to gain valuable information, for example, about an actual or potential competitor, market prices, or new possible terms. Again, there is no intention of reaching an agreement. Rather, the aim is to obtain information which otherwise would not be available. For example, if a company does not want to make further concessions in its negotiations until it is able to learn the terms that are to be offered by a competitor, then it may use delay in order to gain time to engage in industrial intelligence gathering. Then, the company will make concessions to bring its offer just below that of the competitor.

Negotiating as a Forum for Expressing Views

The strategy of acting for purposes other than agreement also encompasses actions that really seek to influence a participant in the negotiation, very often the negotiator's own client. Generally speaking, **influence** refers to the act or power of producing an effect in someone or in some situation without the direct and clear exertion of force or authority. Actions may be taken to impress the client or to vent feelings which the client wants expressed in the negotiation. Such posturing may include justifications of the client's position, statements with inflammatory rhetoric, the use of personal characterizations, debate, and taking extreme positions. By expressing the client's feelings for him or her, the negotiator makes the client feel a sense of unity and appreciation for the negotiator.

Case in Point 3-10: Influence and an Organized Labor Negotiation_____

A labor negotiation has begun with the union's representative haranguing management over perceived wrongs which may not even be negotiable. The labor negotiator complains about management's general attitude. The purpose of that behavior is not to influence or inform management regarding the union's actual grievances. Rather, the negotiator seeks to impress the union's membership (that is, the client), with her understanding of the membership's feelings, and with her willingness to express those feelings in a powerful and aggressive manner. By doing so, the negotiator hopes to enhance her credibility with the membership. Also, she wants to acquire a greater degree of influence when actual issues are submitted later for a decision. Enhanced credibility can be a crucial factor in obtaining approval of provisions that would be unacceptable to a membership which had doubts about the effectiveness of their negotiator. Similarly, if the membership is angry or frustrated, a vivid expression of those feelings at the outset of the negotiation can help defuse them. Tempering emotions can make it easier to have a more reasonable discussion within the membership group than could otherwise occur. Management and other negotiators sometimes use similar approaches with their constituencies.

Influence can also be applied to business situations or to other kinds of clients. For this reason, the presence or absence of clients at the negotiation is an important consideration. Their presence may impede the negotiation by causing the negotiator to act differently in order to favorably influence or impress the client. There are times, however, when a strategy to influence one's own client is appropriate and perhaps even necessary in order ultimately to be able to obtain authorization for a reasonable agreement.

Caution: Engaging in this strategy, even if it successfully impresses the client, is not in the client's best interest if it leads to a failure of the negotiation process. Failure can occur if the negotiator's attempts to impress his or her client so offend or frustrate the other negotiator that the process breaks down.

Negotiating to Influence a Third Party

A negotiator might also endeavor to influence **third parties.** Third parties are parties or entities not directly involved in a negotiation, but who can nevertheless bring power to bear on the outcome. One type of setting in which this occurs is a business, labor, or governmental negotiation in which the parties want either to use or to avoid public pressure. In this instance, the public is considered the third party. Strategies are developed to influence the public's perception of both the negotiation and of the parties themselves. Rather than acting to directly attempt to resolve the subject of the negotiation, actions are devised that are aimed at creating a public image.

For example, a strategy might seek to portray one's client as acting responsibly, fairly, and in the public interest. At the same time, the strategy portrays the other side as irresponsible, unfair, and without regard for the public's interests. An ultimate objective of this approach might be to build public pressure to help one's side obtain a favorable agreement in the negotiation. Note that the appearance of fairness and public concern should be based on real facts persuasively presented. However, since all sides might be using the same strategy, the portrayal of honesty or dishonesty can be subject to serious and heated debate.

Third parties can themselves be the objects of this strategy. A variety of reasons exist for such targeting. Family members, business associates, and friends may be targeted in order to bring their influence to bear on the client or on the other party. The other party's clients, customers, referral sources, and suppliers could be the targets in order to cause economic injury to or apply pressure on the other party. Care must be taken, in such instances, to avoid actions which could be the basis of economic interference with a contractual relationship.

Sometimes, this strategy consists of just threatening to employ it, rather than actually implementing it. The decision to employ or to threaten is dependent on a number of factors. These factors include the severity of the threatened consequences and the other party's potential reaction to the threat. Furthermore, the negotiator must evaluate whether carrying out the threat will cause continuing pressure on the other party, or instead create an adverse consequence to the other party that a subsequently negotiated agreement will not cure. If the latter is true, then, once it is carried out, its usefulness for the negotiation is ended. It even may make a negotiated agreement more difficult to reach by creating a revenge motivation for the other party. For instance, powerfully adverse publicity that a negotiated settlement will not ameliorate falls into this category.

Strategy 8: Moving for Closure

Key Concept 36

The move-for-closure strategy consists of acting to close the deal by creating a firm agreement.

Closure is acting to finalize a particular issue or the overall negotiation with a firm agreement rather than risk losing the available terms. The move-for-closure strategy follows the use of other strategies which have brought the negotiation to a point at which it is preferable to gain a firm agreement based on the offered terms rather than to continue negotiating and risk losing the agreement.

In most, if not all negotiations, the risk of losing an available deal is a real one. People can change their minds from meeting to meeting. Cashflow needs or cashflow capabilities, competition from other potential parties, alternative transactions, and a variety of other factors can change over time. Prior evaluations may be altered because of fluctuating emotional and psychological beliefs or feelings. It's an unfortunate basic fact of negotiating that the agreement which can be made today may not be available tomorrow.

Balancing the Risk of Losing Agreement With the Opportunity of Doing Better

The closure strategy requires deciding whether to accept the offer at present or to continue negotiating with the hope that an even better agreement can be achieved. This issue requires weighing several factors, including the following:

1. *Value:* The value of the agreement that is presently available.

2. *Risk:* The likelihood that the offer will be withdrawn while holding out for even better terms.

3. *Potential:* Potential terms that are judged to be better than the ones presently available.

4. *Odds:* The chances of achieving those better terms.

One must decide whether negotiating for potentially more valuable terms is worth the risk of losing an acceptable but less advantageous agreement.

Issues and Answers on When to Involve the Decision Maker

The negotiator should be very cautious about risking an agreement the terms of which the client authorized to be accepted. If lost, client dissatisfaction is the natural and inevitable consequence. Therefore, before the negotiator decides to risk losing an agreement that is acceptable to the client, he or she should discuss both the risk and the potential benefits of continuing to negotiate. The negotiator should provide a detailed explanation so that the ultimate decision is made by the decision maker. Remember, decisions about whether to agree at any point during the negotiation must be made by the client.

The foregoing discussion assumes a risk of some significance. One need not and should not always stop negotiating whenever the other party offers minimally agreeable terms. Indeed, to do so might show more interest in the offer than is appropriate. Also, by trying to immediately accept minimal terms, the negotiator might signal weakness to the other party, thus motivating it to raise its expectations and to take a harder line than it originally planned. The negotiator's chances of attaining the best agreement would then decrease. In other words, to *always* accept, or to always stop to check with the decision maker as soon as the first agreeable offer is obtained, can be a very poor negotiating strategy.

The necessity of a consultation with the client is, therefore, a matter of judgment. If there is a real risk of losing an acceptable agreement by continuing to negotiate, the client should decide whether there should be immediate closure.

Techniques for Moving the Other Side Toward Closure

For the other side, of course, the same requirements and principles are applicable. Thus, to successfully reach closure on one's proposal, it must at least meet the minimum requirement of the other party's bottom line. In addition:

1. The less the other party believes that it can obtain further concessions,

2. And the more the other party fears that failing to accept will result in no agreement being reached,

3. The greater the likelihood that the move for closure will succeed.

Therefore, a negotiator may need a persuasive presentation in moving for closure to convince the other side that these factors exist, unless all that is needed is to accept the other side's last offer.

Expressing Understanding That Agreement Exists

Sometimes, a party will signal its agreement indirectly. Its assent or acquiescence to a settlement proposal might be implied rather than forthrightly expressed. In this situation, closure can be accomplished in a bona fide way by expressing an understanding that there is, in fact, an agreement. Provided that this is a fair conclusion, this approach has the benefit of not asking whether there really is an agreement, since that question may cause the other negotiator to have second thoughts. If the other negotiator responds that there is no agreement, feedback should be requested with an explanation of the reasons preventing agreement.

Concession-Based Inducement to Close

A different type of move for closure consists of an inducement to act now through the offer of some additional concession. It can be presented through many of the tactics outlined in the following chapters. The additional concession may sometimes involve either a unilaterally large concession by one party, or one or more reciprocal, large concessions by both parties.

At other times, moving for closure may involve a purposefully short negotiation because of a relative lack of value and significance, or because one or both sides are particularly anxious to settle. Under these circumstances, moving for closure may involve anything from relatively small concessions to large concessions, and the concessions may be reciprocal or more one-sided.

Minimizing the Danger of Repudiation Between Closure and Execution

Moving for closure means creating a firm agreement. It can include completing all of the attendant documentation as well as having the parties execute those documents. Usually, where the agreement is to be reduced to writing, however, there is a gap between the close of the negotiation and the execution of the documents that finalize the agreement. Sometimes, a substantial danger of repudiation exists during this time. If so, the closure strategy also includes taking reasonable steps to guard against repudiation during that interim period. For example, a letter confirming the agreement can be transmitted.

Closing Issues Within a Larger Negotiation

Movement for closure is applicable not only to the entire negotiation, but also to settling a particular issue within a negotiation. Final agreement on one issue is reached so that the parties can move forward and focus on the remaining issues. Incremental closure of the various issues that are involved in a negotiation can be very helpful. In this context, the more easily settled issues are closed first, while the more difficult issues are deferred. This strategy can promote a more favorable atmosphere for an overall agreement and can encourage the parties to reach agreement due to the commitments of time and effort that they have already made.

Drawbacks of Moving for Closure

One caveat concerning the move for closure is to be careful that this does not interfere with executing another strategy, such as problem solving. As discussed above, because of the different values that the parties may attach to different issues, problem solving sometimes can involve exchanging concessions on one issue for concessions on another to the mutual satisfaction of both parties. Thus, before moving for closure on an issue if a problem-solving or other strategy is being used to gain trade-offs, negotiators should carefully consider whether a different use of that issue could be made to more favorably resolve other issues and affect a better overall agreement.

Strategy 9: Combining Strategies

Key Concept 37

Using different strategies at different stages of the negotiation or for different issues is usually the most effective method of negotiating.

So far, this chapter has outlined eight different negotiating strategies. However, in negotiating it often is not effective to use a single strategy throughout. Furthermore, the concede-first and closure strategies can only be used during particular portions of a negotiation. By their very nature, they must be used in conjunction with other strategies. A typical combination of strategies might be HRESSC and moving for closure. Another blend could be problem solving, concede-first, and move for closure. There are many possible combinations of strategies.

Why Change Strategies?

The need or desire to change strategies can arise for a number of reasons. A strategy may be tried and discarded because it failed. Since this is not unusual, a willingness to change strategies can and should be part of the overall plan of a negotiation. Also, even with careful planning, unforeseen events during the negotiation can justify changes in strategy.

Categories of Strategy Changes

Strategy changes may be either sequential or issue-oriented. **Sequential changes** are those that occur over time during the negotiation based on a continual reevaluation of the process. **Issue-oriented changes** occur in multiple-issue negotiations in which there are different strategies for different issues. For this reason, negotiations should be planned on both an issue-by-issue basis and an overall basis.

Case in Point 3-11: Sequential Strategy Changes_____

After some initial sparring, ZQ Inc. makes a very low opening offer. Later, it makes some small concessions (HRESSC). The other party's offer is below ZQ's bottom line, and consequently is rejected. ZQ then switches to a no-further-concessions strategy. Negotiations break down. Later, using a rationale of cost changes to save face, ZQ switches to a concede-first strategy, followed by the HRESSC strategy. Happy to receive concessions, the other party moves toward agreement, and a deal is made.

Case in Point 3-12: Issue-Oriented Strategy Changes_____

A purchaser of equipment has a competitive goal of getting the lowest possible price for certain types of machinery, and a self-centered goal of having good service promptly available if there are any malfunctions. Accordingly, these two goals are analyzed as separate issues for which separate strategies are chosen. To minimize the price, the HRESSC strategy is selected. With regard to future service, a problem-solving strategy is chosen. While the strategies and their implementation are closely related, the goals may or may not be achieved without employing distinct strategies to deal with them.

Pitfalls When Shifting Strategies

Strategy changes may not be successful if a prior strategy has undermined the current one. This can happen if the other negotiator has come to believe that one is being disingenuous. For example, a negotiator may not be successful in moving from a no-concessions strategy to a problem-solving strategy. The other negotiator might not believe that the problem-solving strategy is being used in good faith, but that it is a ploy in light of the earlier use of the hard-line strategy of no concessions.

Furthermore, clear signals must be given for the change in strategy (unless the negotiator deliberately chooses to disguise them). Mixed messages or unclear signals will often cause the other party not to recognize the shift in strategy, thereby reducing its effectiveness. The other party's failure to recognize a strategy change differs from the problem of lost credibility. The former problem stems from a lack of clarity in presenting the new strategy and is purely a communications failure. By contrast, the latter is a more substantive dilemma.

Comprehension Checkup

The answers to these questions appear on page 331.

1. Choosing a strategy requires consideration of goals, short-run and long-run interests, particular facts and the nature of the matter, the characteristics of the other negotiator, anticipated countermeasures, and two other primary factors:_____ and _____.
   a. closure and deception
   b. power and alternatives to agreement
   c. trust and manipulation
   d. gamesmanship and concession size

2. Personal credibility is enhanced by _____.
   a. bluffing
   b. expressing anger
   c. understanding the other side's interests
   d. none of the above

3. With either cooperative or defensive goals, one normally should not use the following strategy: _____.
   a. no concessions   c. concede first
   b. HRESSC   d. problem solving

4. A good countermeasure to deadlock is _____.
   a. HRESSC   c. closure
   b. creation of movement   d. yelling

5. The most generally useful strategy is _____.
   a. no further concessions   c. deadlock
   b. concede first   d. HRESSC

6. Both parties have genuinely identified a common problem which is in their mutual interest to solve so that each will receive a win-win benefit. The best strategy is _____.
   a. HRESSC   c. concede first
   b. problem solving   d. closure

7. One party fears that the other will perceive that it is weak and seek to exploit that weakness. It should not use the _____ strategy.
   a. HRESSC   c. concede-first
   b. problem-solving   d. closure

8. Problem solving can be used effectively if the parties have identified a common problem but do not have true mutual interests.   T   F

9. The concede-first strategy can almost always be countered by refusing to reciprocate.   T   F

10. Different strategies must be considered for each goal and issue.   T   F

4
Tactical Control of the Information Exchange Process

Key Concepts

38. Negotiation is a process of disclosing, creating, withholding, obtaining, and analyzing information.

39. Informational tactics are critical to every negotiation. They involve creating, obtaining, and/or disclosing information.

40. Information disclosure can be used tactically to influence the other side's perceptions, expectations, and positions.

41. Whether analyzing the other side or trying to persuade it, nonverbal information is critical.

42. Information gained from verbal slips should be given the most favorable reasonable interpretation as a working assumption.

43. The proper timing of information disclosure is critical to achieving an optimally successful negotiation.

44. As with any kind of presentation, persuasive negotiating is enhanced by visuals and demonstrations.

45. Deflecting or refusing to answer questions are legitimate tactics, but must be used carefully to avoid creating distrust.

46. The snow job is a tactic that seeks to obscure an issue by introducing an overwhelming mass of information.

47. Altering the factual situation by creating new facts is a legitimate negotiating tactic.

48. To avoid being perceived as a bluff or wrongfully aggressive, a threat must be credible, and made only with reasonable justification.

49. The abilities to discover and elicit information are strongly related to the abilities to listen and receive information.

50. The funnel approach consists of asking broad initial questions, followed by increasingly specific ones, to obtain information.

51. Effective negotiating calls for creatively seeking sources of information.

52. Information can be bargained for with general or explicit trade-offs.

53. Discussion is a common means of exchanging information.

The Language of Negotiating

To make full use of the key concepts, you must understand the following terms:

Selective disclosure	Snow job
Nondisclosure	Fact creation
Nonverbal communication	Funnel approach
Verbal slip	Discussion
Deflection	

Introduction

Key Concept 38

Negotiation is a process of disclosing, creating, withholding, obtaining, and analyzing information.

Sir Francis Bacon, the seventeenth-century English philosopher, perceptively regarded negotiation as a process of discovery. While negotiation is more than that, discovery is an important aspect of the process.

Each party seeks to discover things from or about the other, and tries to influence the discoveries made by the other party by controlling the information given. In many ways, negotiation is a process of giving, withholding, and analyzing information.

For all negotiations, information about the other party is critical. The information may be explicit or implicit. For instance, even the refusal to disclose information can provide knowledge that is as significant as facts learned in other more direct ways.

Information about the other party can help a negotiator decide whether an agreement is or is not feasible. If an agreement is believed to be feasible, this judgment becomes a type of information that affects the negotiator's understanding of how to structure the optimal agreement. Thus, it is through information exchange that negotiators create a framework within which to settle a deal or to conclude that an agreement is not possible, and therefore terminate the negotiation.

In this process, negotiators seek mutual interests and common ground, since agreement requires that their respective needs be met. In this way, negotiators also decide whether contemplated strategies and tactics should be followed or altered. The types of information sought include knowledge concerning the needs, interests, and positions of the other party, as well as any other facts which bear on an assessment of the minimum offer that is likely to be agreeable to the other party.

In any negotiation, knowledge of the other party's strategy can influence both the negotiator and the party represented by the negotiator. For instance, if the negotiator knows that the other party's strategy is to make no concessions, the analysis of the negotiation will be quite different than if the strategy is problem solving.

Key Concept 39

Informational tactics are critical to every negotiation. They involve creating, obtaining, and/or disclosing information.

Informational tactics fall into three major categories:

1. Disclosing information.
2. Creating facts through actions that alter the existing facts.
3. Obtaining information.

Before proceeding with a detailed discussion of these specific tactics, it should be noted that their use is both essential and pervasive. Informational tactics are critical in every negotiation, regardless of the goals,

the strategy, and the other tactics being used. There can be no negotiation without engaging in informational tactics.

Negotiators always engage in some disclosure of information. They
are also always involved in obtaining information. Indeed, even an initial offer itself is sometimes, at least in part, an information-seeking tactic. Frequently, seeking and disclosing information will begin as part of
the preparation for the actual negotiating. This may be an integral part
of the planning process, because obtaining information may be necessary in order to choose a strategy and set of tactics. Less obviously, disclosing information before any actual bargaining occurs may be a useful
way for a negotiator to influence the other party's planning and choice
of strategy and tactics.

There is a wide range of information tactics. Some will seem familiar,
while others will be new to you. Negotiators in the United States are
generally accustomed to relatively short negotiations, and are skilled at
argument, but they often lack skill in:

1. asking questions.

2. obtaining information.

3. listening.

4. using questions as a tool of persuasion.

In addition, American negotiators tend to ignore or dismiss practices
accepted in other countries, such as establishing rapport and exchanging pertinent information in the first stages of a negotiation. Sufficient
time and energy should be expended on those stages, since they can affect the later stages of persuasion, concession, and, ultimately, agreement or the termination of negotiation.

Informational Tactic 1:
Disclosing Information

Key Concept 40

*Information disclosure can be used tactically to influence the other
side's perceptions, expectations, and positions.*

Information disclosure can change the entire course of a negotiation.
It may stimulate fresh analysis by introducing facts that one side knows

which would otherwise be unavailable to the other side. The information can alter the analysis of a negotiator or a party either because it was previously unknown or because the side hearing it thought that the speaker was unaware of it.

Selective Disclosure

Negotiators are expected to be truthful in their statements but not to disclose all that they know. A key negotiating skill is **selective disclosure**, that is, the ability to determine what information should be disclosed during the course of the negotiation. Being selective means being conscious and in control of the information that is communicated. Otherwise, the wrong information may be disclosed, creating a disadvantage rather than an advantage. Selective disclosure is one of the most important tools available for persuading the other negotiator or the other party to change position. It requires judgment in balancing:

1. The likely intended and unintended effects of the disclosure.
2. The likely intended and unintended effects of nondisclosure.

Nondisclosure

Nondisclosure, or the intentional withholding of information, becomes even more significant when information is either explicitly or implicitly sought by the other party who will then draw inferences if their requests for information are refused. Negotiators should expect these inferences and decide whether they are more helpful or harmful than disclosure.

Using Information Disclosure to Reveal Beneficial Alternatives

Disclosure may be designed to motivate the other party or its negotiator to accept a particular position. It also can be structured to create previously unknown alternatives. In many negotiations, the lack of information can result in a lower gain for both parties. This can occur when each party tries to maximize its own gains but fails to realize that alternative compromises exist which might lead to a better result for each of them. In this instance, nondisclosure kept each side from discovering new facts or ideas that could have helped the negotiation process. This dilemma is illustrated in Figure 4-1. The parties are designated as A and B. VA represents value to A and VB represents value to B, on a scale of 1 (lowest value) to 10 (highest value).

Known compromise:	A's first choice:
VA 3 and VB 3	VA 10 and VB 1
B's first choice:	Unknown alternative:
VA 1 and VB 10	VA 6 and VB 5

Figure 4-1

As the figure illustrates, the known compromise has less value for either party than the unknown alternative; lack of information has prevented the parties from discovering a preferable alternative. At times, only the disclosure of information can help parties to discover the most mutually satisfying alternatives.

A negotiator may need to reveal some or all of his or her side's goals, needs, or interests as long as the disclosure does not reveal one's own bargaining weaknesses. By selectively disclosing information, the negotiator may be able to establish for the other party that any agreement must be structured within certain parameters (a situation that is helpful regardless of what strategy is being followed). In addition, disclosure may reveal the relevant issues, which is particularly helpful with the problem-solving strategy. Without knowing the goals, needs, and interests of the parties, the parties and negotiators may not be able to identify or solve the problem that impedes an agreement.

Staying Attuned to Inconsistencies Between Verbal and Nonverbal Signs

Key Concept 41

Whether analyzing the other side, or trying to persuade it, nonverbal information is critical.

Selectively disclosing information includes not only verbal but also nonverbal communication. **Nonverbal communication** is conveyed by means other than through the use of words, including graphical representation, body language, tone of voice, and so on. Negotiators should take care to ensure that verbal and nonverbal information correspond.

For example, one's physical actions or tone of voice may be inconsistent with the message that is being transmitted. Selectivity extends both to information that is given directly and to information that is transmitted indirectly through the inferences that the other party draws from the communication. Accordingly, you should be acutely aware of how the other negotiator may perceive a nonverbal communication.

Case in Point 4-1_____

The purchaser listens very carefully to a long proposal made by a vendor. As the vendor is explaining the entire proposal, the purchaser appears to be taking almost verbatim notes. At the end, however, the purchaser says smoothly: "We do not have the slightest interest in that proposal or in anything like it."

If there really was no possible interest in the proposal, then why did the purchaser take time and care to listen, and why take so many notes? While it is possible that the purchaser was initially confused about the direction the proposal was headed, it is unlikely he would have listened and taken so many notes unless there was at least some interest in the plan. At best, the purchaser has sent a confusing, or mixed, message. At worst, the purchaser has unintentionally disclosed information that he wanted to conceal: that the proposal was of some interest. Thus, one should be attuned to any inconsistency between verbal and nonverbal signals from either oneself or from the other negotiator.

Negotiating Mileage From Verbal Slips

Key Concept 42

Information gained from verbal slips should be given the most favorable reasonable interpretation as a working assumption.

A **verbal slip** is an inadvertent transmission of information through a slip of the tongue or some other unconscious accident. As the following dialogues illustrate, the selective disclosure of information also means studiously avoiding verbal slips which might indicate your true position when attempting to project a different one.

BUYER: "Would you take eighteen, I mean, fifteen thousand?"

Although the "eighteen" could just be a mistake, it also can be a verbal slip prematurely disclosing a willingness to make a $3000 concession. Or,

> BUYER: "We would consider paying $15,000 to $18,000."
>
> SELLER: "Well, at $18,000 you are at least getting closer to a price that we could accept."

In this example, the buyer has not selectively disclosed information and has made a slip by communicating that $18,000 would be an acceptable price. The listener always should proceed on the basis of the most favorable reasonable interpretation of the speaker's position, unless it is proved wrong by further information. In this case, the seller can reasonably dismiss the lower offer and assume that the buyer is actually willing to pay $18,000.

Avoiding Inadvertent Disclosures

Related to verbal slips are inadvertent disclosures. An example of an inadvertent disclosure is keeping documents with crucial information in plain view. Generally, negotiators should assume that their counterparts can read upside down, and will read anything in view. Indeed, negotiators must at times consider the possibilities of surveillance, espionage, electronic eavesdropping, and so on, and take measures to guard against them.

Controlling the Timing of Disclosure

Key Concept 43

The proper timing of information disclosure is critical to achieving an optimally successful negotiation.

In addition to the selective disclosure of information are decisions regarding the timing of those disclosures. The negotiator must determine:

1. What information should be disclosed at the outset of the negotiating process.

2. What information ought to be withheld until the negotiation focuses on a particular fact, issue, or argument.

3. What information is to be saved in case the parties become deadlocked.

The timing of the disclosure should be calculated to either maximize or minimize its impact, depending on which of those effects is sought.

The total amount of time available for the negotiation is also a subject requiring a conscious decision about disclosure. Information about the amount of time available for the negotiation should be withheld if that fact forms an apparent constraint which could force the negotiator to accept a less favorable outcome. On the other hand, it should be disclosed if it creates a useful deadline that pressures the other side to concede more.

Case in Point 4-2_____

Mr. Field has traveled to a foreign country to negotiate a deal. He has a deadline by which he must depart for home. If that fact indicates time pressure to accept the best available deal before having to depart, Field should avoid revealing the departure deadline.

When Disclosure Is a Legal Matter

At times, disclosure of certain information is legally required. For instance:

1. In many securities matters, state and federal laws mandate that certain disclosures be made.

2. Required franchise disclosures similarly are governed by law.

3. A seller of real property may be liable for not disclosing known defects, depending on the circumstances of the transaction.

Where disclosure is legally mandated, the degree of selectivity is limited, and the categories of information required to be disclosed must be recognized.

The Optimal Approach to Disclosure

The most persuasive type of disclosure can be to reveal just enough to get the other negotiator to draw conclusions without realizing that they were, in fact, subtly suggested. In contrast, direct conclusions should be stated where:

1. The other negotiator may not understand a more subtle approach.

2. The other negotiator has already drawn the conclusion.

Countering Potentially Negative
Perceptions Through Disclosure

Some disclosures are intended to counter apparently significant, negative factors. This should be done where such factors are known to the other party. Consider these model statements:

> "If I were in your place, I'd be concerned about that aspect. I think, however, you will find that in practice it actually functions to..."

> "Although you probably think that creates a disadvantage, it really doesn't work out that way. Any disadvantage is more than balanced by the four positive factors..."

By anticipating factors which the other party might view as problematic, a negotiator may be able to restructure a planned proposal and explanation to defuse the potential problem. The restructuring can eliminate the undesirable factors, or portray them in a less negative or even in a positive light. Not only can such forthrightness enable one to give a more persuasive presentation, it also can lower the defenses of the other party and promote an atmosphere of trust. It demonstrates to the other party that its needs are being comprehended, acknowledged, and responded to realistically.

Often, it may be normal and expected for one or both parties to disclose a substantial amount of factual data to the other party. For instance, in negotiating a merger, a joint venture, or a partnership agreement, information that might be expected could include:

1. Itemized records of past and present revenues.

2. Itemized records of past and present expenses.

3. Records of accounts receivable.

4. Information concerning anticipated income in both the short term and the long term.

5. Data regarding anticipated expenses for both the short term and the long term.

6. Figures showing the past and present salaries, bonuses, and fringe benefits of partners or executives.

7. Indications of who the key employees are.

8. Information regarding the retirement, or other pertinent personal plans, of partners or executives.

9. Data concerning assets, credit, and capital investments.

10. Information about financial obligations and liabilities, including pension and profit-sharing plans.

You must be concerned about whether and how such information should be disclosed to protect against or defuse potential claims by the other party. The claim may be misrepresentation because of failure to disclose, or because of a misleading disclosure. Concern means that legal and business judgment must be made on the nature and extent of any risks, and on the appropriate measures to be taken.

Disclosure by Means of Visual Aids

Key Concept 44

As with any kind of presentation, persuasive negotiating is enhanced by visuals and demonstrations.

Verbal or written narratives are the most common forms of disclosing information. However, charts, graphs, drawings, photographs, videotapes, financial statements, and any other type of visual communication can be used when appropriate. Visuals may be necessary for situations in which there is reason to believe a narrative approach will not be received, or understood, or motivate the desired response. Even where it is not a matter of absolute necessity, it can be more persuasive to supplement narrative presentations with tangible displays.

Similarly, tours of facilities and other demonstrations can be an effective means of persuading the other party of the value of a business, service, or product. "Seeing" may be far more persuasive than reading. The same is true when trying to convince the other party of a factual issue where litigation might be involved. Although such techniques often are thought of as "sales" ploys, they are effective negotiation tools in a variety of contexts and should not be overlooked.

Techniques for Avoiding Disclosure

Key Concept 45

Deflecting or refusing to answer questions are legitimate tactics, but must be used carefully to avoid creating distrust.

Substituting Favorable Information or Giving Only Partial Answers.
Avoiding disclosure without creating distrust and without any misrepresentations is a crucial part of the selective disclosure of information. Some inquiries can be responded to by answers that are carefully and clearly framed to include only the most favorable information. However, it is essential that these partial answers not constitute misrepresentation.

Note: To preserve credibility as well as to avoid potential charges of fraud, the negotiator should not disclose information as fact unless relatively certain that it is. Unless openly acknowledged, guessing or speculating can easily lead to inaccuracies which will be discovered later. If information requested by the other negotiator is not known, you either should:

1. Admit a lack of knowledge.

2. Deflect the inquiry.

Deflecting.   **Deflection** refers to a negotiator's intentional response to a question in a way that moves slightly or completely off the direct line of inquiry. Deflection techniques include:

1. Answering a question that was not asked as if you understood it to be the question that *was* asked.

2. Refusing to agree with a portion of or an assumption within a question.

3. Appearing deliberately ignorant of the answer to a question so that the response simply indicates a lack of knowledge.

Unless used carefully and selectively, deflection can create distrust. For that reason, it should be used sparingly during any negotiation.

Outright Refusal to Answer.   At times, a simple and direct refusal to disclose information can be appropriate, for example, if the requested information is either:

1. Sensitive and, at least in the perception of the party being asked to make the disclosure, not of legitimate concern to the party requesting it.

2. Simply not a subject for disclosure at all, such as the amount of one's authority.

In deciding which technique to use to avoid a real answer to an inquiry, the following factors must be balanced:

1. The need to be perceived as honest and candid, rather than disingenuous, in order to create or preserve trust.

2. Whether the information should be disclosed in part or avoided directly so that the negotiation proceeds in a desired direction.

3. How the other negotiator and the other party will react to a deflection or a direct refusal to answer, including any inferences they may draw.

A direct refusal to answer often should be accompanied by an explanation of why the inquiry is believed to be unfair or improper. In this way, potentially adverse reactions to the refusal to answer may be defused.

If it happens that the other negotiator remains silent when asked a specific question, the negotiator has good reason to assume that the question contained elements that the other negotiator believes dangerous. This assumption can then become the basis of further discussion or investigation. Silence on the part of one negotiator or another may have other motivations. By remaining silent, a negotiator may subtly be compelling the other negotiator to keep talking and thereby reveal information that was not intended to be disclosed.

Key Concept 46

The snow job is a tactic that seeks to obscure an issue by introducing an overwhelming mass of information.

An entirely different type of information disclosure is the **snow job.** Here, the negotiator attempts to obscure important information within a mass of other information. The major countermeasures are:

1. To demand carefully drawn categories of information.

2. To painstakingly peruse all the information with sufficient time allocated to allow an effective review.

Informational Tactic 2: The Creation of Facts

Key Concept 47

Altering the factual situation by creating new facts is a legitimate negotiating tactic.

Communication by action can be effective and persuasive. The tactic of fact creation consists of actions that legitimately add to, or alter, an existing factual situation. It does not involve dishonesty or deceit; instead, it is a bona fide enhancement of a party's factual posture or presentation. For the purpose of persuasion, a fact does not exist until the other party either believes it or is sufficiently convinced to take it seriously.

Case in Point 4-3_____

A house is for sale. To improve its appearance and increase its value and the price that can be asked, it is painted. The increase in price is much greater than the cost of painting. Thus, the result is a greater net profit.

Case in Point 4-4_____

A party, seeking to sell its business, is concerned that a potential buyer will be skeptical of the financial data which was compiled by the seller's in-house bookkeeper, even though the data is both attractive and accurate. Accordingly, the seller creates a new fact by obtaining a financial statement from an independent, reputable accounting firm. This statement presents essentially the same financial information as the party's own bookkeeper's statement. The independent confirmation adds the *fact* of the accuracy of the information.

Case in Point 4-5_____

A verbal description of a new product has been presented during the negotiations, but the potential purchaser does not accurately comprehend the description. Therefore, prior to any further bargaining, the seller demonstrates the product. The demonstration thereby "creates" a new, persuasive fact of the realities of the product since, in the negotiation, that fact did not previously "exist" in the potential purchaser's mind.

Painting or even cleaning a house that is for sale may display the same building in an entirely different way. An internal bookkeeper's financial information may be discounted or considered with great skepticism, whereas the addition of an audited financial statement that verifies the economic data can change the posture of the negotiation. A written or verbal description of a product or service may contain its attributes, but still leave an unpersuaded audience. An effective demonstration can impress that same audience far more than the most eloquent and clever written or verbal description. In this sense, each of the cases in point portrays a fact which, in effect, did not exist before.

Creating a New Factual Situation

Another type of fact creation relates to win-win offers that are based on "new facts."

Case in Point 4-6

Discounts for early payment are offered to secure a sales contract. The discounts are important to the buyer but cost the seller relatively little.

Case in Point 4-7

Guaranteed tonnage is very significant to a carrier because it reduces the possibility of serious cashflow problems. The guarantee is offered by the shipper to secure more favorable terms for a shipping contract. The guarantee has no cost to the shipper, which needs to have that much of its product transported anyway.

Case in Point 4-8

In the lease of an office building, the future cost of insurance is uncertain. Rather than raise the rent to cover the potential future cost, the parties agree to pass through any increase in insurance costs so that the tenant pays any increase. Both sides benefit by having a formula that ensures fairness and avoids a protracted dispute about the correct dollar estimate of future cost increases.

These three cases in point consist of possible new facts which can be created during a negotiation. Cases in Point 4-6 and 4-7 create win-win results, because while the new facts have significant value to one party, the offer entails nonexistent or small costs to the other. Case in Point 4-8 illustrates a resolution that equitably solves a problem for both parties. All three cases involve the creation of new facts which permit making new, more attractive offers that in turn lead to agreements.

Disclosing information to outside parties can create new operative facts. For example, public pronouncements demonstrate commitment to a position. Unless it is considered a bluff, a publicly announced position forces the other party to consider whether to agree with the public position or to at least make further concessions. The persuasiveness of the public position comes from the knowledge that:

1. There is a natural reluctance to accept the loss of face entailed by compromising a public position without receiving a valuable concession.

2. The position has greater value to the party stating it than was previously understood by the other side.

3. Contrary to the other side's prior belief, the party's position is either less flexible or inflexible.

Litigation, or the persuasive threat of it, creates new facts. These include potential fees and costs that may not be recovered, as well as an uncertain outcome if the matter is decided at trial or on appeal. The uncertainty of a judge's ruling or a jury's verdict provides a powerful incentive for settlement. Changes in bargaining rules also constitute new facts which can have a tremendous impact on negotiations.

Case in Point 4-9_____

Through free agency, a professional sports athlete can negotiate with different teams for the best possible player contract. In 1975, an arbitration ruling altered the rules of free agency for baseball players. Four years later, players' salaries had more than doubled.

A significant part of effective negotiating consists in presenting facts persuasively. Thus, it is clear that the creation of facts which the other party finds convincing and significant can be a vital tool to improve one's position in the negotiation.

Making Credible Threats

Key Concept 48

To avoid being perceived as a bluff or wrongfully aggressive, a threat must be credible, and made only with reasonable justification.

Threats of potentially adverse change can be new facts that create uncertainty. The following model statements reveal how threats can create uncertainty for the other party.

> "We cannot prevent some of our union's members from engaging in a wildcat strike, if they decide to go out."

> "We believe that you—a key employee wanting to buy the company—have been misappropriating certain funds. If this deal is not made on our terms, we will audit and investigate fully and perhaps bring charges against you. On the other hand, if you buy the business on these terms, we'll consider the matter closed."

> "If it's not resolved today, we'll institute litigation. My attorney has an emergency temporary restraining order and the other papers ready, and we'll see you in court tomorrow. But let's see what we can do together to prevent that."

Threats can be based on matters totally controlled by one party. They also may involve matters outside the control of the party making the threat, such as in the wildcat strike example. Either way, the fate of the threatened party is in its own hands. The threatened party can either accept the offered terms and avoid the threatened consequences, or accept the risk posed by the threat.

To be credible, threats (or indeed, any kind of potential action) must appear as genuinely dangerous, and not as a mere bluff. Personal credibility and historical precedent often are the key factors in determining whether the danger is viewed as real or not.

Threatening Without Being Aggressive.   Depending on what precipitates them, threats need not be presented from a hostile posture. A party may wish to avoid appearing aggressive, either to:

1. Maintain a relationship with the other party.

2. Impress interested third parties, including the media or the public.

To avoid the appearance of aggression, a threat can be presented coolly—as a matter of fact. The other party can respond by being reasonable. The same purpose can be achieved by expressing some reluctance to make threats, but explaining that the other side's refusal to fairly compromise has forced this position to be taken.

Where a threat is a hostile gesture, it may be presented along with an explanation as to why it is justified, as the following statement shows.

"Given the agreements and promises that you have violated, we have no choice but to file suit, unless we receive provisions ensuring penalties for such conduct in the future."

Countering Tips for Threats

Countermeasures to threats include:

1. Counterthreats.
2. Being indifferent to the threat.

Effectively Discovering and Receiving Information

Goals Compatibility

Like the other types of informational tactics more often used, fact creation can be used for all goals, strategies, and other tactics. However, it is important to remember that in many negotiations the fact-creation tactic will not be appropriate because the opportunity to legitimately alter the factual context does not exist.

Key Concept 49

The abilities to discover and elicit information are strongly related to the abilities to listen and receive information.

A corollary tactic to the selective disclosure of information is the effective acquisition and comprehension of information. This is a two-stage process. First, the information must be elicited or discovered. Second, it must be received and understood.

Regarding the latter point, spoken information can be far more difficult to receive and understand than written information. It cannot be focused on or studied as something in writing can. People often are more interested in talking than listening. Consequently, they frequently are thinking more about what they are going to say next rather than about what is being said by someone else. They may also have preconceived ideas about what they expect to hear from the other negotiator. They then fail to perceive what is really being said, and instead think that they heard what they wanted or expected to hear.

Informational Tactic 3:
The Funnel Approach to
Obtaining Information

Key Concept 50

The funnel approach consists of asking broad initial questions, followed by increasingly specific ones, to obtain information.

The **funnel approach** is a structure for obtaining broad information from a totally or somewhat willing source. It begins by asking general questions which seek a narrative response. After learning as much as possible from broad questions, the negotiator asks narrower and narrower questions to discover more specific or detailed information.

Business executives and managers, attorneys, and other negotiators often unintentionally cut off information which they would like to know. Even when broad information is needed, they focus their questions too narrowly, even when someone is willing to disclose more. Rather than attempting to elicit a complete narrative, they launch into a cross-examination style of questioning. That is, they ask yes-or-no, leading-type questions. This approach is a much more difficult and less effective means of obtaining complete information. Anyone who doubts this should attempt a simple experiment:

1. Ask someone to think of an interesting or exciting experience.

2. Attempt to learn all about that experience by asking only questions that can be answered yes or no, and instruct the person responding to answer only yes or no.

3. Then, for comparison, attempt to learn about the same or a different experience by encouraging the person to explain in his or her own words what occurred. Instruct the other person to be cooperative. Speak only to encourage the person to continue, to give guidance if the account becomes confusing, or to stop an irrelevant digression.

The appeal of the old television show *What's My Line?* came from its premise that the panelists could only ask yes-or-no questions in attempting to determine a guest's occupation. The yes-or-no question often failed to generate sufficient information, which made deducing the occupation difficult. If broader, narrative-type questions could have been asked, determining the occupation would have been easy. No one can anticipate all situations. Narrow questions can miss important details or unexpected portions of a story. Such questions should be saved for un-cooperative sources, or to fill in missing details from an initial account.

Getting High Returns From Casual, General Questions

In many situations, a seemingly casual general question such as "How's business?" may not be so casual at all. Rather than just being perfunctory and polite conversation, it can be a highly effective information-gathering device for the negotiation. Being placed off guard, the other party may disclose key information. Eliciting information in this way can be extremely valuable for analyzing one's own position. The information can help to avoid either undervaluing or overvaluing your side's position, as well as to establish the appropriate settlement range.

Case in Point 4-10

Prior to an upcoming negotiation, the negotiators for the two sides happen to meet.

NEGOTIATOR A: "How's business?"

NEGOTIATOR B: "We're basically doing very well. With our expansion, our profits next year should skyrocket. But right now, the expansion has caused real cashflow problems. If anything happens to interrupt our present production, we would be in serious trouble."

NEGOTIATOR A: "Well, hopefully you can avoid that."

Obviously, this dialogue is exaggerated. However, it demonstrates a significant lesson. If Negotiator A represents a union, for example, and Negotiator B represents management in an upcoming labor negotiation, then Negotiator B has disclosed vital information that will allow Negotiator A to accurately set high realistic expectations for the union. Negotiator A can also accurately assess management's settlement point and know how to pressure management. This example illustrates just how informative the simple "how's business" type of inquiry can be.

The general, less direct form of probing is the first stage of the funnel approach. Often, the first stage is done as a low-key, apparently unimportant part of the conversation. The inquiry is made to sound as if it is not part of the real negotiation, but just routine conversation. In this way, the other party or negotiator may be less alert to guarding against inadvertent disclosures of important information. This casual first stage should be followed by more narrow, direct questions.

Probing More Directly

The funnel approach also can start with more direct, but still general probes, as the following model statements illustrate:

"Have you ever had a bad or an unsatisfactory experience in this type of deal before? What happened?"

"To help me structure the best deal for both companies, tell me your objectives and needs."

"How do you judge the success of this kind of program?"

"Do you basically like the present offer? Do you require some changes? Or are we operating in totally different areas?"

"Maybe I don't understand. Explain how you see it." (*An opening may be created by acknowledging a lack of understanding, and then framing the inquiry in terms of the other's perceptions.*)

These types of direct inquiries can be made when either:

1. The other negotiator or the other party wants to respond in an attempt to influence the structure of the proposed arrangement.

2. The negotiator wants to place the burden of not being able to consider restructuring the existing proposal, or of not being able to consider any further concessions, on the unwillingness of the other side to provide the requested information.

The latter usually is triggered by two types of situations. In the first, the negotiator who chooses direct inquiry believes the information is such that the other party will not divulge it. The negotiator wants to precipitate a refusal to disclose the information in order to create a rationale or pretext for blocking further movement in the negotiation. This is effective only if the request for information is reasonable, so that the inquiry appears to be legitimate. Clearly, asking for the other negotiator's bottom line or ultimate authority, and then refusing to negotiate further without that disclosure, will not be viewed as legitimate.

In the second type of situation, a negotiator is willing to proceed but needs the requested information to do so, and wants to be able to blame the other party for creating an impasse if the information is withheld. This can be especially important if the parties want to influence the other negotiator's client or client's constituency, allies, or other third parties.

Using the Funnel Approach for Fact Verification

The funnel approach can be a response to volunteered information, permitting you to explore the true content of the information.

Case in Point 4-11

A proposed lease from a landlord contains a proportionate pass-through of all building operating expenses and real estate taxes in excess of $750,000. The tenant first inquired into the operating expenses using broad questions.

"What expenses are included in operating expenses?"

"How are operating expenses expected to rise during the four-year lease term?"

"Are any real estate tax reassessments scheduled during the lease term?"

She next followed up with narrower questions, including:

"How have operating expenses risen recently?"

"What were the total operating expenses in each of the last three years, and what was the amount of each category of the operating expenses in that time?"

"Are there any items of deferred maintenance, or expected major maintenance, replacement, or repair that may occur during the lease term?"

Finally, she sought to verify the figures that were reported.

"Can we have a copy of the building's profit and loss statement for the last three years, or at least that portion that shows the operating expenses?"

In this way, the funnel approach is used to explore a factual issue. For many uses of the funnel approach, the negotiator must be aware of issues and problems from previous experience or from prenegotiation information. Without the necessary substantive knowledge, important matters may be overlooked. For instance, in a lease negotiation, if the negotiator does not know the difference between usable and rentable space, an entire area of concern may be missed.

Information should be checked, rather than blindly accepted. A degree of skepticism is healthy. Statistical analyses, computer models, and other significant facts (including those that are not self-evident) should at least be probed using the funnel method. Even so, other, more concrete verification techniques should be employed if they are warranted and feasible. These include getting references, samples, demonstrations, affidavits, inspections, warranties, opinion letters, and so forth. Proof or confirmation of asserted "facts" may be demanded from the other party or obtained independently.

Countering Tips for the Funnel Approach to Questioning

The countermeasure to the funnel approach is selective information disclosure. Guarded responses are necessary. At times, a full and open response is fine. At other times, requests for information must be resisted.

Informational Tactic 4: Finding and Using Credible Sources of Information

---

Key Concept 51

Effective negotiating calls for creatively seeking sources of information.

Your Own Client Party as a Source of Information

The first sources of information are the people closest to you: your client party and staff. Generally, these people will remain available to you as sources throughout the negotiation. When the client is an entity, potential sources of information should not be limited to the key decision makers and the top staff. For instance, there are times in a labor negotiation when the best source of information can be the line supervisors, who may have insights into problems, issues, costs, facts, or analyses that are unknown to higher levels of management. Similarly, supervisors, technical staff, or other workers may have information that the top levels of management lack. In negotiations, one naturally and properly fo-

cuses on the other party and its negotiator as major sources of information. They certainly are important sources of information in every
negotiation.

Other Sources of Information

Other sources of information can also be important. Indeed, in many
negotiations, the preparation for the negotiation will begin by gathering
information from these other sources. As previously noted, this investi-
gative work may be critical to the eventual success of the negotiation.

Previous Negotiations. Previous similar negotiations can provide
facts, standard or specialized terms, or market values. Also, by investi-
gating factually similar negotiations with the same party, a negotiator
may learn that party's true needs, interests, and intentions. Even factually dissimilar negotiations can impart significant insights into the strategies normally employed by the same party or the same negotiator. Precedents can also be established to determine the credibility of the party
and negotiator of the other side.

Other Negotiators. Other negotiators, both inside and outside of one's
own office, who have interacted with the same party or the same negotiator, can provide valuable information and insights about them. Similarly, parties with prior interactions also can be valuable sources.

Reference Sources. Reference sources may be utilized to learn information about the other party, depending on the nature of the situation
and the type of information sought. University or association studies
and reports may be available. Professional societies, their publications,
and other periodicals can reveal facts about a party, the market, and so
forth.

Of course, these are only the starting points for the analysis of the
negotiation. Each situation must be evaluated independently in light of
the needs and the positions of the parties. Prior agreements must be
viewed with special caution. These almost inevitably are the product of
compromise rather than the ultimate structure with all the terms that
either party wished it could have obtained in the agreement. They must
be scrutinized for ways to improve the terms.

Consultants and Experts. Consultants and experts also are sources of
information. For example, in the transportation field, a consultant may

know the most cost-efficient mode for shipping; the strengths and weaknesses of specific carriers; and the market rates. Appraisers, contractors, and engineers can be used to determine the value of a particular building. The possibilities are almost limitless.

Government Studies. The government is another fertile source of information. Governmental studies can contain important data or other facts. In negotiating with a governmental agency, its own rules or rulings can reveal limitations on its negotiating authority. In any industry or profession in which there is government regulation, those regulations and the record of their promulgation may be helpful. Moreover, information about the other party may well be available from the government through a freedom of information request. However, these requests are subject to the relevant privacy and freedom of information restrictions.

Physical Inspection. For some types of transactions, inspections are a source of information for the buyer. These include purchases of:

1. Real estate.
2. Businesses.
3. Machinery, equipment, and other goods when their quality or quantity should be verified before an agreement is reached and/or prior to making full payment.

Investigators. In more unusual situations, investigators can assist as a source of information. These types of investigators include "corporate intelligence" and "competitor intelligence" firms. To decide whether to employ an investigator, one must consider:

1. The potential benefits from the information sought.
2. The likelihood of obtaining that information.
3. The risk of embarrassment, or of offending the other party, if the investigation is discovered.
4. Any danger that illegal acts may occur during the investigation.
5. The costs of the investigation.

These considerations must be balanced in deciding whether the use of a private investigator is sound or not.

Informational Tactic 5:
Bargaining for Information

Key Concept 52

Information can be bargained for with general or explicit trade-offs.

A reluctant or recalcitrant source of information may be persuaded by astute reasoning. Sometimes, however, a negotiator must bargain for information. In such instances, the information itself becomes the subject of negotiation, as something of value that is traded for specific information.

With third parties, the trade can involve anything from goodwill to money. The means of obtaining the information are confined only by legal and ethical restrictions, such as the laws regarding bribery; insider trading; the theft of corporate and business secrets; the disclosure of various categories of information by government officials; and privileged information.

Implicit Bargaining

In the negotiation itself, there can be either explicit or implicit trades of information. With implicit trades, disclosure may be made with the clear, albeit unstated, expectation that it will lead to a reciprocal release of information from the other negotiator. This is analogous to the concede-first strategy. If the other side fails to respond, one can try to demand a reciprocal disclosure. If that fails, the negotiator should, at least for a period of time, refuse to make any further disclosures unless there is a specific agreement on mutual disclosures.

Explicit Bargaining

In an explicit trade of information, a party may forthrightly offer to disclose certain information if information held by the other side also is revealed. At times, parties are reluctant to make disclosures because they fear that one-sided disclosures will lead to an imbalance in the information known to the parties and a corresponding disadvantage in the negotiation. When such a problem arises, the explicit trading of information can open up productive communications between the parties. Assuming that the parties are acting in good faith, trading information can alleviate the fear that the flow of information will only be in one direction.

Informational Tactic 6:
Information Through
Discussion

> ## Key Concept 53
>
> *Discussion is a common means of exchanging information.*

One of the most common methods of exchanging information is through discussion. **Discussion,** or the consideration of a question or issue, can take the form of a conversation, debate, or argument. The form the discussion takes will depend on the situation, the parties, and the negotiators.

Keeping Discussions Nonadversarial

Except to the extent that an adversarial posture is required, a less adversarial discussion is more likely to produce information. A less adversarial form of discussion allows negotiators and their parties to focus more easily on the content of the message, rather than on its style of delivery (conversation, debate, or argument). The key is to find the style, phrasing, and tone that persuasively convey selective information to the other party and its negotiator while simultaneously eliciting from them the information that you need.

When the Adversarial Style Is Appropriate

An adversarial debate or argumentative style is appropriate in some situations. For example, an adversarial position is appropriate when the other negotiator can be overwhelmed; however, this is the exception rather than the rule. Any attempt to overwhelm an opponent can be counterproductive since failure to do so often serves to increase resistance and, sometimes, to create resentment.

Debating or arguing in an adversarial style also is fitting when the other negotiator is determined to interact on that level and when initial efforts to engage in a less adversarial manner have been futile. Under these circumstances, a more adversarial style is necessary to avoid creating the impression that you or your side can be intimidated.

Furthermore, the need of the client or other important parties to witness a more adversarial posture can make the use of such a style appropriate. The negotiator, however, must function as an advisor. He or she should not adopt an antagonistic manner just because the client has hostile feelings toward the other party or its negotiator. The client's desires may be skewed by highly charged, emotional misconceptions. One of the functions of a negotiator in representing a party is to act without the animosity that can cloud the judgment of clients who are caught up in their personal feelings. Indeed, that is one reason why it is sometimes difficult to represent oneself in a negotiation. Zealousness should be based on an objective assessment of the situation and on what actually will benefit the client. For a negotiator to fail to properly advise the client and to feign antagonism only because it reflects the client's desires without regard to consequences is poor representation.

Releasing Information

Releasing information in a discussion should not necessarily be resisted. One of the reasons parties with basically the same goal can disagree on how to achieve it is a difference in the information they possess. Thus, particularly where cooperative goals or a problem-solving strategy are involved, it may be important to discuss and to share data and information about needs, opinions, and so forth. Indeed, in such situations, brainstorming sessions that seek creative solutions can be an effective means of discussion.

During the discussion portion of a negotiation, there may be facts or other information that should not be disclosed. Commonly, negotiators do not want to disclose their authority or any weaknesses in their positions. In these situations, generalities and deflection can be used to avoid disclosure to the other party. (In addition, questions about authority can be handled in several specific ways. One could respond with astonishment that anyone would ask such a question and expect a serious answer. Alternatively, inquiries about authority can be met with an outright refusal.)

The Use of Principles and Policies

Principles and policies are especially useful tools for discussion in negotiations with governmental or other entities which:

1. Have a goal that is a policy objective, or is premised on certain principles.

2. Have a decision maker and/or a negotiator who is truly influenced by that policy goal or principle.

Examples of policy goals and principles include protecting or enhancing the environment, or preventing or redressing age, race, sex, religious, or handicapped discrimination. When such policy considerations or principles constitute a key motivating factor for the other side, a good opportunity may exist for discussion to be used to shape or to explain offers and positions. The discussion should seek to influence the other party through the use of its own policy or principle.

Case in Point 4-12

"I realize that as an EEOC attorney, you are trying to protect the rights of blacks whom you believe should have been but were not hired. However, in protecting those rights, you have proposed a backpay award which would be devastating to the company. I'm sure this is inadvertent. Perhaps you are unaware of the company's precarious financial position, especially with regard to debt and its relationship with its lenders. In fact, even if the government were to prevail at trial and win a large backpay award, the result would bankrupt the company. So the real result would be a loss of work for everyone. That result will not advance the government's policy objectives. But, I think there is a middle ground, if you are willing to be flexible without abandoning any of your policy objectives."

Off-the-Record Discussions

Off-the-record, or informal, discussions can lead negotiators to an unexpected degree of candor. Their guard may drop because of the spontaneity, the informality, and the feeling that a higher degree of candor is expected in talking outside of the formal negotiation as one professional to another. A negotiator should initiate informal discussions whenever they will be advantageous, but be extremely wary of being drawn into one. There are times, however, when the ability to candidly comment off-the-record to the other negotiator provides a face-saving or less threatening means of disclosing information.

Goals Compatibility

Since discussion is often a useful general method for selectively disclosing information as well as for eliciting information, it is an option that can be used for all goals and strategies.

Comprehension Checkup

The answers to these questions appear on page 331.

1. During the negotiation, you realize that the other party does not understand your company's cashflow issues. Although clearly solvent, the company needs to have at least 45 days to make payments, instead of the customary 30; you should use _____.
   a. nonverbal communication
   b. snow job
   c. selective information disclosure
   d. deflection

2. The other negotiator says, "We'll sell for $305,000 – I mean, $355,000."
   You should _____.
   a. ignore the $305,000 figure.
   b. assume that a $305,000 offer is acceptable, but that even a lesser offer
      may be possible.
   c. offer $305,000 and move for closure.
   d. ask if the $305,000 really was an error.

3. You are asked a question that you do not want to answer, but you also want
   to avoid creating distrust. You can use _____.
   a. a refusal to answer
   b. deflection
   c. snow job
   d. all of the above

4. You want to get information from the other negotiator. Initially, you
   should use _____.
   a. threats
   b. specific questions
   c. the funnel approach
   d. deflection

5. You ask a question. The other side changes the subject. You should
   _____.
   a. feel frustrated.
   b. assume the answer would be unfavorable to the other side.
   c. use threats.
   d. respond with a snow job.

6. When seeking to sell a physically unattractive building in need of cosmetic
   repair, you should use _____.
   a. fact creation
   b. lowering the price
   c. discussion
   d. concede first

7. The other party refuses to reveal certain information which you need to proceed, and then claims that you are the one who is holding back on information. You should use _____.
   a. indifference
   b. public posturing
   c. bargaining
   d. a and b
   e. b and c

8. A good negotiator discloses as little information as possible.   T   F

9. Informational tactics are used in every negotiation.   T   F

10. If your information is correct when you say it, your expression and tone of voice are unimportant.   T   F

11. Being a good listener is more important than being a good talker.   T   F

5
Situational Tactics— Part 1

Key Concepts

54. It is generally better to keep concessions as small and unpredictable as possible.

55. A precondition, regardless of whether it is based on power or reasonableness, is a nonnegotiable concession required for a negotiation to proceed.

56. Avoid making the first offer, unless you are forced to by time constraints or you are in a position to set a realistic bargaining range.

57. Always demand a clear response to an offer or position before modifying it.

58. Reciprocity is a tactic whereby a party demands a concession in exchange for one given.

59. The win-win tactical approach involves creative thinking to discover or create mutual gain or a low-cost or no-cost concession.

60. When structuring concessions, take into account the fact that two parties will not necessarily place the same value on a concession.

61. Trial proposals are offers that involve sudden shifts in focus, with great uncertainty as to the other party's reaction.

62. Bargaining is an explicit offer to exchange one thing for another.

63. As a negotiating tactic, debate is more than mere argument. It is an exchange of views designed to persuade the other negotiator to accept your position.

64. Offers are most persuasive if the stated reasons for making them show how they meet the other party's interests or needs.

The Language of Negotiating

To make full use of the key concepts, you must understand the following key terms:

Preconditions	Risk preference
Procedural preconditions	Trial proposal
Substantive preconditions	Bargaining
Realistic first offer	Debate
Norm of reciprocity	

Introduction

Negotiators have a wide range of tactics available to help accomplish their goals. Using information accumulated through informational tactics (outlined in Chapter 4), negotiators implement strategies using tactics presented in the next chapters. For your ease of reading, these situational tactics have been numbered consecutively.

The situational tactics described in this chapter provide a variety of ways to advance a negotiation. A range of tactics is offered to maximize the negotiator's choice and effectiveness. The tactics will be explained and, when applicable, related to the strategies to which they are best suited. It will also be pointed out when a tactic is particularly unsuited to support a particular strategy.

Key Concept 54

It is generally better to keep concessions as small and unpredictable as possible.

A number of the tactics described below involve making concessions. Many negotiators tend to repeat patterns in making concessions. The most successful negotiators tend to make smaller concessions and to avoid predictability by using a more varied pattern of concessions. Using concession patterns as a clue during the negotiation will be analyzed in the sections on the implementation and adjustment of a negotiating plan in Chapter 12.

Situational Tactic 1: Demanding Preconditions

Key Concept 55

A precondition, regardless of whether it is based on power or reasonableness, is a nonnegotiable concession required for a negotiation to proceed.

Preconditions are demands which must be agreed to by all participants before the negotiation can proceed. Although often articulated as demands, preconditions are often, in fact, just the first stage of some negotiations. In addition, preconditions can be used as the first stage of a particular phase or issue within a negotiation.

Preconditions are chosen unilaterally by a party and presented as nonnegotiable items. In many respects, their use is like the no-concessions strategy, except that they are limited to gaining initial agreement on certain points. In this way, they differ from simply deciding that an issue should be negotiated with compromises first as part of establishing an agenda. Although minor adjustments can sometimes be made to preconditions, their basic premises are not negotiable.

The nature of preconditions may be procedural, substantive, or a combination of the two. **Procedural preconditions** are ground rules that will govern all or part of the negotiation. They could include:

1. An understanding that audited financial statements will be provided to verify financial conditions.

2. The presence or absence of the clients at the negotiation.

3. Whether or not the negotiations will be conducted secretly.

4. The place where the negotiating will occur.

Substantive preconditions are items which one party or the other ultimately seeks to gain. They can also be items that one party or the other refuses to include in the negotiation. Examples of substantive preconditions include:

1. Price terms that are not negotiable.
2. The assurance that the parties will (or will not) be equal partners or shareholders if an agreement is reached to form a new partnership or corporation.
3. The agreement that a party is ready to pay realistic damages, not merely nominal damages or the cost of defending a lawsuit.
4. The understanding that installment payments will be permitted.

Sometimes procedural and substantive preconditions can be combined. For example, when negotiating with a group, a leader of a nation insists that the willingness to negotiate does not mean any recognition of the legitimate status of the group.

Exercising Preconditions

There are two common situations in which the use of preconditions is especially appropriate. The first arises when the demanding party has sufficient power to unilaterally impose a prerequisite as a trade-off for the other party's right to even negotiate the remaining issues. In the second situation, preconditions are necessary to clarify an essential issue for which there can only be total agreement or total disagreement. In this case, preconditions are reasonable from the perspective of both parties. Since the issue is critical and no middle ground exists, preconditions avoid the possibility that the parties will be wasting their time by attempting to negotiate.

Demanding preconditions is a tactic that should be employed with caution; in fact, it should not be used in most negotiations. The other side in the negotiation may resent the imposition of preconditions. They may view it as a form of coercion, or an attempt to unfairly gain concessions without relinquishing anything in return. Whether resentment will occur depends on the custom and practice for that type of negotiation, whether the precondition is presented harshly or gently, the personalities of the other negotiator and party, and whether the precondition seems fair or appropriate. Preconditions based on reasonableness are less likely to cause resentment than those that rely on the imposition of power.

To decide whether or not to demand preconditions, the possible resentment of the other party must be weighed against the potential benefits for your side. This analysis should include whether one party will refuse to negotiate at all, retaliate, or adopt a harder line on the remaining issues to compensate for acquiescing to the preconditions. A careful analysis of possible unintended effects is especially important in the following situations:

1. When the goal is cooperative.
2. When the plan for the negotiation includes the use of a problem-solving strategy.
3. When a long-term relationship between the two parties is at stake.

In these instances, a congenial atmosphere is more likely to result in a successful negotiation. Demanding agreement on a precondition can prevent or destroy that type of atmosphere.

Countering Tips for the Demanding-Preconditions Tactic

Countermeasures include direct refusal to meet the demand, which is a no-concession strategy applied to the precondition. Unless the other party will be intimidated, this technique usually should be combined with a face-saving tactic (see Chapter 6) so the party demanding the precondition can continue gracefully without having won it. Under some circumstances, another countermeasure is to demand a reciprocal precondition.

Situational Tactic 2: Making or Avoiding Making the First Offer

---

Key Concept 56

Avoid making the first offer, unless you are forced to by time constraints or you are in a position to set a realistic bargaining range.

A negotiating myth — one which used to be heard more often — is that a good negotiator always tries to avoid making the first offer. But consider what would happen if everyone engaged in negotiations stopped making the first offer: there would be no negotiations! Obviously, someone must make the first offer. In fact, sometimes it is better to make the first offer than to wait for the other side to do it.

The term **realistic first offer** refers to an offer that is neither so high that it is absolutely disregarded by the other negotiator or party, nor so low that it concedes too much. In other words, a realistic first offer can establish the "ball park" range in which the negotiation will be played out. When a negotiator is in a position to make a realistic first offer, it can be advantageous to do so in an attempt to control the parameters of the negotiation. In this way, the negotiator might be able to influence the other side's perception of what is possible or reasonable for them to achieve in the negotiation. Care must be taken to leave room to maneuver during the remainder of the negotiation.

Whether you are in a position to make a realistic first offer depends on the amount and the quality of information you have. Making the first offer can be counterproductive if it is so unrealistically high that the other side either believes that no agreement is possible (when that is, in fact, not true), or judges that the offer cannot be taken seriously. Making the first offer also can be counterproductive for you if it is so low that it concedes too much or discloses more about your bottom line than is prudent. Avoiding these pitfalls requires having sufficient information to properly assess the negotiating situation.

If you are uncertain about whether you have adequate information to make a realistic first offer, it is advisable to wait for the other party to make the first offer. Their offer will provide additional information for assessing the bargaining range and the potential outcomes. One exception occurs when time constraints force you to make the first offer. In this instance, time factors outweigh the risks of making a first offer with insufficient knowledge. When pressed for time, it is better to err on the side of aiming too high than too low.

Goals Compatibility

Generally, the first-offer tactic can be used with any goal or strategy. One caveat is that in some types of negotiations, the accepted norm may be for one side to virtually always make the first offer. For example, in the sale of real estate, the seller typically sets an asking price which usually is understood as negotiable. This assumes, as is normally the situation, that the seller is seeking a buyer, rather than that a buyer is approaching an owner to convince that owner to sell.

In some fields, custom permits the imposition of bidding or written proposal procedures. When appropriate, a party can thereby force the

other party to make the first offer by requiring written bids or proposals. The bids may constitute the entire negotiation, or at least the major
portion of it.

Situational Tactic 3: Demanding Responses to Offers and Positions

---

Key Concept 57

Always demand a clear response to an offer or position before modifying it.

Two very experienced business negotiators once attempted to demonstrate an effective negotiation. One had planned extremely carefully,
with a series of positions and reasons for each position. He did most of
the talking. The second person never responded in a definite way to
any of the first negotiator's positions. Instead, she would look incredu-
lous, question the seriousness of his reasoning, and smile or laugh quietly as part of her response. Although she did not refuse his offers outright, he kept making more and more concessions in an attempt to
achieve agreement. In fact, he went so far in his concessions that he actually exceeded his settlement authority! It is ironic and interesting that
all this occurred in a demonstration designed to show how to negotiate.

In this example, the first negotiator (a lawyer) neglected to utilize a
basic tactic: to get clear and absolute responses to his offers. Rather, he
assumed that the other negotiator's vague reactions to his positions were
refusals. Instead of demanding that she accept or reject his proposals,
he just kept making further concessions. In effect, he was bargaining
against himself. If the situation had been real, the first negotiator would
have been guilty of malpractice because he made too many concessions
and exceeded his settlement authority.

To avoid unnecessary concessions when the negotiator believes that
an offer (or certain terms) has been accepted, the negotiator should
summarize the negotiation to that point. The following model statement illustrates this tactic.

"At this point, let me review what we've agreed on and what is still
open."

You must pin down that terms are actually accepted, and not just that they are understood and will be considered. These two types of responses can sometimes be confused in the vagaries of a discussion, as the next model statement shows.

"That's an interesting idea that we haven't considered before. I think I like it."

Generally, one should clarify an ambiguous response by stating forthrightly your understanding that there is agreement on the point, as long as that is a fair interpretation. Avoid questioning the other negotiator about whether there is agreement. The rationale here is that a question might unnecessarily generate doubts. The other negotiator might interpret your questions to mean that serious issues still remain on whether there should be an agreement.

Keeping Positions and Their Rationales Separate

Demanding definite responses to offers or positions is very different from demanding agreement on the reasons for them. The other side may either be absolutely set against agreeing with your reasoning, or just unwilling to admit agreement. Acknowledging the correctness of your reasoning may involve a separate psychological, political, or business loss to the party beyond the issue being discussed. For example, such acknowledgment may be viewed as an important precedent to avoid. Or, it could be perceived as a factual admission that could be used for other issues in the negotiation. Also, it might involve the loss of face or prestige.

Regardless of the motive underlying the refusal to agree with the reason for the offer, the important concept is that disagreements on reasons rarely need to be resolved, provided the parties agree on the terms of the offer itself. In sensitive situations, a party should be allowed to tacitly agree to the terms for the reasons stated by the other party, even if it refuses to acknowledge that those are the reasons which led it to agree. It is substantive agreement that is crucial.

Agreement on the reasons for a position should be sought only in those relatively infrequent situations when it is difficult to separate the reasoning behind the agreement from the manner in which it will be implemented. If the manner of implementation cannot be absolutely specified and is subject to dual interpretation, then it may be important to agree on the rationale of the agreement. This will help to avoid or minimize future problems in interpreting the accord, or at least provide some objective guidance if questions do arise.

As a negotiator, you must try to be aware of any tendency on your part to expect or demand that responses be direct verbal ones. Of course, the response still must be sufficiently clear and definite to proceed with, or subtle clarification should be sought using informational tactics. The response to an offer or position can also be revealed indirectly or nonverbally. Similarly, a fear of silence, or a corollary tendency to break silences, may interrupt the other side, thereby preventing it from considering how to respond and blocking the opportunity to learn important information.

Goals Compatibility

The tactic of demanding responses to offers and positions applies to all goals and every strategy, with one exception. If the purpose of the negotiation is something other than agreement, then the response becomes irrelevant. Normally, however, without clear responses from the other side, the negotiator cannot properly evaluate that party's positions.

Note: In many negotiations, the negotiator lacks final authority, but exerts considerable influence over the ultimate decision maker. In that situation, an agreement to recommend acceptance to the decision maker is a definite response. On your part, a key question to secure a definite response could be: "Will you recommend acceptance of this proposal?"

Countering Tips for the Demand-Response Tactic

Countermeasures to demands for the acceptance or rejection of offers include:

1. Citing a lack of authority.

2. Expressing a need for clarification, factual information, or exploration of other issues before responding.

3. Remaining silent, if that is likely to force the other side to keep talking and thereby make additional concessions, disclose more information, or explicitly or implicitly withdraw a demand for feedback.

4. Using silence as a form of refusal to the demand for a response, unless it will counterproductively antagonize the other negotiator.

To deter unrealistic expectations by the other party, normally it is better to clearly reject an unacceptable offer than to simply not respond. When your opponent presents a totally unrealistic proposal, the four most useful responses generally are to:

1. Probe to discover the other side's perception of the benefits in order to:
   a. Uncover previously unknown or undervalued aspects.
   b. Gain insight into the other party's true needs, interests, values, and goals.
   c. Obtain an understanding of the other side's perception of the needs, interests, values, and goals of one's client and oneself.
2. Reject the position firmly with an explanation of the reasons why the offer is unrealistic.
3. Make an equally unrealistic counteroffer as protection against an attempt to use the split-the-difference tactic (see page 153).
4. Present a realistic counteroffer, specifying that any suggestion to split the difference will be rejected because the other party's offer was completely unrealistic.

You can use one or more of those responses as needed.

Situational Tactic 4: Setting Up Reciprocity

Key Concept 58

Reciprocity is a tactic whereby a party demands a concession in exchange for one given.

Related to the concept of demanding definite responses to offers and positions is the idea of reciprocity. The reciprocity tactic is to demand a concession in return for a concession. The demand is made on the premise that to make a concession after receiving one is only fair, and that the other negotiator now "owes you one." The demand might also be made in terms of a legitimate need for feedback on whether the other side is willing to further modify its position. Feedback might also be needed on what the other party believes is a reasonable range of items to discuss. The point of reciprocity is to avoid repeated concessions without obtaining anything in return.

Reciprocity can also take the form of requiring a counteroffer by the other side in response to making the first settlement demand. Initial offers by the parties are not concessions per se, but the principle is the same. You want to avoid bidding against yourself by requiring some reciprocal movement by the other side.

Of course, this tactic may not work if the demand, offer, or concession does not present a reasonable enough position to justify reciprocity. Even if a negotiator makes a mistake and, on reevaluation, determines the position to be unreasonable, an effort still should be made to
obtain reciprocity on the basis that the position was taken in good faith.
In this situation, reciprocity also might be sought on the basis that one
needs to know what the other side considers to be reasonable. This is
particularly applicable when an initial counteroffer is sought in response to a first demand.

Goals Compatibility

With three exceptions, this tactic can be used for all goals and with all
strategies. The exceptions are aggressive goals inconsistent with concessions, and the strategies of no concessions and no further concessions.

Countering Tips for the Reciprocity Tactic

Regardless of whether you're on the giving or receiving end of this tactic,
you must realize that negotiators often feel compelled to respond to an offer with a counteroffer, and to respond to receiving a concession by giving
a concession. This feeling or tendency to respond in kind to offers or concessions is often called the **norm of reciprocity.** Although these responses
are frequently reasonable, the norm of reciprocity sometimes operates
blindly. Negotiators often believe that this is the customary or normal way
of proceeding. That inclination must be resisted. There is no rule that negotiators blindly respond in kind. Counteroffers should be extended only
if it is appropriate to the situation and consistent with your strategy. You
need not automatically make a concession just because one is received. The
countermeasure is simply to be aware and to use judgment in consciously
deciding whether to reciprocate.

Situational Tactic 5: Crafting Win-Win Proposals

Key Concept 59

*The win-win tactical approach involves creative thinking to discover
or create mutual gain or a low-cost or no-cost concession.*

As described in Chapter 2, the problem-solving strategy consists of working with the other party to discover mutually beneficial approaches or low-cost or no-cost concessions that eliminate the other party's objections to an offer. Mutual gain is achieved either by expanding the pie or through concessions that are valued by one party but cost the other little or nothing. Similar types of mutually beneficial proposals can result from the creative analysis of the parties by one negotiator, with or without input from the other side. Offering win-win proposals is such a tactic.

Of course, win-win possibilities do not exist in every case. The potential for discovering them depends on being able to capitalize on differences between the parties' beliefs, values, needs, goals, and risk preferences. The term **risk preferences** refers to a party's willingness or reluctance to live with various degrees and types of risk.

Win-win proposals can take a wide array of forms, limited only by the goals, situational constraints, willingness, and creativity of the participants. The following scenarios illustrate possible ways to craft win-win situations.

Negotiating Scenario_____

An agreement is reached to handle billing in a way that will first reduce costs and then split the savings among the parties to the negotiation.

Negotiating Scenario_____

A transaction is structured in a way that increases the tax benefits for one party while proportionately reducing the cash cost to the other party.

Negotiating Scenario_____

In the sale of a business, uncertainty about liabilities has created a dilemma for a potential purchaser that could compel the seller to lower the price. To achieve a win-win outcome, the seller considers changing the deal to sell the assets rather than the corporate stock (along with its liabilities) of the present business. The buyer avoids the dilemma involved in the business's liabilities and the seller, who would have had to face the liabilities without the sale, makes the sale.

Negotiating Scenario_____

Two parties are interested in entering into an agreement for the licensing of technology. The potential licensee dislikes the customary terms of a minimum royalty for the item. In fact, the licensee does not want any royalty arrangement. Taking this into account, the licensor structures an appealing offer that omits those terms. Instead, payment is to be based on a simple formula using a shared cost savings with an inflation index (which, in fact, leads to a higher total income than the normal royalty fee). This was a win-win proposal because it removed all risks from the licensee, since payment was only required if the licensee achieved a cost savings from the use of the technology.

Goals Compatibility

The win-win tactic can be employed to advance any goal or strategy, except two. The exceptions are negotiating for purposes other than agreement, and certain aggressive goals in which a win-win proposal would be inconsistent with weakening or destroying the targeted person or entity.

Win-win proposals are especially useful with cooperative goals, the problem-solving strategy, and the HRESSC strategy. Even when the HRESSC strategy is employed in what appears to be a competitive negotiation, win-win proposals can be used tactically.

Negotiating Scenario_____

Another method for structuring the win-win sale of a business is to set a flexible price based on future operations. This technique creates a win-win proposal by making payment to the seller fluctuate, depending on the revenue generated by the buyer after assuming control. Usually, the price is a percentage of revenue for a set period of time.

The win-win tactic is discussed further in Chapter 11 in the section concerning planning win-win outcomes.

Situational Tactic 6: Leveraging the Difference Between the Values of a Concession for Each Side

---

Key Concept 60

When structuring concessions, take into account the fact that two parties will not necessarily place the same value on a concession.

Negotiations result in agreement because parties place different values on whatever each side is giving and receiving. People are not going to expend time and energy negotiating a trade of five undistinguishable $100 bills for five similarly undistinguishable $100 bills.

The tactic of concessions of greater value to one party focuses on these differences in value to structure a concession. Individual needs, interests, goals, information, and so on, can cause one party to place far greater value on a particular concession than the other party.

Even the same number of absolute dollars can have different subjective, psychological, or business values for each party, depending on its economic status, cashflow requirements, or the emotional impact of either having to pay or being the recipient of the funds.

Negotiating Scenario_____

In a commercial transaction the buyer knows that the seller is having serious cashflow problems and experiencing excess production capacity. Accordingly, the buyer makes an offer substantially less than would ordinarily be acceptable, but which includes payment in 10 days instead of the customary 45 days. This is sufficient to solve the seller's cashflow crisis. The seller makes a business decision in which the benefits of accepting the low offer now outweigh the detriments of having to wait much later to receive a higher price.

Many businesses emphasize short-run financial results. So if you are negotiating with such an entity, you may be able to trade long-run concessions of greater value to your side for short-run concessions that are valued more by the other side.

It is usually advantageous to disguise the value of an item which is the object of bargaining. If the other party believes the item to be of less value to your side than it actually is, they may demand less in a trade-off. In some instances, however, revealing the item's value to you may be necessary in order to obtain it.

The ideal concession is one that involves conceding something that is not essential for your side and is of far greater value to the other side. This item can therefore be used as a direct trade-off, or as a means to extract a concession for something else that your side holds in greater value. In this situation, the concession of greater value tactic resembles a win-win tactic, because gains are made by both sides at relatively little cost to either. However, this is only a possibility. It is important to realize that one side can gain what it wants by using this tactic without any corresponding advantage for the other. To use the pie analogy again, this tactic differs from the win-win tactic in that it does not involve expanding the size of the pie.

Variations of the Concessions of Greater Value Tactic

One variation of this tactic that is applicable to multiple-issue negotiations is to purposely include demands that one is willing to trade off for other concessions. To be effective, the demands must appear reasonable. In reality, however, they are included merely as disposable concessions that the other side perceives as more valuable than they are, and which your side can trade for something of greater value.

Another variation is to use a number of small concessions to demand a single concession of greater value than all the smaller concessions combined. This tactic works as long as the aggregate value of the smaller concessions granted to the other party are valued by them more than the value of the single, large concession being demanded by you. In this situation, it might be useful to point out the relative advantages for both sides, as demonstrated in the following model statement.

> "I agreed to your demands on delivery, guarantees, and discounts. All I'm asking in return is for the terms for servicing. That's certainly less than what I've given you."

Goals Compatibility

The tactic of using a concession of greater value to the other party can be used with most goals and strategies. There are, however, some exceptions. Obviously, this tactic is not applicable to the no-concessions or no-further-concessions strategies because those strategies do not permit offering any concessions. The tactic also is inconsistent with a strategy of negotiating for purposes other than agreement, for a party then is merely using the negotiation as a pretext for a different objective. Finally, if the other party in the negotiation is the target of an aggressive goal, a concession of greater value to that party would be inconsistent with the objective of weakening or destroying it. This tactic, however, is not always inconsistent with aggressive goals. It depends on the particular situation.

Negotiating Scenario

You have the aggressive goal of acquiring one of your competitors. Offering a concession of greater value to the competitor in this case would be consistent with the aggressive goal. For example, if the competitor's owner places a far greater value on one of your race horses than you do, then the horse may be the perfect concession.

Situational Tactic 7: Trial Proposals

> ### Key Concept 61
>
> *Trial proposals are offers that involve sudden shifts in focus, with great uncertainty as to the other party's reaction.*

A **trial proposal** is an offer made as a sudden shift to a new type of arrangement, or to terms significantly different from those which were previously proposed. This sudden shift is distinguished by the fact that it is not part of a logical sequence in a series of offers. Trial proposals are made with great uncertainty as to whether there will be acceptance or rejection by the other party. The purpose is to attempt something different in order to gauge the reaction of the other negotiator or the other party. Even if rejected, a trial proposal may still elicit a reaction that provides important information about the other party's vital interests or its real position.

If a trial proposal involves a large concession, it should be offered only after careful evaluation. When you suddenly make a large concession, you run the risk of giving away more than is necessary to achieve an agreement. In addition, a sudden large concession may lead the other party to believe that rejecting the offer or making additional demands could result in even greater concessions. Therefore, it also is essential that trial proposals involving large concessions be phrased especially firmly, with persuasive reasons given for the position being taken. This carefulness minimizes the possibility that the trial proposal will be perceived as a sign of weakness or a willingness to make further large concessions.

Trial proposals are commonly referred to with certain slang expressions such as, "floating a trial balloon" or "running it up the flagpole to see who salutes." Despite these colloquialisms, the trial proposal tactic should be taken seriously.

Goals Compatibility

Trial proposals can be used with any goal or strategy except the no-concessions or no-further-concessions strategies. When combined with the win-win tactic, trial proposals are especially effective. They are, however, less applicable where the only issue is an amount of money to be paid. They are often helpful in creating movement in stalled negotiations.

Situational Tactic 8: Bargaining

Key Concept 62

Bargaining is an explicit offer to exchange one thing for another.

Bargaining consists of an offer to exchange one specific item for another. It may be a certain amount of money in exchange for merchandise, property, or a settlement agreement. In a business negotiation, bargaining might involve increasing the price to obtain agreement by the seller for more liberal payment terms. In professional football negotiations, the bargaining might involve the offer of a tackle and a draft choice for a speedy and strong wide receiver. In whatever situation, the essence of bargaining can be stated as: "I will give you X for Y."

Usually, bargaining becomes a series of offers and counteroffers. To avoid the appearance of unbridled "horse trading" or just throwing numbers back and forth, it is especially important to state reasons for your bargaining position.

People often appreciate items more when they perceive them as having been earned or won, rather than merely given away. In the context of some negotiations, the value of a particular concession will be clear; at other times, it will be unclear. A negotiator must always carefully avoid giving the impression that a concession has little value. This can be done by requiring the other party to bargain or otherwise work to obtain it. Avoid bargaining this way in those cooperative negotiations in which it is more important to demonstrate goodwill than to secure a specific concession.

In bargaining, it also may be helpful to set a point somewhat above one's bottom line for use as a check point. Once this point is reached, the negotiator should reevaluate the negotiation before agreeing to any further bargaining concessions. This may help the negotiator avoid having to retreat to the actual bottom line, or it may provide the chance to adjust a previous plan on the basis of new information acquired during the negotiation. Much of the writing on negotiating underemphasizes the better-known tactic of bargaining and concentrates on the lesser-known cooperative and problem-solving areas, perhaps in order to appear to be imparting new wisdom.

Goals Compatibility

Bargaining is useful for reaching many goals, especially competitive ones. It can also be used with any strategy that employs concessions. If used for the strategy of purposes other than agreement, a negotiator must offer proposals that are either seemingly attractive but actually unacceptable, or ones which lead to a willingness to continue negotiations but without creating a final agreement.

Situational Tactic 9: Debate

Key Concept 63

As a negotiating tactic, debate is more than mere argument. It is an exchange of views designed to persuade the other negotiator to accept your position.

Debate is an exchange of views designed to persuade the other party or its negotiator to agree or acquiesce to a proposal, position, or reason. A debate might persuade the other side to withdraw or desist by influencing their values, facts, principles, needs, or interests. A debate might also convince the other side of the futility of continuing along a particular line or approach.

Because the debate tactic functions to influence the other party to move in a specific way, it is essential to place the action or other response that you seek clearly in the mind of the other side. Equally essential, is to persuade the other side to accept it. Persuasion is accomplished by altering the other's perception on the merits of the subject and the usefulness of a position for the purpose of the negotiation.

Negotiating Scenario

In the debate phase of a negotiation, a negotiator seeks to demonstrate that the market value of an item is different than the other party believes. The negotiator attempts to convince the other party of the correctness of the different assessment without pressing for an explicit acknowledgment, thereby allowing the other side to save face. Because the other side may not be convinced of the "facts" being argued, the negotiator also seeks to convince the other side that its assessment of the market value will not be accepted by the other party's company. This corollary has the beneficial effect of forcing the other party to realize that its concept of the market value will not be the basis for an agreement.

Making Persuasive Offers

Key Concept 64

Offers are most persuasive if the stated reasons for making them show how they meet the other party's interests or needs.

If possible, the persuasive argument should be aimed at showing how your position will meet the underlying requirements, wants, and goals of the other party. If an offer is met by skepticism or an objection, the negotiator should:

1. Restate it in the form of a question, if needed for clarity and to avoid any misunderstanding. For example, a negotiator may say: "You agree, don't you, that this approach creates a cost savings which our clients can divide?"

2. Respond directly to the perceived problem with proof, if possible.

3. When appropriate, restate and stress the overall benefits of the proposal while minimizing any drawbacks.

Indifference to an offer may require probing to discover or clarify the other party's needs. The funnel approach can be very helpful in this process, allowing one to elicit areas of general need and then focus in on the details.

Productive debate requires concentrating on specific substantive or procedural items to cause a modification or reversal of the other side's views.

It is usually not productive to engage in personal attacks or conflicts by charging bad faith or attitude problems. There are two exceptions:

1. When doing so is useful as part of focusing on the process.
2. When the explanation of a demand or a rejection of an offer requires that type of rationale.

Turning Your Weaknesses Into Strengths

Persuasive arguments for the debate tactic include:

1. Weaving factual themes into a coherent and credible whole.
2. Presenting one's strengths and facing or minimizing one's weaknesses.
3. Forcing the other side to argue its weaknesses.
4. Presenting one's weaknesses as strengths.

One of the most powerful argumentative techniques is to take a point considered by the other side to be one of your weaknesses and to present it as a strength. A willingness to discuss the point, combined with a reasonable argument that it is not a weakness, can be very discouraging to the other negotiator who thought that a persuasive flaw had been discovered. This technique is a popular one with politicians and has been described as the central principle of political jujitsu.

Structuring the Debate

Whether the debate will be formal or informal, it is important to plan the issues you will address, your manner of presenting them, and your responses to the other side. How issues are defined can determine the direction of the debate. Issues must be implicitly or explicitly agreed on for the process to progress. Nevertheless, they should be defined as favorably to your side as possible. The best definitions of issues tend to lead to positions with unassailable premises from which to begin arguing.

Backing Positions With Objective Criteria: Pros and Cons

It may be useful to rely on objective criteria as the basis for the reasons of your position. With government officials, the objective criteria should focus on justice and the specific principles that they are supposed to be seeking as part of their official duties. Objective criteria may be drawn from any number of sources, including:

Precedent and common practice.

Knowledge (or technical expertise) generally recognized by those in the field.

There are times, however, when a negotiator must not place too much emphasis on objective criteria. For example, care should be taken when arguing from precedents. The other negotiator could succeed in arguing that the precedent you are using concerned a situation which had important differences from the present negotiation. In this case, the validity of your objective criteria becomes suspect. In a similar way, appeals to reason or principle can be countered by challenges to their validity or applicability, thereby neutralizing their effectiveness as a basis of argument.

Using Debate to Appeal to the Personal Interests of the Other Negotiator

At times, to create the necessary motivation for the other side to modify or reverse its position, it is essential for the argument to appeal to the other negotiator's personal interests. When all else fails, debate and persuasive argument can sometimes cause a change in the other side's personal attitude which, in turn, might change the direction of the negotiation. See page 193 for more information on appealing to personal interest.

Overcoming Emotionally Based Deadlocks

There are times when difficulty in reaching an agreement may be due to differences in how the participants perceive the issues. This deadlock can result from the differing and conflicting emotions of the parties and negotiators. One clue that emotional forces are stalling the negotiation is that the debate has degenerated into counterproductive argument. In such instances, discussing the perceptions or the emotions may help resolve the differences.

When the deadlock is caused by strong feelings of anger, steps need to be taken to defuse the tension. These include:

1. Changing the tone.
2. Focusing on the process while acknowledging the legitimacy of the feelings.
3. Responding in kind, if that will shock or intimidate the other side into refraining from angry argument, rather than intensifying the anger.

However, if a highly charged, argumentative form of debate is being attempted as a ploy to intimidate, an effective countermeasure is to calmly ignore the violent tone. Regardless of the verbal or nonverbal communication selected in response to an angry argument, it is crucial that the negotiator remain poised and inwardly calm in order to think clearly.

Goals Compatibility

Debate can be used for all goals and strategies. A reasonable debate can be an especially effective tactic for persuading parties that a proposed term or a complete agreement is fair and worthy of acceptance. Persuasion based on fairness is most important with a cooperative goal or with the problem-solving strategy. In those situations, it often combines using informational tactics with an exploration of the needs of the parties.

Because debate involves an exchange of views, it differs from the informational tactics discussed in Chapter 4, in which one negotiator gives, or seeks to obtain, information. However, in actual negotiations, debate often is combined with informational tactics, especially selective disclosure or the funnel approach.

Countering Tips for the Debate Tactic

Countering tips for the debate tactic include:

1. Presenting contrary facts.
2. Attacking the other side's interpretation.
3. Revealing purported facts to be mere assumptions.
4. Acknowledging a mistake in an argument but promptly replacing it with a new point.
5. Admitting an argument's validity, but showing its limitations.

6. Using or distinguishing analogies.

7. Permitting the other side to abandon positions gracefully, thereby allowing them to avoid or minimize a loss of face.

Comprehension Checkup

The answers to these questions appear on page 331.

1. You only want a contract for services from William Ltd. if emergency services will be available on 2-hours' notice from the same company. You should choose _____.
   a. debate   c. preconditions
   b. bargaining   d. trial proposal

2. You are sure that any agreement will be in the range of $10 to $15 per unit, and decided to initially demand $16. You should _____ the first offer.
   a. be willing to make   b. avoid making

3. When the other negotiator presents a precondition, one good countermeasure is to _____.
   a. demand reciprocity   c. use trial proposals
   b. use the funnel approach   d. avoid making the first offer

4. You just received a concession. The other negotiator says, "It is only fair that you reciprocate with a concession of equal value, since you haven't made any concessions yet." You normally should _____.
   a. refuse   c. terminate
   b. agree   d. a or b

5. You carefully explained your offer, giving reasons which show the benefits to the other side. However, your offer is met by silence. You should _____.
   a. create a deadlock   c. demand reciprocity
   b. demand a response   d. offer to split the remaining difference

6. For a competitive goal using the HRESSC strategy, the win-win tactic is _____.
   a. appropriate   b. inappropriate

7. You encounter a deadlock in a negotiation. A wild idea enters your head, but the other party may not be interested. You should use _____.
   a. caution and wait   c. trial proposal
   b. debate   d. bargaining

8. An offer is most persuasive if the reasons stated include how it _____.
   a. is firm   c. meets your needs
   b. was calculated   d. meets the other's needs

9. In every negotiation, you should try to create win-win proposals. T F

10. A trial proposal with a large concession that is more likely to be accepted is better than one with a small concession that is less likely to be accepted. T F

11. Bargaining is less effective than most other tactics. T F

12. During a debate, you should argue but avoid discussing the other negotiator's personal interests. T F

6
Situational Tactics— Part 2

Key Concepts

65. Conditional proposals are offers that are contingent on the resolution of other issues.

66. The effective tactical use of power depends on a number of considerations, both long-term and short-term.

67. Bluffs are positions stated as nonnegotiable which actually are negotiable. Bluffs also refer to adverse consequences which one side supposedly will cause to occur, when, in fact, it will not really do so.

68. Tone is the general mood in which negotiations occur. Tone can affect whether an agreement is reached as well as its terms. It should be controlled to yield the desired effect.

69. The presence of alternative opportunities gives a negotiator added leverage when negotiating.

70. Split the difference when (a) the gap between positions or offers is small, (b) other tactics have failed and each side's position is reasonable, or (c) time pressure dictates, and (d) closure will result (e) without a harmful precedent that outweighs the gain.

71. Focus and downplay are used to learn the other party's real interests and, if appropriate, to mislead the other party about your own.

72. Whenever possible, a negotiator should try to create a psychological commitment for agreement in the other side.

73. Allowing the other side to back down without embarrassment may entail ignoring a position, providing new information, granting a token concession, offering a different interpretation, or changing the tone or the negotiator.

74. Sometimes, failure to move a negotiation forward is due to the people involved, not the terms under consideration.

The Language of Negotiating

To make full use of the key concepts, you must understand the following key terms:

Conditional proposals	Precedent
Power	Focus and downplay
Bluff	Psychological commitment
Tone	Work group phenomenon
Alternative opportunities	Supercrunch
Whipsawing	Lowball
Splitting the difference	Face saving

Situational Tactic 10: Making Conditional Proposals

Key Concept 65

Conditional proposals are offers that are contingent on the resolution of other issues.

Conditional proposals are offers that depend on the resolution of some or all of the remaining issues in the negotiation. This differs from bargaining in that the tactic involves an offer of X for Y, but only after points A, B, and C have been settled. The following model statement illustrates a conditional proposal.

"I'm willing to meet your price on the initial shipments if we resolve the volume discount on the subsequent orders."

The use of conditional proposals is appropriate for goals and strategies that involve the following circumstances:

1. Multiple issues.

2. A relationship between some or all of the issues so that trade-offs between issues are possible.

3. A concern that the other party may make high demands on issues being negotiated later so that there may be a legitimate need to reexamine earlier issues (and subissues) in view of the emerging totality of the overall agreement.

Case in Point 6-1_____

A hospital wants a doctor who is finishing her residency in cardiology to relocate to a different state and open her practice in the hospital's area. There are numerous issues involved in the potential agreement. The negotiable benefits for the doctor include:

1. The amount of money which the hospital will pay the doctor.

2. The time over which that amount will be paid.

3. The nature and extent of various fringe benefits, including professional liability insurance, life insurance, disability insurance, and moving expenses.

4. The length of time for which these benefits will be provided.

5. Whether free office space will be provided, and if so, how much and for how long.

6. Whether loans will be given to provide the doctor with working capital, and if so, how much and on what terms.

As to the doctor's obligations under the potential contract, the issues include:

1. The length of time that the doctor is obligated to maintain her practice in the hospital's area.

2. The definition of the boundaries of that area.

3. The circumstances under which the doctor would not be obligated to maintain her practice.

4. The extent, if any, to which secondary offices could be opened outside the hospital's area.

5. The amount of the hospital's damages and of the physician's obligations should she breach the contract.

6. The definition of maintaining the physician's practice, including such considerations as vacations, time spent on continuing medical education, and maternity leave.

The hospital presents a relatively comprehensive proposal which appears to be a reasonable first offer. The situation warrants the use of conditional proposals because the three criteria that justify the use of this tactic are present (multiple issues, possible trade-offs between issues, and a need to reexamine tentative subagreements as new issues that are agreed on shape the total package). Part of the hospital's offer would obligate the physician for a period of 4 years. In structuring a counteroffer, the doctor seeks, among other things, higher pay and more money in loans. In presenting the counteroffer, the physician informs the hospital that the inclusion of the 4-year time period in the counteroffer is conditional upon the acceptance of the rest of the counteroffer.

Situational Tactic 11: Power

Key Concept 66

The effective tactical use of power depends on a number of considerations, both long-term and short-term.

Generally speaking, **power** refers to the amount of control, authority, or influence one party exerts over another, or over circumstances. In international negotiations, for example, the tactic of power can be exercised through such means as granting or withholding economic assistance, trade sanctions, or the threat or actual use of military force. The use of power is effective for addressing immediate issues to the extent that one party truly has power over the other to force an agreement on its terms. However, when long-term relationships are at issue, power must be exercised with a comparably long-term view. The effective exercise of power over time requires the careful consideration of both intended and unintended effects.

The party with less power often resents the use of power to force it to acquiesce. That resentment can lead to overt or covert resistance, attempts at sabotage, or other forms of retaliation. To determine whether to use the power tactic, the potential adverse effects must be weighed against the benefits of exercising power. Both long-term and short-term effects must be anticipated.

In addition, the potential ramifications for constituent groups (such as union members) or third parties (such as customers or suppliers) must be examined in two respects. First, one must decide whether the views of these entities, individuals, or groups have a sufficiently significant impact to be taken into account. Second, if their views are to be taken into account, one must evaluate which views are likely to emerge from an exercise of power in light of historical positions, short-term and long-term vital interests, and any immediate situational pressures. The questions to consider include whether the exercise of power will be:

1. Perceived as legitimate or illegitimate.

2. Felt as intimidating and cause an immediate counterreaction.

3. Viewed as creating a precedent for the future, or just as a one-time event.

If the exercise of power is tied to a legitimate rationale, and therefore is perceived by the other side as justified but unwelcome, the use of power is less likely to provoke a hostile reaction. A related factor is that this perception may alleviate the other side's problem of self-esteem; its acceptance (in terms of a legitimate rationale) might minimize its need to save face by resisting. For the same reason, if one party uses power to threaten another, it often is better to issue the threat in a non-threatening style. This proviso assumes, however, that a threatening manner will cause the other party to react to save face, rather than become intimidated. If the other party might be intimidated by a threatening style, that style should be considered in light of any long-term effects. In summary, the potential benefits from exercising power must be weighed against the likelihood of serious unintended and adverse effects that might occur. One must consider the potential pitfalls that can arise from anger, jealousy, or resentment by the less powerful side.

Power can take many forms. A party may have effective control in various ways, such as by:

1. Offering extremely attractive economic benefits to the other party.

2. Causing the other party to incur extremely high costs unless there is an agreement.

3. Delaying the resolution of a claim.

4. Threatening noneconomic sanctions which constitute an unacceptably high risk to the other party.

There are legal and moral restrictions on the use of power that one needs to consider. For example, it is not only immoral to threaten to dump toxic waste on someone's property to force them to sign an agreement, but it is also illegal, and provides grounds to void any such "agreement" on the basis of duress.

Usually though, issues of legality and morality are not relevant because the types of power being contemplated are neither illegal nor immoral. In most instances, the key factor in deciding whether to employ power is effectiveness. Ordinarily, the decision to exercise, or to refrain from exercising, power is made on the pragmatic grounds of long-run and short-run usefulness.

Goals Compatibility

Due to the negative reactions that can result from the exercise of power, it should be chosen as a tactic only after an especially cautious analysis of goals and strategies. Cooperative goals generally are inappropriate for the power tactic. At a minimum, it will be perceived as inconsistent with a cooperative attitude. Competitive and aggressive goals usually are ideal for the use of the power tactic, assuming that sufficient power exists and that there's an absence of conflicting goals. It also can be useful for self-centered and defensive goals.

The power tactic is ideal for the strategies of no concessions, deadlock-breaking concessions, and HRESSC, since it eliminates or decreases the need to make concessions. The power tactic also may be helpful with the strategies of negotiating for purposes other than reaching agreement and of moving for closure, again depending on the specific factors in the particular negotiation. For the problem-solving strategy, however, the negotiator may decide to refrain from, or temper, the use of power to avoid the perception of being uncooperative.

Countering Tips for the Power Tactic

To counter the use of power, one must try to create a realistic adverse effect to wield against the party that is using or contemplating the use of power. These effects may be either short-term or long-term. Remember, the potential gain from the use of power must be outweighed by the potential loss. The countermeasure must convince the party contemplating the use of power that its exercise is not worth it. This can be done directly by the targeted party itself, or indirectly through allies. In order to constitute an effective countermeasure, the threatened counter-effect must be known or communicated to the party employing or considering the use of power.

Situational Tactic 12:
Bluffing—A Two-Edged Sword

> ## Key Concept 67
>
> *Bluffs are positions stated as nonnegotiable which actually are negotiable. Bluffs also refer to adverse consequences which one side supposedly will cause to occur, when, in fact, it will not really do so.*

Bluff simply refers to taking a position as if it were absolutely fixed and without any possibility of modification, when that is not really true. Instead, the negotiator is prepared to back down if strongly challenged. A bluff may take two forms. The first is a purportedly nonnegotiable offer or counteroffer. The second is a threat to cause an adverse consequence for the other party if it refuses to agree to certain terms, when the negotiator knows that he or she can not or will not do so.

The obvious dilemma in bluffing is that if caught, the negotiator risks losing credibility. Also, the other negotiator is compelled to push harder on all remaining issues to determine whether other bluffs are being attempted. Being caught in a bluff will affect not only that negotiation, but also all future negotiations with that party or negotiator. It also is likely to affect negotiations with other negotiators and parties, since one's reputation tends to become known.

Do negotiators ever try to bluff? Of course they do. What can go wrong? Consider Case in Point 6-2, taken from an actual negotiation.

Case in Point 6-2

The negotiation is to buy out the interest of one partner in a very successful business. On Monday, the parties negotiated and reached an agreement on the price and on other basic terms. By late Tuesday morning, the buyers' lawyer prepared a draft agreement and transmitted it to the seller's attorney in time for a scheduled 2 p.m. closing. Each lawyer remained in his office. The negotiation of some remaining terms continued through a series of telephone conferences and exchanges of draft agreements. By 6:30 Tuesday evening, the attorneys were still negotiating the drafting of the terms. The seller had agreed that the mutual releases would not bar the buyers' potential indemnification claim against the seller if customers sued because of certain specified actions of the seller. However, the seller's attorney suddenly inserted a paragraph which, in the event of such a third-party suit by a customer, would require the buyers to assert that the seller had acted properly in the buyers' defense of the action. Previously, the buyers had adamantly refused to agree to such a term, and it negated the indemnification exclusion agreed to earlier that day. The buyers' attorney (BA) then telephoned the seller's attorney (SA). Later in the discussion, the seller (SL) also speaks.

BA: Paragraph seven has to come out. You know that my clients won't take that position with their customers.

SA: Tell them I assure them that it won't hurt them to do it.

BA: They aren't interested in assurances. They won't do this, and they really can't be expected to do something so detrimental to their long-run relationships with their customers.

SA: It can't come out.

BA: Are you saying that it's nonnegotiable? You stuck it in after we've agreed to the contrary and now it's nonnegotiable? Is that your position now?

SA: Yes. You tell them that they're fools if they blow the deal over this!

BA: I'm not going to debate who's behaving like a fool! But, if this has been your plan all along, then you've wasted everyone's time. If it's nonnegotiable, then that's it. I'm going home. I'm telling my clients to tear up the certified check which has been sitting here most of the day and I'm going home. Good-bye.

SA: Wait. Byron [the seller] is standing right here. Let me put him on. Byron, talk to Gerry about paragraph seven.

SL: What about paragraph seven?

BA: Byron, your lawyer says it's nonnegotiable. You know that my clients can't agree to this. If this was nonnegotiable, then you've just wasted two days of your time and money.

SL: O.K., then take it out. Now we have a deal.

In this process, the seller's attorney grossly miscalculated his position. He lost all his credibility by his unsuccessful bluff. In addition, by placing his client in the position of having to personally admit the bluff and back down, he certainly did not enhance his standing with his own client.

Damage Control When Caught Bluffing

One method of extricating oneself from an unsuccessful bluff is to seek "new information." In planning what to do if caught, the negotiator should consider whether anything can be referred to as new information which apparently became known after the bluffed position was taken. If so, the negotiator can attempt to escape from the dilemma by acting as though the change of a previously unalterable position (or the threat) was due to having learned some new and totally unanticipated information. The feasibility of this maneuver depends on the plausibility of the new information cited. Also important are one's demeanor and the level of skepticism of the other party and its negotiator. The successful use of the new information ploy will prevent a loss of face and credibility from a bluff that is called by the other party.

Countering Tips for the Bluff Tactic

Countermeasures include calling the bluff with an outright refusal to acquiesce. This may or may not involve creating new facts which could alter the threatened consequences of the bluff. A negotiator may also use selective information disclosure, debate, and face saving to persuade the other negotiator to back out of the bluff.

Situational Tactic 13: Controlling the Tone of the Negotiation

---

Key Concept 68

Tone is the general mood in which negotiations occur. Tone can affect whether an agreement is reached as well as its terms. It should be controlled to yield the desired effect.

The **tone** of a negotiation is the general mood in which it occurs. It may be:

1. Relaxed or tense.
2. Friendly or hostile.
3. Trusting or suspicious.
4. Cooperative or competitive.

Tone is an unavoidable and ever-present element in every negotiation. Perhaps more than any other factor, tone will affect the direction and results of the negotiation. The negotiator who can control the tone of the negotiation has an important advantage in controlling the proceedings.

The tone can help determine whether the negotiation actually will progress to an agreement. Even when the parties' bottom lines overlap, negotiators must often be willing to spend time exploring each other's positions. If the negotiation has an unpleasant or unnecessarily difficult tone, a negotiator may decide that a satisfactory offer is unlikely. This then can become a self-fulfilling prophecy.

Unless, in light of long- and short-run interests, it will be productive to intimidate or overwhelm the other side, the negotiation should not be conducted in such a way that one side feels it is being manipulated. This feeling can create a defensive or hostile reaction that will make it more difficult to achieve a good agreement.

You must anticipate and observe the other negotiator's reactions to the tone of the negotiation. It is difficult to be persuasive if the other negotiator is concentrating on retaliation, face-saving ploys, or scoring debating points.

Tone is especially significant if the negotiator contemplates some relationship beyond the present negotiation. All other factors being somewhat equal, people prefer dealing with people they like. Negotiators are no different. In deal making, a negotiator who is liked has an advantage in the negotiation. Furthermore, when a long-term working relationship between negotiators (or their parties) is an objective in the negotiation, difficulty or unpleasantness experienced during the negotiation may be interpreted by the other party as a sign of unpleasant things to come in future dealings. The tone then becomes a strong negative factor in deciding whether to enter into an agreement at all.

In most deal making, the tone of the negotiation should be professional and pleasant. Normally, the parties have come together without coercion and have authorized the negotiation because of their mutual interests in reaching an agreement. They have not sent their negotiators to do battle, although at times very tough negotiating stances need to be taken. Even if one party is, or desires to appear to be, less interested in making a deal, a disinterested or more distant tone need not be unpleasant.

Applying Pressure

Generally, a negotiator should avoid pressuring his or her counterpart. That does not hold true, however, if pressure is likely to succeed because of the needs, constraints, or even the personalities of the other parties' negotiators. Frequently, a low-key, but assertive posture is best. This means:

1. Avoiding the hard sell.
2. Coaxing the other party into appreciating one's point of view.
3. Adopting a modest attitude while at the same time being quietly forceful whenever necessary or appropriate.

Tone also can be useful in encouraging the other party and its negotiator to be psychologically committed to making a deal. Taking on a tone of enthusiasm, for example, while showing the inevitable benefits of a particular deal for both parties, can be effective in motivating the other party and its negotiator to move toward agreement.

Using an Adversarial Tone

Sometimes a more adversarial tone is appropriate. It can be used to counter an aggressive tone on the part of the other negotiator or party, and to demonstrate one's resistance to intimidation or pressure. Also, a more adversarial tone should be used when it is very likely to succeed in intimidating or pressuring the other party or its negotiator without off-setting negative effects. Finally, an adversarial tone can provide a temporary display of emotion to underscore and reinforce a particular point, argument, or reaction. Its use may even be necessary to ensure consistency between the negotiator's words and demeanor, thereby preserving his or her persuasive power.

Changing the Tone

A temporary change of tone can be effective to convey or emphasize the message being articulated. Whereas constant or predictable displays of emotion tend to be viewed as personality-related or as tactically motivated, a temporary, controlled, appropriate display of anger, skepticism, amusement, bewilderment, or other emotion can indicate the depth and sincerity of the statements being made. It even may be the persuasive factor necessary to convince the other side of the truthfulness of the statements.

Using an unexpected tone can be an effective way to deliver a message. If loudness is expected, soft intensity may be used to capture the listener's attention, avoid prepared psychological defenses, and take the listener off guard. Similarly, increased volume can make a point if only moderate tones are expected. The loudness should not be so extreme that it is offensive, but sufficient enough to make the listener feel the speaker's deep belief.

Although professionals should usually avoid dramatics, sometimes a little drama can be effective. However, one's flair for the dramatic must not overwhelm good judgment. It may simply cause the other side to react equally dramatically, or with some other response that neutralizes the original dramatic gesture.

Countering Tips for the Tone Tactic

One method to counter a strongly emotional tone is to indicate understanding of the person's feelings, and yet remain focused on the facts. The factual explanation should demonstrate that one's position is reasonable and fair. The following model statement demonstrates this countering tip.

> "I understand your frustration. But you must not realize the ramifications of what you're asking. First of all..."

Some negotiators' effectiveness is affected by the other negotiator's establishing a tone of personal like, respect, or approval; they might drop their guard or tone down their aggressiveness. In dealing with such an individual, one should use that fact and behave in a personable, friendly, respectful, and approving manner. Conversely, a negotiator must have the self-awareness to realize his or her own vulnerability, which may be due to a need to be liked or feel approval. It does not matter whether the other negotiator's conduct is genuine or manipulative. In no event should momentary personal emotional gratification prejudice one's own true interests.

Goals Compatibility

There is a complex relationship between goals, strategies, and the tone in which they occur. For example, in shifting from a competitive goal, HRESSC strategy to a cooperative goal, problem-solving strategy, a negotiator often must also shift the tone of the negotiation. However, many negotiators confuse the tone of the negotiation with the negotiator's goal of being competitive or cooperative. This error can create a significant flaw in the analysis of the negotiation. A cooperative tone of voice does not necessarily indicate a cooperative goal.

Case in Point 6-3_____

In a lease negotiation, the lessor started with a basically unreasonable position, but articulated it as if she were cooperatively engaged in problem solving. The other negotiator sounded mildly adversarial, but really tried to engage in problem solving. His opening position was quite reasonable. As the negotiation continued, the lessor continued to use a cooperative tone, and initially refused to make any concessions. The lessee made a large initial concession. During the balance of the negotiation, the two engaged in bargaining. The lessor, with the more cooperative tone, made fewer and smaller concessions, while the lessee, with the adversarial tone, made more and larger concessions.

This scenario was demonstrated at a National Institute for Trial Advocacy Negotiation program. A postsimulation discussion produced predictable results. In general, the audience's reaction was that the lessor had been cooperative, while the lessee had been competitive. Yet, from an analysis of the behavior of each party, the audience discovered that it had been deceived by both negotiators' tones. A quite different picture emerged when the audience focused on the actual behavior and concession patterns.

Positions, process, concessions—all within the context of tone—must be considered before a decision can be made about whether a negotiator is engaged in competitive or cooperative negotiating. This is essential to properly analyze the other party and its negotiator during the negotiation. Only in this way can effective adjustments be made that are based on the true intentions and behaviors of the other party and its negotiator, rather than on mere tone and style.

Situational Tactic 14: Using Alternative Opportunities

Key Concept 69

The presence of alternative opportunities gives a negotiator added leverage when negotiating.

In the background of some negotiations, there are known opportunities with outside parties that are alternatives to the positions being presented by the other party. Such **alternative opportunities** are mutually exclusive with the deal being presented. You can do only one or the other. The opportunity may involve a different building, a different supplier, a different business or investment opportunity, a different opportunity for partnership or shareholding, and so forth. In these situations, the alternative to reaching an agreement is not the absence of agreement, but possibly entering into an agreement with a different party through a separate negotiation.

When pursuing a negotiation, a negotiator must not neglect alternative opportunities. At times, multiple, simultaneous negotiations are essential to maintain all options and maximize results.

Case in Point 6-4

A professional practice was for sale. Because of the limited market for the practice, there was a significant danger that a viable, potential purchaser might back out of the deal. The seller negotiated simultaneously with several possible buyers until the best available deal was identified and a written agreement was executed.

As shown in Case in Point 6-4, alternative opportunities provide a negotiator with leverage over the other party. It is permissible to present and use the alternative, since one cannot be reasonably expected to accept terms inferior to those clearly available from a different source. Furthermore, alternative opportunities provide a negotiator with both a measure of the market value and the market terms for a transaction. They also create a bottom line beneath which no transactional agreement will be considered because a better deal awaits elsewhere. If there is any uncertainty regarding the firmness of an alternative opportunity, the situation must be analyzed, weighing the potential benefits against the risk that the opportunity could fail to materialize.

In examining the market, the alternative opportunity need not presently exist, although it certainly is a more powerful bargaining chip if it does. However, past history, which reasonably indicates that similar opportunities might currently be available, can be used to formulate an alternative opportunity position.

Alternative opportunities can result from legitimate fact creation. By successfully searching for, or having a client explore, genuine alternative opportunities, a negotiator creates a new operative fact in the negotiation. This new fact must be responded to by the other party and its negotiator. They cannot ignore it completely, even if they refuse to match or exceed it. Employing this tactic necessitates planning and preparation, since the negotiator must be aware of specific alternative opportunities. It requires knowledge of the market and its prices, customs, values, and practices. The requisite knowledge may be already known to the negotiator, or may come from some other source, including the client.

The alternative opportunity tactic differs from the bluff tactic since the assertion that an alternative opportunity exists is true. If you strongly suspect that the alternative opportunity claimed by the other side is a bluff, you may weigh the risks of being mistaken and call the bluff, or you may demand verification that the purported opportunity exists. The following model statement demonstrates how to respond to this dilemma.

"If I am going to get my people to take this offer seriously, I will need a copy of the written offer from this other source."

Such a direct challenge can be appropriate, although it does create the danger that the other party will be unwilling to relent because of a fear of losing face, even if it wants to retract the bluff. Generally, a less aggressive, but nonetheless firm, approach will be more effective in leading to the retraction of a bluff, without requiring any overt or embarrassing admission that the other party was bluffing. This approach always includes some statement that provides an opportunity for the other side to escape from the bluff without a loss of face. The following model statement demonstrates how a negotiator can provide the other side with a way out of a potentially embarrassing situation.

"If you can really get the same thing, especially when quality is really taken into account, and get it at that price, then you should do business with them instead of with us. We cannot, and will not, sell at that price because there is no margin for a reasonable return. Before you make your final decision, however, you should closely evaluate the qualitative factors. There is no way they can come close to our quality at that price, unless they're selling below cost just one time before they raise the price on you. From what I know, I don't think you'll find the quality to be the same. In fact, you're going to find out that all you've bought are new headaches. But, obviously, it's your decision."

This firm, face-saving approach ignores the bluffed assertion that the position was fixed and final. Instead, the approach affords a method for further reconsideration and modification of the position. Although every negotiation will be different, the basic principle is to not act as if the other negotiator's position (that is, the bluff) was stated as fixed and final, to present a face-saving opportunity for the other negotiator to move away from that position, and to proceed with the negotiation.

Evaluating Alternative Opportunities

Because of the possibility of a bluff, the alternative approach tactic often leads to the debate, funnel approach, or informational bargaining tactics. Furthermore, apart from the question of a bluff, the negotiators may discuss or argue about whether the other opportunity is truly comparable. You may first need to make inquiries to determine whether the alternative opportunity is certain, tentative, or illusory.

Case in Point 6-5_____

A medical practice was for sale. One potential purchaser probed during the negotiation to ascertain whether any legitimate, serious rivals existed with the means to make a comparable or superior offer to the one being planned.

Once the status of the alternative opportunity is determined, differences in the opportunities are identified and explored to evaluate whether the opportunities are really comparable, or whether one is distinctly advantageous. Quantitative or objective differences can be disposed of relatively quickly once they are identified. However, qualitative and subjective differences often are difficult or impossible to measure. For this reason, qualitative or subjective differences usually are the focus of the most difficult portions of a discussion to determine whether the opportunities are equivalent, or whether one is better than the other.

Deciding to Adopt Alternative Opportunities

A negotiator must be sensitive to two reactive factors in deciding whether to employ the alternative opportunity tactic. In some situations, the relationship between the parties is such that the loyalty is a positive negotiating factor with real value to the other party. Reliance on an alternative opportunity will undermine that loyalty factor. If it is appropriate or necessary to use this tactic despite the negative effect it may have on loyalty, the negative impact should be tempered by a suitable explanation. The following model statement demonstrates how to offer an explanation to preserve loyalty.

"You and Fred have done business together for a long time. You know that he has remained loyal to you, even when there have been some disadvantages for him. And he knows that you've been good and fair with him, at times going out of your way for him. He appreciates your loyalty, as I'm certain you do his. But look at the choice that he's facing. It would be irrational and virtually suicidal to throw away such a great opportunity out of loyalty. And he's not even asking you to match it penny for penny. All that he's asking is for you to come close enough to offer a rational opportunity for a business decision in your favor."

The explanation should be framed in terms of a loyal but reasonable person or entity who is being driven away by the other party's unwillingness or inability to present a rational alternative in the negotiation. The second reactive factor in deciding whether to employ the alternative opportunity tactic is how the other party will perceive it. Will the alternative opportunity be viewed as either an unfair threat or as the equivalent of asking competitors to bid back and forth against each other in a setting where such bidding is considered inappropriate. This process of back-and-forth bidding is sometimes derogatorily referred to as **whipsawing.** Some parties may resent being whipsawed, and refuse to participate in it. Resentment can be based on the nature of the parties' relationship, the qualitative or personal nature of the product or service, or the fact that it is not customary to operate in this manner. For many negotiations, however, matching, or at least responding to, a competitive offer or position, is the custom rather than the exception.

These two potential, unintended, negative effects must be weighed against the often powerful leverage created by a realistic and legitimate position that no agreement will be entered into that does not favorably compare with specific alternative opportunities.

Goals Compatibility

The alternative opportunity tactic can be utilized with any goal or strategy. It can demonstrate reasons for, and justify a range of, positions. The following negotiating scenarios illustrate some of these positions.

Negotiating Scenario_____

A manufacturer decides to employ the no-concessions strategy in making an offer to purchase raw materials from a potential supplier. The appropriateness and fairness of the offer is explained by the willingness of a different supplier to accept virtually the same offer.

Negotiating Scenario_____

In a commercial transaction involving financing, one of the unresolved issues is the rate of interest that will be charged. Utilizing problem solving, an agreement is sought by resolving the issue based on the terms available from alternative opportunities. "Let's see what interest rates are commonly used in these types of deals, and we'll match the best one commonly available."

Negotiating Scenario_____

In a different commercial transaction, one of the issues is the base price of the unit. The alternative opportunities provide a basis for a necessary concession. "If that's the price they're quoting, I will meet it. And you'll know that you're still getting superior workmanship."

Situational Tactic 15:
Splitting the Difference

Key Concept 70

Split the difference when (a) the gap between positions or offers is small, (b) other tactics have failed and each side's position is reasonable, or (c) time pressure dictates, and (d) closure will result (e) without a harmful precedent that outweighs the gain.

One of the most frequently invoked negotiating tactics is to split the difference. **Splitting the difference** means that the negotiators agree to an equal division of the item in question. The difference may be in dollars, the date for closing a transaction, or anything else that is capable of being split.

Splitting the difference is effective when:

1. The parties have reached a point at which the difference between their positions is relatively small.

2. Each party realizes that the other's position is at least somewhat reasonable so that the split is fair.

3. Time limitations are so pressing that each side agrees to split the difference in order to meet a deadline.

4. Closure will result rather than the other side demanding further concessions.

5. No harmful precedent will occur to outweigh the gain.

Under these conditions, splitting the difference is an appropriate method for resolving the issue. Since each party has a reasonable position and the difference between them is relatively small, it may be difficult or impossible to bridge the difference in any other way. In most cases, neither party may be willing to move more than halfway, either out of a fear of losing face, a desire for a fair agreement with equal compromises of good faith disputes, or both. The split preserves fairness while avoiding embarrassment.

The optimal time for splitting the difference is when, in addition to the conditions described above, the other party's position is already within the range acceptable for agreement. At this time, a split can improve an already acceptable offer.

Avoiding Harmful Precedents

When the difference between the parties is relatively small or proportionately unimportant, even unreasonable differences can be appropriate to split. It just may not be worth either the cost in time and energy, or the risk of losing a potential agreement, to refuse to split what, in context, is a minor but unreasonable difference. In doing so, however, one must guard against establishing an unacceptable precedent. A **precedent** is a statement or action that serves as an example or rule used to justify or authorize a similar future statement or action. A precedent can become unacceptable if it leads the other party to become unreasonably stubborn on remaining issues. Avoid allowing the other party to expect always to be able to resort to splitting differences.

Harmful precedents can be avoided in two ways. One way is to explain at the time of the split that it is being agreed to on this particular issue for certain stated reasons, but that such a split should not be expected on future issues. Another method is to refuse to agree to split the difference on future issues if the other party attempts to establish a pattern of extracting small, last concessions by haggling and then demanding a split of the difference. The consequences of failing to avoid such a pattern are what is commonly known as being "nickeled and dimed to death."

Splitting Large Differences

Generally, negotiators should avoid splitting large differences. A narrow exception to this rule is appropriate when all of the following conditions are present:

1. The result of the compromise is still within the range for an acceptable settlement.

2. Other tactics have been tried without avail.

3. The parties are deadlocked.

4. A further negotiation using other tactics appears futile, or there is a time problem so that immediate closure is important.

The apparent fairness and ease of splitting the difference often creates considerable impetus for its use. However, the analysis must not be superficial or automatic.

The splitting-the-difference tactic should not be used because of laziness or as a method to bypass proper negotiation. Relatively large differences should not be split, because other tactics can be used to explore resolutions in the more favorable area of the bargaining range. By splitting the difference, a negotiator ignores the potential for a more favorable agreement when considerable latitude still exists. Cost effectiveness is the key.

A Caution Regarding This Tactic

You must guard against an opponent who manipulates the negotiation so that splitting the difference results in a more favorable outcome to the other party. This can occur in two ways. The other side may set its initial position artificially high, planning to resort to a split of any remaining difference. This ploy leads to a better outcome for the other party because the artificially high initial position has unduly skewed the bounds of the difference toward one end of the bargaining range. The other method is to make consistently smaller concessions than are extracted, leading to a more advantageous position at the time a split occurs. While guarding against such manipulation, you should use these maneuvers as countermeasures if they are likely to be successful.

Goals Compatibility

Splitting the difference can be used with all goals and almost all strategies. It *cannot* be utilized with the strategies of no concessions, no further concessions, or of negotiating for purposes other than an agreement (except as a ploy, since ploys are not concerned with resolving differences through compromise).

Splitting the difference is especially useful for three strategies. It can be used as a deadlock-breaking concession. Second, in problem solving, splitting the difference can be a "reasonable" method of resolving the difference between the parties' positions. Third, this tactic can be the method for closing the agreement by splitting the only remaining difference that has been preventing a complete agreement.

Situational Tactic 16: Focus and Downplay

Key Concept 71

Focus and downplay are used to learn the other party's real interests and, if appropriate, to mislead the other party about your own.

In analyzing a negotiation, you should consider the subjects on which the other party focuses and those which the other party avoids. These subjects and patterns can provide clues to that party's real interests.

The tactic of **focus and downplay** consists of giving a false clue whereby, for a time, the negotiator focuses on items of less interest and downplays items of real interest. That pattern of behavior makes it appear that the item of real interest has less value than it actually does. If successful, it leads to obtaining the item at a lesser cost because the other party underestimates its value to your side.

A basic example of this tactic can be found in the following purchase of transportation by an entrepreneur in the Old West.

Case in Point 6-6_____

In the Old West, one Mr. Suggs decides he wants to buy a new mule. As a prospector, he knows that mules are more useful than horses. Mr. Suggs reports on how he made his deal:

"I jest didn't want to be without four-legged transportation. The mule looked about the best of the lot. Having dealt with the stable owner before, I carried on about wanting to buy the Apoolosa horse, which he didn't own. A disappointed look crossed his face as he said that he only had the mule for sale."

In this way, our western entrepreneur purchased the mule, which was what he really wanted, while manipulating the seller into believing that he preferred a horse. By creating an appearance that the most desired object is less desirable, the purchaser tends to minimize its cost.

The converse can also be true for a seller. By playing up the value of the less valuable item, a seller with two items of unequal value for sale puts himself in a position to demand more if the buyer prefers the alternative item.

Focus and downplay should not be used if it is important that the other party realize your real interest or need in order to elicit the best possible response. Then, selective information disclosure is the proper tactic.

Countering Tips for the Focus and Downplay Tactic

Countermeasures consist of informational tactics to avoid being misled, such as using other sources, the funnel approach, informational bargaining, and discussion.

Situational Tactic 17: Creating a Psychological Commitment for Agreement

---

Key Concept 72

Whenever possible, a negotiator should try to create a psychological commitment for agreement in the other side.

In some negotiations, it is possible to encourage the other party and its negotiator to have a psychological commitment to reaching an agreement. A **psychological commitment** refers to a mental predisposition toward favoring an agreement. For this tactic, the "carrots" or "sticks" are not directly important; rather, the negotiation process itself is used to create a strong motivation for the other negotiator to achieve agreement. The commitment must occur within the absolute and final limits of the negotiator's authority. If the motivation is sufficiently powerful, this tactic can lead the other negotiator to seek more flexible authority from the party they represent in order to reach an agreement. Similarly, using the negotiation process to create strong motivations to reach an agreement also can be directed against the other party (regardless of whether the other party is representing himself or herself). If successful, it leads the other party to increase its negotiator's authority and to lower its own bottom line. The most effective use is a subtle one, so that the other party and its negotiator are not aware of the psychological commitment being created. By the same token, you must guard against being manipulated in this way yourself.

One method to create a powerful psychological commitment is to focus on, and even be enthusiastic about, the benefits that an agreement will mean for both parties. The emphasis is on the benefits flowing from the general concept of the agreement, without regard to the details of the terms. A second method is to focus on the benefits from the points already resolved. Even conditionally resolved points can be used in this effort.

While in some negotiations apparent coolness and disinterest are necessary to avoid being perceived as overly eager and therefore weak, in other negotiations, that perception is less of a concern. If your side is in a position of relative strength with the other party, you may be able to afford to display enthusiasm without creating a perception of weakness. In many transactional matters, some degree of enthusiasm about the end result for all parties can encourage the other party and its negotiator to more vigorously and flexibly seek to resolve any differences and to find a way to reach agreement.

At times, it might be useful to demonstrate enthusiasm over how the deal will personally benefit the negotiator, particularly when the negotiator represents a party other than himself or herself. The following model statement shows how to apply this type of enthusiasm.

> "You know, if we can pull this off, you will have made one of the largest deals that they're going to see. It certainly won't hurt you a bit in the company."

Using the Work Group Phenomenon

The **work group phenomenon** is another factor that can create a psychological commitment to reaching agreement among the negotiators; it refers to the divided feeling some negotiators experience when the interests of the parties they represent conflict with those of a group with whom they regularly interact. When negotiators repeatedly deal with each other, they can become dependent on one another to facilitate their work. The group may consist of members who either regularly or only periodically interact. Each of the negotiators in the group has a load of assignments, responsibilities, and personal goals. Since no one member of the group can make agreements happen without some cooperation from the others, they are to some degree dependent on each other. Often, they ask each other for small accommodations or favors. To some extent, an unconscious divided loyalty emerges when the negotiators represent parties, not themselves, since each of the negotiators becomes a part of the group of negotiators, with feelings for the group as well as for the party which they represent.

The work group phenomenon raises two points for such negotiators who find themselves part of a group. These points consist of awareness and opportunity.

First, they must be aware of the tendency to act against their own or their party's best interests in order to assist another negotiator from the group who requests a personal favor. This does not exclude giving personal favors to other negotiators which will benefit their side in the long run because reciprocal favors will be granted. It *does* exclude those favors, however, that will not be returned for the present client, although the negotiator personally or other clients may benefit from reciprocity. This restriction is limited, however, to favors that negatively impact on the present client, since only those favors create a prohibited conflict of interest.

The second point is that when it is advantageous, the negotiator should exploit any opportunity created by the work group phenomenon. The decision to use this tactic must be made only after consideration of both the long-term and short-term effects, since reciprocity is likely to be demanded.

Sometimes within, and at other times apart from, an actual work group, an agreement is negotiated with someone with whom there are likely to be future negotiations. The future negotiations may involve either the individual negotiator, or the negotiator's client. To encourage a psychological commitment toward reaching future agreements, one should act appreciatively about the current deal, with as much professional respect and camaraderie as appropriate. Be aware of the other negotiators' personalities and the way they behave during the negotiation. The negotiator who leaves a negotiation feeling good about the outcome will be far easier to deal with in the future than one who feels disappointed or upset about the result. Upset negotiators might wait to use the next negotiation to make up for previous losses or to get even. This antagonism creates an additional burden which should be avoided whenever possible.

Causing the Other Party to Invest Valuable Resources in the Negotiation

Another method for creating psychological commitment to reaching agreement is to cause the other party to expend a great deal of time, energy, and effort toward reaching an agreement. The greater these investments, the more reluctant the other party and its negotiator will normally become to cease negotiating without achieving some form of agreement. To do so is to admit failure and that all the time and effort spent on the negotiation was wasted. This is especially likely to occur if the time and effort also involve a substantial out-of-pocket cost so that a monetary loss is created by the failure to achieve an agreement. In a multi-issue negotiation, the other party may be induced to invest more time, energy, effort, and expense by deferring the more difficult issues until last and reaching at least conditional agreement on the easier issues.

The higher the investment of resources in the negotiation (whether economic or noneconomic), the more anxious a party is likely to be to attain an agreement. Consequently, any negotiator must guard against becoming too committed to agreement. One must be wary of performing less assertively or of making unnecessary concessions because of undue fear that no agreement will result from all that has been invested in the negotiation.

In deal making, especially in acquisitions, the general mood can tend toward the feeling that the deal is wanted, so "let's get it done." The negotiators and the parties may become unduly concerned with losing the deal rather than with either achieving the best possible deal or avoiding a bad deal. Overeagerness to gain a deal can lead to an unwarranted emphasis on a cooperative approach and on the problem-solving strategy, when the party would achieve a more favorable agreement by using other strategies and tactics.

Using the "Supercrunch" Tactic

Another means of establishing psychological commitment has been called **supercrunch.** Supercrunch refers to creating great pressure by bringing competitors together to, in effect, bid against each other. For example, a group of competitors are invited to a meeting by a party with whom they wish to do business. They are presented with difficult demands or requirements by that party. The party using supercrunch then tries to get each of the competitors, in the presence of the group, to commit to its demands or requirements. If a substantial number of commitments are attained, pressure is placed on the competitors to return with favorable bids or proposals that do, in fact, meet the demands or requirements.

Timing and Psychological Commitment

In disputes, an attitudinal issue might arise whereby a party and its negotiator may be ambivalent about whether to settle or to fight. This confusion leads to an issue about the timing of the negotiations. It also can induce an undue psychological commitment *against* settlement, even when a favorable result could be reached that is unlikely to be exceeded. The negotiator must guard against an inappropriate psychological commitment not to settle because of a belligerent or aggressive predisposition, as well as against an inappropriate psychological commitment to settle due to an unwillingness to fight. A negotiator must be wary of losing perspective by being overly disposed toward either battle or peace.

Making a Lowball Offer

Some negotiators attempt to cause the other party to become psychologically committed to a deal through a **lowball** offer. The lowball offer consists of a very attractive initial price, but one which has hidden costs, generally through extras that come to light once the basic price has been accepted.

The lowball is more likely to be successful if disguised by a presentation that makes the hidden costs appear customary, or otherwise fair.

The lowball maneuver is an extreme, short-run measure. It can cause such resentment and distrust that the other party terminates the negotiation. If it works but is discovered, the other party or negotiator is unlikely to seek future negotiations. Unless the other side is composed of complete fools, once is more than enough to teach the lesson and to create either a very guarded approach to any future interactions, or a refusal to negotiate with the party, its negotiator, or both.

The long-run loss of credibility often outweighs any short-run gain from this ploy. Depending on the circumstances, it also may be considered unethical, deceptive, or, in extreme cases, fraudulent.

Countering Tips for the Lowball Maneuver. A countermeasure to guard against the lowball maneuver is to demand full information about the items that are included or excluded before indicating acceptance of the deal. By having all the facts, one cannot be deceived about terms and conditions.

Situational Tactic 18:
Allowing Your Opponent to
Save Face

Key Concept 73

Allowing the other side to back down without embarrassment may entail ignoring a position, providing new information, granting a token concession, offering a different interpretation, or changing the tone or the negotiator.

Face saving involves an action or statement that permits the other party or its negotiator to back down from a position, or to make additional concessions, without being embarrassed. Creating an opening for further movement without losing face can motivate concessions or other shifts in position which would otherwise never occur. It is not at all unusual for a party or a negotiator to stubbornly refuse to act even when that may be costly, rather than suffer personal embarrassment or a potential loss of respect.

The problem of keeping a need to save face from impeding movement is inherent in the nature of negotiating. It has been observed that negotiators face an innate contradiction by simultaneously needing to be firm without appearing rigid and willing to yield without appearing too conciliatory. This makes the need for ways to save face part of the basic fabric of negotiation.

One method of implementing this tactic is to simply ignore the other party's assertion that this is a final or nonnegotiable position. The negotiator continues to proceed as if that position were never stated. If, of course, the other party reasserts that its position is final, it will have to be treated as such. The other party, however, may be secretly relieved to have its threat of finality ignored so that it can change its position without embarrassment or humiliation.

Another method of allowing the other party to save face is to provide new information about the matter at issue. This can save face in two ways. First, the information may provide a new and *real* reason for the other party to alter its previously fixed position. Alternatively, the information may function as a *pretext* that permits the other party to act as though it received new knowledge which justifies a change in its previously fixed position. Either way, the new information effectively allows the other party or its negotiator to save face.

A third method of saving face for the other party or negotiator is to offer what is, in reality, a token or meaningless additional concession in return for the other side making a meaningful change in its position. This allows face to be saved by creating the fiction that the other side improved its bargain or engaged in a reciprocal trade, rather than stating the reality that it made a concession.

A fourth method is to interpret the other side's position differently than it was really intended, so that the other side does not have to indicate that it is changing its position. Such an interpretation must be expressed in a way that is neither condescending nor unfair.

In the following cases in point, the other negotiator has just made a "final offer." The responses are designed to permit additional movement without forcing an implicit admission that the assertion that the offer was "final" was a lie or a bluff.

Case in Point 6-7_____

You know that the other side's "final offer" was not intended to include the inventory. Nevertheless, your response is: "That offer is acceptable as long as it includes the inventory." To allow face to be saved, you act as if you did not know that the other side intended not to include the inventory. Your response, therefore, is actually a demand for an additional concession.

Case in Point 6-8_____

You know full well that the other side has all the information it needs to make its decision. Its offer is ridiculously low. In response, you suggest that the other side lacked information or misinterpreted it.

"I think that you either misinterpreted, or were not given some critical information. Let me try to explain it to you, because I think then you will agree that it wouldn't make sense for us to accept the last offer given the way that it is structured. However, an adjustment to the structure will make it work for both of us."

By providing the information in this manner, you establish a pretext of ignorance which the other party can use to save face. It is better to appear misinformed than to lose a deal by being too rash.

It is important to recognize a subtle request from someone who is either too embarrassed or reluctant to ask directly. If it will create movement in the desired direction, a negotiator can grant an implied request without explicitly referring to it. Again, the other party can save face and the negotiator achieves an important goal. Further, an unspoken agreement might compel the other party to feel gratitude that can pay dividends in the future.

In general, the less threatening, intimidating, and aggressive one appears, the easier it is for the other party and the other negotiator to save face. This is particularly true where the other negotiator or party perceives an approach to be unfair or unjustified. Conversely, the easier it is for the other side to justify its decision to concede or compromise as the most effective choice under the circumstances, the less it feels threatened with a loss of face. To the extent that a proposal can be made consistent with the other side's values and self-image, it will be easier for them to accept the proposal without a loss of face.

Techniques to break an impasse while allowing the other side to save face include altering the terms, tone, or the participants, such as:

1. Modifying the payment terms.

2. Changing the negotiator or the negotiation team leader.

3. Altering the allocation of risk.

4. Modifying the time of performance.

5. Changing or adding guarantees of satisfaction.

6. Altering or adding a grievance mechanism.

7. Changing strategy with a concomitant change in tone.

8. Modifying or adding options.

9. Changing specifications.

10. Adjusting terms.

11. Using a mediator, an arbitrator, or some other outside means of resolving a dispute.

12. Creating a joint study committee.

13. Focusing on the lack or inaccuracy of information on which the other negotiator, through no fault of his or her own, has been relying.

14. Telling a funny story, as long as it is appropriate.

Goals Compatibility

Face saving is not used with an aggressive goal if that goal includes intentionally embarrassing or humiliating the other party or its negotiator. That type of situation, though, is rare. For other types of aggressive goals, and indeed, for *all* other goals and strategies, face saving can be used to avoid or break deadlocks that arise when one side has backed itself into a psychological corner from which it does not know how to escape.

Situational Tactic 19: Identifying People as the Problem

Key Concept 74

Sometimes, failure to move a negotiation forward is due to the people involved, not the terms under consideration.

One very important general principle of negotiation is that normally one should avoid presenting the problem being negotiated as a problem of the people involved. Once people are identified as the problem, they are likely to become defensive and seek to save face, react with personal counterattacks, and so forth. All those reactions can create serious impediments to productive negotiation. By articulating issues objectively and impersonally, the dangers of those reactions are minimized.

Furthermore, unless it is realistic to think that the person who is viewed as part of the problem will change through negotiation, making him or her the focus of the problem is useless. If such a change is realistic, however, it can come about in one of two ways. First, the problem person can be removed by transfer, the reassignment of duties, promotion, or demotion. Second, the problem person on the other side can alter his or her personal behavior in response to the negotiation, thereby eliminating the problem behavior. Either type of change is difficult, if not impossible, to create because of personal traits, psychology, intercorporate relationships, alliances, managerial bureaucracy, and the like. In many situations, therefore, it is unrealistic to negotiate an issue of specific people as the problem because the desired change is impossible or too difficult to achieve.

However, an important exception exists where such change is feasible, or the problem cannot be solved without a change in the people involved. Examples of the latter include the following:

1. A negotiator whose highly antagonistic style or lack of understanding makes progress impossible, after all realistic alternative tactics have been exhausted.

2. An employee of the other party whose personal style, behavior, or incompetence creates very significant problems that are (a) necessary to solve, and (b) cannot be solved by alternative tactics. In these limited circumstances and despite the inherent serious risks, one cannot effectively negotiate by avoiding making people the problem or stating the problem in purely objective terms. Of course, this is a tactic of last resort, to be used as diplomatically and sensitively as possible. Face saving should be used, whenever possible, in combination with this tactic.

Comprehension Checkup

The answers to these questions appear on page 331.

1. You have the power to force the other side to accept certain terms for a short-run contract. These terms provide some financial benefits to you, although the amounts are minor compared to the overall benefits from the contract. The terms are very costly for the other side. You want to develop a long-run relationship with the other side and seek a long-run contract. However, the other side presently resists any commitment to a long-run contract, and favors that a short-run contract be negotiated. You should _____.

   a. immediately press for agreement on the terms
   b. decide now not to demand these terms
   c. make a conditional proposal which concedes the terms if they switch to a long-term contract during the short-term contract

2. You miscalculated and were caught bluffing, a risk you thought was minimal. You should _____.
   a. confess   c. use new information
   b. use power   d. terminate the negotiation

3. During the morning negotiation session, the first three of five issues were considered. There were trade-offs among issues, and there remain potential trade-offs among those issues and the last two issues. At lunch, you decide that the other party's positions on those three issues are acceptable. You should use the tactic of _____.
   a. focus and downplay   c. bluff
   b. conditional proposal   d. power

4. The negotiation has been in progress for most of the day. The difference between the positions of the parties on the key issue has narrowed. The other party now states, "If you do not agree with the last offer, we will make a deal with Rafeco," one of your competitors. You now should use the tactic of _____.
   a. funnel approach   c. bargaining
   b. agreement   d. bluff

5. The tone of the negotiation is one of goodwill and cooperation. Your concessions therefore should _____.
   a. be faster   c. be slightly larger than the other side
   b. match the other side   d. still be as few and slow as possible

6. You anticipated that the negotiation would take most of the day. Shortly after lunch, the other negotiator offered to split the difference on a key issue. The positions of the parties are far apart. You should _____.
   a. agree
   b. refuse

7. The other negotiator has taken positions that have created a deadlock. The situation developed so that the other party can not make a concession without a serious loss of face. You switch to the face-saving tactic to break the deadlock utilizing _____.
   a. new information   d. all of the above
   b. token concession   e. none of the above
   c. interpretation

8. The other party has been focusing on certain points, while downplaying others. You should use the countermeasure of _____.
   a. HRESSC   c. problem solving
   b. information tactics   d. bluff

9. You often negotiate with the same parties and negotiators. You must beware of the effects from _____.
   a. work group   c. lowballing
   b. supercrunch   d. committees

10. Your company has a contract with a construction company and construction has commenced. However, you have totally lost confidence in their architect, who is involved in negotiating certain design modifications. Your immediate tactic of choice is _____.
    a. psychological commitment   c. make people the problem
    b. alternative opportunities   d. conditional proposal

7
Situational Tactics— Part 3

Key Concepts

75. It is sometimes possible and advantageous to hold in reserve one or more issues to create new opportunities for trade-offs.

76. Focusing on the negotiating process can be a helpful tactic when procedural, personality, or tone issues have caused a breakdown in progress.

77. The creation-of-movement tactic can help avoid the loss of a potential agreement that has become stalled during a negotiation.

78. Deadlock is a risky tactic that can be used to test the other side's strength or to cause delay.

79. Threaten to or actually terminate a negotiation when less dramatic means fail.

80. Adjourn to regroup, change mood, obtain authority, give the other side time to reconsider, or give yourself time to deal with other matters.

81. Patience prevents one from being pressured into premature concessions or agreements.

82. Reasonable deadlines are used to avoid being tied up in a negotiation. Deadlines also help prevent the loss of alternative oppor-

tunities and can neutralize any procrastination on the part of the other side.

83. Deal with negotiators who lack authority by preconditions, demanding replacement, reliance on an influential negotiator's recommendation, informational tactics, trial proposal, changing tactics, withholding concessions, and bypassing the negotiator.

84. If appropriate, use surprise by unveiling startling new, apparently attractive terms during the negotiation to catch the other side off guard and prevent a thorough analysis.

85. Appeal to the personal interests of the other negotiator or nonparty decision maker when that will cause disregard for the other party's interests.

The Language of Negotiating

To make full use of the key concepts, you must understand the following terms:

New issues	Adjournment
Focusing on the process	Deadline
Procedural dilemma	Real control
Movement	Bypassing
Linkage	Personal interests
Termination	

Situational Tactic 20: Injecting New Issues

Key Concept 75

It is sometimes possible and advantageous to hold in reserve one or more issues to create new opportunities for trade-offs.

When negotiations begin, the negotiators normally already know or quickly learn the issues. This often is done with generalities and assumptions about the common meaning of what is included in the issues.

In a sale of a home, it is assumed, without discussion, that the issues will include such items as the amount of the purchase price, a
sum to be held in escrow, the date by which the transaction will
close, and the terms of the mortgage contingency clause. Whether
other matters are issues, such as a liquidated damages clause regarding the amount forfeited if one party defaults (that is, fails to
proceed under the agreement), or the inclusion of certain fix-
tures, is quickly determined.

In planning a negotiation, one may decide to save certain issues for
possible use later in the negotiation. The purpose of this tactic is to
be able to trade off on the new issues to gain concessions on other
issues, if the need arises. In negotiating, **new issues** refers to those
issues held in reserve to be introduced later as "new." The new issues
tactic differs from setting an agenda. Establishing an agenda means
having certain issues negotiated before others, in order to deal with
the easiest or the hardest first, or to see how the negotiation of certain issues unfolds before reaching other issues. Under the inserting
new issues tactic, one or more issues are purposefully withheld until
another issue or a certain problem is reached regardless of when in
the negotiation process that point occurs. The withheld issue then is
injected into the process while the other issue or a problem still is
being considered. At that point, the new issue then can be bargained
away for greater concessions on the issue or problem already being
negotiated.

Case in Point 7-1_____

Corporation A is negotiating with Corporation B for the acquisition of B's wholly owned subsidiary, Corporation C. The manner
in which certain aspects of the transaction are structured will affect the potential tax benefits and liabilities of each company.
Prior to beginning the actual negotiation, A already knows basically how B wants to structure those aspects of the transaction. In
planning its approach to the negotiation, A purposely decides to
create and save an issue concerning B's accounts receivable to see
what develops regarding structuring the transaction and the resulting tax consequences. The accounts receivable issue can later
be injected and then traded off to obtain concessions on the tax
issues.

Disassembling Proposed Package Deals

A different version of the injecting new issues tactic is to disassemble a proposed package deal. The parties then bargain about the component parts of the deal. The final agreement may be limited to one or some of the components, rather than the complete package. The new issue consists of imposing a more limited scope on the negotiation than originally existed.

Case in Point 7-2

Mr. Bains seeks to purchase machinery and equipment with installation and servicing. The original issue is the price and other terms for the package; however, it is possible to purchase the various components of the deal separately. In order to probe the seller for further concessions, Bains inquires into whether he can purchase each component separately. Since the components can be bargained for separately, Bains then negotiates for the lowest possible price for each component. Next, he compares these prices with the original price for the entire package. Bains can now attempt to obtain discounts for buying either the entire package or a combination of components. If advantageous, a portion of the desired items may be purchased from the seller with the remainder obtained from other sources.

Even if the use of the new issues tactic has not been planned, a negotiator must remain aware of its potential use in the event that a suitable opportunity arises. Such an opportunity can occur spontaneously through creative thought. A negotiator may suddenly think of an issue that can be effectively used with this tactic. Also, the actions or positions taken by the other party can create a new issue which had not been included when originally planning the negotiation. The issue may be one which the other party purposely injects into the negotiation as a separate issue, or it may arise inadvertently as a result of the actions or positions taken by the other party.

Case in Point 7-3

The Smith & Brown Company owes money, but has financial difficulties that prevent it from being able to pay the full amount it owes. In order to save litigation and collection costs, as well as to be more confident that it will actually receive payment, eXecCorp is willing to compromise on the amount that is owed by Smith & Brown. It is not, however, willing to compromise on the amount nearly as much as Smith & Brown had hoped. Accordingly, a negotiator for Smith & Brown introduces a new issue to ease the cashflow problem; she suggests spreading the payment through installments rather than making one total payment.

Injecting New Issues to Save Face

Injecting new issues sometimes can be used to save face while settling a losing negotiation when outside parties are of concern. This occurs when a party believes that its real goals cannot be achieved, but that it needs to win something so that it can save face. Usually, a party resorts to creating a new issue which it can win. The party then uses the newly won issue to claim that the negotiation was successful. The claim of success is directed toward the public, business associates, or whoever else has an opinion or reaction that is of concern to the party.

Goals Compatibility

The new issues tactic can be employed with any goal or strategy. However, care must be taken to inject the new issue in a manner that appears to be legitimate and fair, especially when cooperative goals or problem-solving strategies are involved. Otherwise, the tactic will be perceived as an attempt in bad faith to use a functionally irrelevant issue as a bargaining chip.

Case in Point 7-4_____

After extensive negotiations and an oral agreement, a draft agreement has been prepared by B and transmitted to A. Certain terms intended by B were implicit throughout the negotiation, and were expressly referred to by B in reaching an oral agreement. The negotiators now are meeting to discuss the draft.

A: In reviewing the draft and looking again at how it will work, we can't live with sections 2.03 and 3.06, unless we receive a 10 percent volume discount. I know we agreed in general, but this just wasn't clear to us.

B: We have spent hours and hours in working out this deal and it always was understood that it would be structured in the manner that the draft reflects. No volume discounts were ever mentioned.

A: That may have been your understanding, but we certainly never intended to agree to do that. And we now realize that the deal is unfair without a volume discount.

B: There have been any number of references to the structure in these provisions and you never once questioned it.

A: Well, it wasn't really clear to us until we saw it on paper. Then the full import hit us.

B: It was discussed sufficiently to be clear. I feel that you are now just trying to get an extra concession because you think that we're locked into this deal. We are *not* locked in, though, and I do not intend to be pressured in this way.

This case in point illustrates the problems and distrust that can arise when a new issue is introduced in connection with issues already resolved. It is critical to inject the new issue for increased bargaining leverage on an existing issue before agreement is reached on that issue. Otherwise, inserting a new issue will likely be viewed as dishonest, or as an expression of bad faith. When considered to be in bad faith, an injected new issue can lead to a breakdown in the entire negotiation. In addition, it may well lead to a loss of the negotiator's personal credibility.

Difficulty can inadvertently arise if the parties or the negotiators honestly differ about whether there was an agreement on the initial issue before a party sought to use the new issue tactic. The disagreement can generate controversy over whether the injection of the new issue is an attempt to renege on a prior agreement. This difficulty usually can be avoided through periodic summaries of the following:

1. Issues completely agreed on at a given point.

2. Issues agreed on only conditionally.

3. Issues that still are totally open.

For the latter two items, the injection of a new issue into the existing issue is a legitimate, proper bargaining tactic to gain increased leverage.

Countering Tips for the Injecting New Issues Tactic

A countermeasure to new issues injected into the negotiation, when agreement is virtually complete, is to treat the demand as though it necessitates reopening all the issues. Other countermeasures include a refusal to negotiate the new issue at all, inserting one's own additional issues, or terminating the negotiation.

Situational Tactic 21:
Focusing on the Process

Key Concept 76

Focusing on the negotiating process can be a helpful tactic when procedural, personality, or tone issues have caused a breakdown in progress.

Apart from substantive issues, the very process of negotiating can impair a negotiation or cause it to break down. The negotiators or the parties may become embroiled in disputes over how to conduct the negotiation. The process itself then becomes disrupted, sometimes to the extent that the negotiation does not proceed productively.

The problem that has blocked a negotiation may be the result of an emotional outburst that locks the negotiators in a power struggle over how the negotiation will proceed. This might involve which issue to negotiate first, some other aspect of whose agenda will control, whether to engage in problem solving, or the extent to which the merits of each party's case should be debated. **Focusing on the process** is used to resolve the procedural dispute, so that the negotiators can return to substantive concerns. The negotiators may bargain and trade concessions on the process to be followed, just as they would for the substantive agreement itself.

The steps to focus on the process are:

1. Stop the negotiating activities and reflect on the situation.

2. Get agreement from the negotiators that the negotiation has been sidetracked by a problem in the process which does not involve the substantive interests of the parties, and that they want to get back on track.

3. Use informational tactics, problem solving, or debate to resolve or ease the blockage or procedural problem and to obtain agreement on a way to proceed with the substantive issues.

4. Return to negotiating substantive issues.

Use a nonthreatening approach if it will help establish a more cooperative atmosphere. Phrase the cause of the problem without making accusations. Similarly, allow other negotiators to save face if that will help them focus on the process. Focusing on the process may address the issues or situations, such as:

1. The causes of past conflicts.

2. The perception each negotiator or party has of the other side.

3. The means to obtain the proper climate for constructive discussion.

Using the Tactic of Focusing on the Process to Clarify Situations

Sometimes a **procedural dilemma** arises when one negotiator becomes distrustful of, confused by, or simply misunderstands the manner in which the other is proceeding in the negotiation. This can lead to a breakdown in progress on the substantive issues because the negotiator becomes concerned about weakening his or her position due to a tactic or strategy that the other side is thought to be using. The dilemma is worsened if the negotiators on both sides engage in this behavior simultaneously.

Case in Point 7-5_____

Jolton believes that progress toward a cooperative goal will happen only if a problem-solving strategy is conducted by both parties. However, she is concerned that the other party is only pretending to engage in a cooperative, problem-solving approach, while actually being quite competitive and using a deadlock-breaking concessions only, or HRESSC strategy. Jolton knows that proceeding with a problem-solving strategy will be ineffective, and could even be disadvantageous if the other party unfairly manipulates it. Therefore, she feels unable to proceed in any direction. To stimulate progress, Jolton switches to the focus-on-the-process tactic, seeking to determine whether problem solving is a viable choice.

JOLTON: I'm trying to think the problem through with you and solve it, but you seem to just want to talk about more concessions. I don't see how we'll get anywhere that way.

GREEN: First, I thought you were just arguing with me. From my standpoint, the problem is a little different. Perhaps we should discuss how we see this point, and try to see if we can agree on the problem.

The tactic of focusing on the process can provide a solution by having the negotiators articulate their concerns, misunderstandings, confusion, or disagreements about how the other negotiator is proceeding. They then discuss or negotiate and agree on the process of the negotiation.

Focusing on the process can consist of identifying certain conduct by the other negotiator, and promising to make the conduct known if it persists. You may halt or restrain outrageous demands or behavior by the other negotiator if there is:

1. A correct perception that the other party does not want a breakdown of the negotiation over its negotiator's excessive demands or offensive conduct.

2. Verbal identification of the conduct.

3. An open record of the conduct.

4. Acknowledgment of an intention to explain to its party, or to interested or influential third parties, the reasons that the negotiation is not feasible.

The likelihood that these actions will help clarify the negotiating situation is greatly enhanced if the parties have a close relationship, so that they communicate other than through their negotiators.

Countering Tips for the Tactic of Focusing on the Process

If confronted by the other side with the tactic of focusing on the process, one must think rather than react rashly. A negotiator should consider his or her objectives in determining how best to react. The reaction should not be based on satisfying some immediate, inner feelings. Before countering, the negotiator must be sure that he or she is not, in fact, contributing to failed negotiations. If faced with the accusation that one has unnecessarily created difficulties in a negotiation, one should first consider, as objectively as possible, the source of the accusation and its credibility. If and only if the source has some credibility, the possibility should be considered that:

1. A mistake about facts has been made.

2. Something has been misinterpreted.

3. Information is lacking.

4. There has been a miscalculation of strategy, tactics, or tone.

A negotiator must not become unsettled or uncertain just because of personal criticism or attack. Neither should the negotiator be blind to the possibility that—since no one is perfect—an error has been made. However, to retain a generally confident attitude, one should not accept such criticism unless one is clearly convinced that it's justified.

When the negotiator is sure that he or she is being targeted by the tactic of focusing on the process, the negotiator can consider these countermeasures:

1. If the comments were justified, switch strategy or tactics, perhaps with an explanation that the problem was not intentionally created.

2. If the comments were justified, change a substantive position.

3. If the comments were sincere but misguided, explain why they were mistaken.

4. If the comments were sincere but mistaken, reject their accuracy, acknowledge the other person's sincerity, and switch strategy or tactics as a good faith effort to proceed.

5. If the comments were just an attempt to manipulate, reject the criticism or attack bluntly.

Situational Tactic 22: The Creation of Movement

Key Concept 77

The creation-of-movement tactic can help avoid the loss of a potential agreement that has become stalled during a negotiation.

Sometimes in a negotiation, the parties may become bogged down or may reach an impasse. The atmosphere can become marred by intransigence and polarization. In many instances, both sides are responsible for the dilemma, while at other times, only one negotiator or party is responsible. Regardless of who created the situation, a negotiator needs to be aware of it when it occurs. The negotiator then must decide whether his or her interests and goals are important enough to warrant assuming the responsibility of trying to get the negotiation unblocked and moving again. The term **movement** refers to the action of assuming responsibility for pushing a blocked negotiation forward, regardless of which participant caused the impasse.

The decision to assume responsibility may be contrary to the negotiator's belief that the other party or its negotiator created the situation and therefore should have the burden of correcting it. Those personal feelings must be set aside, though, and the issue should be analyzed on the basis of your side's best interests. Sometimes the decision to take responsibility will necessitate consultation with the client. At times the decision to act requires the use of dramatic steps.

If the decision is made to create movement, the analysis begins with an examination of the reasons for the lack of progress. Often, this will lead to the use of other tactics. Tactics which tend to be particularly useful in these situations include the following:

1. Information disclosure.
2. Fact creation.
3. Face saving.
4. Injecting a new issue.
5. Focusing on the process.
6. The use of allies.
7. The use of media or community pressure.
8. Alternative dispute resolution.
9. New instructions for the negotiator.
10. Changing negotiators.

Deciding to Use the Creation-of-Movement Tactic

Although other tactics often are used to help generate progress, the creation of movement merits separate consideration because it arises in response to a particular problem and becomes of paramount importance. Despite the existence of any zone of agreement (because the parties' bottom lines overlap), many negotiations fail because impasses arise and neither negotiator assumes responsibility for generating movement. They are insufficiently creative, or inadequately skilled to find a way to create movement. Through proper planning and knowledge of negotiation strategy and tactics, negotiators should be able to create movement when it is in their side's best interest.

The analysis of the impasse and the creation of movement may involve recognizing and understanding one's own emotions, as well as those of the participants from the other side. In this regard, it may be that one participant's perception of another's intentions or of the facts is not accurate. If so, that participant's perception may need to be altered through persuasion. It also may be necessary to let the other party or its negotiator "let off steam" before further progress can be made. One should also consider whether negotiations have broken down because of a failure in communication or from substantive or procedural problems. The negotiator should be sure that each side understands what it wants and what it seeks from the other.

When a single issue in a multiple-issue negotiation causes the impasse, the creation of movement can involve a decision to temporarily agree to disagree on that portion while attempting to make progress on other issues. If progress is made, there may be more flexibility on the bypassed issue. It may also be possible to circumvent the issue that has deadlocked the entire negotiation by agreeing to resolve it in the future.

Situational Tactic 23: Deadlock and Termination

Key Concept 78

Deadlock is a risky tactic that can be used to test the other side's strength or to cause delay.

The Deadlock Tactic

As defined in Chapter 3, deadlock is the creation of an impasse; it can occur during a negotiation either intentionally or unintentionally.

It occurs unintentionally when you are at your bottom line and the only alternatives are capitulation by the other party or termination of the negotiation. As an intentional tactic, deadlock can function as a temporary means of testing the other side's strength and resolve. Therefore, as a tactic, deadlock should only be used when there is:

1. A good chance of success.

2. A relatively low risk that the other party will react so strongly that it terminates the negotiation or causes serious long-run problems.

3. A plan to save face and create movement to break the deadlock.

4. An awareness that closure is inappropriate, or not feasible.

One method to produce a temporary deadlock is to insist on unspecified concessions. The following model statement illustrates this point:

"At this point, I've done all I can. You'll just have to do better if we're ever going to reach an agreement."

Using Deadlock to Force Delay. A second function of the deadlock tactic is to implement a strategy of negotiating for delay rather than for agreement. A party may welcome a deadlock where a delay produces its own benefit. For instance, management may welcome a deadlock, and even a strike, if they resulted in a reduction of large inventories without having to pay fixed labor costs or the saving of wages which could then be used to help fund the wage increase that will eventually be agreed upon.

The dynamics of a prolonged deadlock are important. Research indicates a highly polarized, unproductive conflict is characterized by the following dynamics:

1. Feelings of anger, resentment, tension, hostility, mistrust, frustration, and futility.

2. Expressions of criticism and blame, and attempts to block criticism and blame.

3. A blurring of the issues.

4. Personalization of the conflict.

5. Focusing on areas of wide disagreement instead of areas of agreement.

6. Each side locking into its positions.

7. Each side tending to unite as a team against the other side.

Countering Tips for the Deadlock Tactic

Some of the countermeasures used to break a deadlock and to create movement correspond to the conditions listed above; these include:

1. Focusing on the process to acknowledge the legitimacy of feelings, enhance understanding, and, if possible, depersonalize the situation.

2. The use of selective information disclosure and information bargaining, instead of making accusations.

3. Calling an adjournment to reduce tensions and to create an environment for a "fresh start."

4. Redefining the issues.

5. Switching to a problem-solving approach.

6. Using a win-win proposal to alter the pattern of the dynamics.

7. Creating facts to demonstrate the resolve to resist the other side's demands and pressure.

Using Linkage.   Sometimes linking more than one negotiation together can help overcome an impasse. In this context, **linkage** refers to the joining together of different negotiations in the hope that the resulting situation will present new conditions with which to overcome the impasse. Although complicated, this maneuver can be useful if the linkage is practical. One may creatively open an entire new series of possibilities by linking the present negotiation to:

1. Other pending or future negotiations with the same party.

2. Other pending or future negotiations with a different party.

Making First Concessions.   Another approach to breaking a deadlock is a variation of the concede-first strategy. One party makes a unilateral concession. The concession is accompanied by an explicit statement that it is a one-time attempt to reduce tension and the other party is asked to reciprocate in a specific way.

The Termination Tactic

Key Concept 79

Threaten to or actually terminate a negotiation when less dramatic means fail.

Termination refers to the complete cessation of negotiations. A threat to terminate the negotiation is the ultimate test of a deadlock. Threats to terminate, or actually terminating, a negotiation may be utilized where less dramatic tactics have failed. Obviously, this is a high-risk tactic and should be used as a last resort.

Goals Compatibility

Because of the danger of actual termination and the hostility or frustration which it can produce, the deadlock and termination tactics should rarely be used with a cooperative goal. They should be used cautiously any time a negotiator is concerned that an undesired termination of the negotiation will result.

Situational Tactic 24: Adjournment

Key Concept 80

Adjourn to regroup, change mood, obtain authority, give the other side time to reconsider, or give yourself time to deal with other matters.

The term **adjournment** means the suspension of a meeting or session. The tactic of adjournment involves the decision to stop the negotiation temporarily and resume it later, either at a specified time or at a time to be established by mutual agreement. This tactic is used to:

1. Regroup.
2. Change the mood.
3. Obtain authority.
4. Give the other side time to reconsider its position.
5. Deal with other matters.

At times the negotiator may need to adjourn the negotiation to regroup. This occurs when the negotiator is unable to gain momentum or is otherwise stymied. It can occur because a decision must be made to proceed or not with further concessions despite approaching or having reached one's bottom line. Or, feeling frustrated, defensive, or angry due to the uncooperativeness of the other party, the negotiator may need a break.

At these times it may be best to adjourn if one believes that having time to analyze the negotiation will enable one to act more effectively when negotiations are resumed. For instance, pressure for an immediate decision usually should be resisted if doubt exists, since the immediate decision generally is not really required. In dire situations, an immediate decision can be required, despite uncertainty and doubts. This will lead either to closure or termination of the negotiation.

At other times, the mood of the various participants is such that it prevents progress in the negotiation. If the negative mood appears to be temporary, a period of adjournment is needed to allow time for it to improve.

Sometimes an adjournment is necessary because a client has to be consulted about the scope of authorized negotiating authority. The length of an adjournment will depend on the client's availability and the amount of time needed to confer with the client to obtain a decision regarding the bottom line. This need can arise from an unanticipated approach being taken in the negotiation to which the negotiator lacks authority to respond. It also can arise if the positions taken by the other party on the anticipated issues require a different kind of authority for agreement than that which was originally planned.

Similarly, adjournment can be used to give the other side time to reconsider a position. The likelihood of a favorable reconsideration must be weighed against unfavorable regrouping, new alternative opportunities for the other side, or other unfavorable changes.

On occasion, scheduling conflicts make adjournment necessary. Since adjournment causes loss of momentum and prevents closure, adjournments due to scheduling conflicts should be avoided if the momentum is good or if closure is near.

In seeking adjournment, you may reveal the real reason, or it may be necessary to use a pretext. The decision on what reason to give should be based on the criteria used for selective information disclosure (see page 85).

Regardless of the actual reason for adjournment, it allows for a clearer assessment of positions and of the process, since there is more time for analysis and less distraction than during the negotiation itself. This may be a positive or a negative factor for each side, depending on which negotiator and party will benefit from more time for analysis and whether the negotiator is so confused or otherwise in trouble that the time is needed regardless of the potential benefits to the other side.

Opting Not to Adjourn

Negotiators will encounter situations when adjournments are inappropriate. Adjournment should be resisted under two conditions. First, if it will benefit the other negotiator more, and you can continue negotiating without losing self-control or the ability to act effectively. And second, if resisting adjournment is not likely to result in hostile feelings which outweigh the detrimental effects of the proposed adjournment.

Demonstrating Endurance. A negotiator may also opt not to adjourn during negotiations that involve marathon bargaining sessions. These sessions are structured to test endurance. Sometimes the side which is less tired, or which can function better under stress, finally prevails in a negotiation. In these circumstances, physical toughness is helpful, and mental toughness is essential. A good negotiator knows when to:

1. Use an endurance advantage.

2. Refrain from exploiting an endurance advantage if the attempt will generate hostility.

3. Refuse to get locked into an endurance test in which there is a significant danger that the other side will prevail.

Scheduling Adjournments

Adjournment often includes setting a specific time and place for the next meeting. This may consist of an agreement to confer within a set time to schedule the next session. However, a different method should be used if the negotiator wants to convey an impression of disinterest or pessimism over the potential for an agreement, or an atmosphere of general uncertainty. Under these conditions, an open-ended adjournment may be useful. An open-ended adjournment leaves undetermined the scheduling of the next session, or whether the negotiation will continue at all. The latter option should not be chosen unless your side is prepared to accept either:

1. A termination of the negotiation, unless the other party initiates further contact.

2. Taking the initiative for further contact and the risk that it may fail.

Goals Compatibility

The adjournment tactic can be employed with any goal and with all strategies, except for closure. In fact, it is the exact opposite of closure; therefore, it should not be considered when closure is appropriate.

Situational Tactic 25:
Keeping Patient

Key Concept 81

Patience prevents one from being pressured into premature concessions or agreements.

Although a negotiator may at times need to be relentless, there are other times when patience is a negotiating virtue. Unless the other party or its negotiator is susceptible to being pressured into the desired decision, pressing too quickly for agreement can in itself lead to resistance. Undue pressure may produce a perception that the pushy negotiator fears that calm analysis will reveal undesirable or hidden information. In addition, "acceptance time" is sometimes needed simply to adjust to new ideas. Only when the new ideas are comfortably absorbed can the negotiation proceed.

Patience also can demonstrate resolve and firmness when rhetoric fails to do so. This increases in importance if a deadline approaches and the pressure increases on both sides to take some action. Patience can convince the other side that a position is real and not subject to change, at least not without receiving a major concession. In this manner, patience can lower the other party's expectations and wear it down.

Patience must be balanced against a danger of mood changes, new alternative opportunities for the other side, or other potential unfavorable outcomes of increasing the time for the negotiation process.

Countering Tips for the Patience Tactic

Patience is most effectively countermeasured with deadlines. The fact that a deadline *must* be met makes moot any tactical use of patience as time becomes short.

Situational Tactic 26: Imposing Deadlines

Key Concept 82

Reasonable deadlines are used to avoid being tied up in a negotiation. Deadlines also help prevent the loss of alternative opportunities and can neutralize any procrastination on the part of the other side.

A **deadline** is a date or time by which something must occur. Deadlines should be used to limit the time period for acceptance of an offer whenever:

1. An open offer may cause the loss of alternative opportunities that cannot be fully pursued while the offer is outstanding.

2. A decision is needed because otherwise costs will be incurred or unwanted actions will be taken.

3. The cost basis or other factors can change and it is awkward or difficult to revoke the offer.

4. They will force a procrastinating party to make a decision.

Negotiating Scenario_____

> A relatively significant offer in the form of a binding estimate is
> made. The estimate takes into account current costs, but those
> costs are liable to increase in the future. Therefore, a deadline for
> acceptance is utilized.

The reason for imposing a deadline should be given to the other
party so that the deadline appears to be both fair and firm. If there is
no apparently legitimate reason for the deadline, except to apply pressure, the deadline *is* unreasonable and arbitrary.

Unfair or arbitrary deadlines can be perceived as high-pressure
power plays, and might lead to resentment on the other side. Assuming
that the other party cannot be overwhelmed or intimidated by a deadline, their resentment will be counterproductive to reaching an agreement. In order to clearly demonstrate its ability to resist such pressure,
the other side may reject any agreement based on the deadline.

Sometimes deadlines are negotiable. If nonnegotiable and credible,
they create a time pressure to increase the speed and/or size of concessions in order to reach agreement. Therefore, deadlines can be used to
speed up the negotiation process, although care must be taken to avoid
deadlines that unnecessarily cause a termination of the negotiation
without agreement or have to be withdrawn with a consequent loss of
face and credibility.

If a failure to agree has greater adverse consequences for one party
than the other, the deadline obviously represents relative strength for
the latter's position. Finally, in protracted or complex negotiations, interim deadlines on certain issues may be set to determine whether it is
worthwhile to expend further time, energy, and cost on the negotiation.

When a client imposes a deadline on its own negotiator and no corresponding pressure is placed by the other party on its negotiator, the
first negotiator tends to be weakened. The negotiator facing an impending deadline from a client then is liable to lower his or her aspirations, soften positions, and increase the rate and the speed of concessions. This has the same effect as a deadline successfully imposed by the
other party.

Countering Tips for the Deadline Tactic

If confronted by a deadline, one should analyze whether it really is advantageous to the other party to force a decision. If not, one should generally be skeptical of whether the deadline is real or a bluff, which one can attempt to change. Deadlines often are more flexible than negotiators realize. The other party may be willing to alter an artificial deadline, especially if offered a face-saving reason to do so. Modifying the deadline to reasonably accommodate the needs and interests of both parties is an example of a face-saving reason.

In addition to utilizing a face-saving demand for modification, another countermeasure is fact creation by changing the benefit or the appropriateness of the deadline. This may involve either increasing the cost to the other party of enforcing the deadline, or reducing the cost to your side if the deadline is enforced.

Negotiating Scenario

The party being confronted with a deadline believes that it has the power to force a withdrawal of the deadline by increasing the cost to the other party of invoking it.

"We will not negotiate at all unless that ultimatum is withdrawn and no further public threats are made while negotiations proceed."

Another version of the fact-creation countermeasure to deadlines is to create an incentive for reaching a prompt agreement. The incentive obviates the other party's need for a deadline.

Situational Tactic 27: Dealing With Negotiators Who Lack Authority

---

Key Concept 83

Deal with negotiators who lack authority by preconditions, demanding replacement, reliance on an influential negotiator's recommendation, informational tactics, trial proposal, changing tactics, withholding concessions, and bypassing the negotiator.

It is not unusual to be confronted by a negotiator who lacks real control over whether his or her client will enter into an agreement. For purposes here, **real control** can be considered either as having formal authority to make binding compromises or sufficient influence on the client to have, in effect, informal binding authority.

This is not a situation in which a negotiator could get traditional negotiating authority to bind the client but has failed to do so. Rather, it is one in which the party or its policies dictate that its negotiator proceed without binding authority and then submit the resulting proposal for a decision. Thus, such a party will insist that the negotiation proceed although its negotiator lacks authority, and that the result be transmitted to the appropriate superior for a final decision.

The approval of concern here is not perfunctory, but rather is that of the real decision maker, who independently analyzes the proposed agreement, even though the negotiator's views may be considered. In such instances, the negotiator without authority functions more to screen and to probe for information, and to shuttle messages back and forth between her or his decision maker and the other side's decision maker.

This situation must be distinguished from one in which the ultimate decision maker is normally or always a perfunctory player in the process and the negotiator's recommendations are normally followed. If that is the case, the negotiator should be treated as having final authority, since, in effect, her or his informal authority is ordinarily final. This principle is adhered to even if the party must personally execute documents, if execution is simply a formality, and if there is not enough time to reevaluate before deciding whether to agree.

The presence or absence of authority may not be immediately apparent. At times, a negotiator may not reveal whether she or he has real authority. If there is uncertainty about whether someone with real authority is present, the question should be pressed. Such an inquiry does not request that any specific authority be disclosed, but is restricted to whether the negotiator has authority to enter into an agreement. In addition, other possible sources of information should be considered to learn the other negotiator's true role.

Confronting a Negotiator Who Lacks Authority

A typical setting in which one is confronted by a negotiator without authority is a government bureaucracy. Many government negotiators are expected to fully negotiate and obtain concessions, but are not empowered to make binding concessions. Of course, not every governmental bureaucracy functions in this way.

Many times, government bureaucracies function in this way because the decision makers are elected boards, elected officials, or high-ranking administrators. For purposes of controlling the demands on their time, they refuse to invest time monitoring negotiations until a possible final result is presented. As a matter of law, however, the result cannot be final until a decision maker at this level approves it.

Analyzing the Situation.   When confronted by a lack of formal authority, one initially must analyze the situation in terms of the following factors:

1. The potential for making the other negotiator's authority a precondition.
2. The other negotiator's influence.
3. The other party's approach toward concessions.

First, can the other party be forced to provide a negotiator with real authority so that this dilemma can be avoided? Can this be demanded as a precondition to substantive negotiations? Second, what is the other side's procedural approach to further concessions? Does it operate merely by approving or disapproving the negotiated proposal, or does it always (or often) demand further concessions so that another stage of negotiation is necessary?

Requiring the Other Negotiator's Authority as a Precondition.   The tactic for dealing with those who negotiate without authority depends on the answers to these questions. When a precondition demanding that the other negotiator obtain authority before the negotiation proceeds appears to be viable, that maneuver should be attempted first. A variation of this, which has the same effect, is to demand that the other negotiator be replaced by a superior who does have authority. If such a precondition is not feasible, or is unsuccessful, then the negotiator should elect a different tactic.

Gaining the Other Negotiator's Support.   The next step depends on the status of the other negotiator's influence. If the other negotiator, either individually or in combination with other involved subordinates (even those who may not be present), has significant influence with the ultimate decision maker, then the negotiation should be aimed at a proposal which the other negotiator will support. A proposal that is supported by the other negotiator is desired under these circumstances because it will make the other party's ultimate approval far more probable.

To obtain support from the other negotiator, some concessions, either real or apparent, may be necessary. In this way, the other negotiator feels that his or her superior will approve of the recommendation that was won from the other party through hard, skillful bargaining. Similarly, appeals to the other negotiator's self-interest also may be employed. One should indicate how the other negotiator will be viewed favorably by others because of a pending proposal, or will benefit from reaching an agreement and having it approved.

In part, one negotiates for a firm commitment from the other negotiator to support a proposed agreement. Unless the answer has already been volunteered, one should directly inquire whether the other negotiator will recommend the tentative agreement. This request is coupled with a demand that the other negotiator unequivocally state that the proposal will be recommended. Unless there is immediate agreement, one should seek a firm commitment from the other negotiator to make a strong recommendation to the other party. The following types of statements may be used:

> "I expect you to make a strong recommendation."
>
> "I trust that you're going to push this to gain approval."
>
> "If I convince my client to go this far, will you do your best to convince your side to accept it?"

Whether to state this as a question or as an expectation depends on the other negotiator's personality and the relationship between the negotiators. These should be considered to anticipate whether the other negotiator will react more favorably to being asked or being told that the recommendation is expected. In either case, definite feedback *must be* obtained from the other negotiator so that a clear commitment or refusal is received.

Facing the Other Negotiator's Opposition.   Even if the other negotiator is influential with her or his client, you must decide whether to demand that a proposal be transmitted to the other party without or against the other negotiator's recommendation. Unless clearly fruitless, the other negotiator's opposition or refusal to recommend should not deter pressing for an appropriate position. The following factors should be considered:

1. Does the position have a reasonable chance of acceptance?
2. Are further concessions completely unacceptable, or unwise at that time?
3. Will an overriding negative reaction occur from the other negotiator or the other party?

If the other negotiator lacks influence on the real decision maker, the viewpoint shifts. Now, the negotiation aims for an acceptable proposal that is likely to be approved by the other side before clear feedback is received. The degree of likelihood is affected by any need for closure at that point. If closure is not needed, informational tactics or a trial proposal can be used to generate feedback for further evaluation. When the alternative is an unduly large and immediate concession, one must sometimes negotiate for the best proposal that seems appropriate at that time, even though it seems unlikely to meet the other side's approval.

Managing the Other Party's Requirement of Additional Concessions. If the other party operates with the expectation of additional concessions after a tentative agreement is submitted, then some potential concessions are withheld for when these additional demands are made. If, however, the other party operates by accepting or rejecting tentative agreements without demanding further concessions, one should submit the best proposal that seems appropriate at that point. Again, this depends on whether a need for closure exists.

When faced with a setting in which no further concessions are likely to be sought, but in which rejection is a significant possibility, it is especially important to begin the negotiation with a relatively high position and make a series of concessions before the proposal is transmitted. This allows the other negotiator to appear to have forced a better agreement for his or her side than you wanted to make. Receiving a proposed agreement that appears to contain concessions which were reluctantly made due to forceful bargaining by the other negotiator can influence the ultimate decision maker's opinion of the proposal. It can cause the real decision maker to think the agreement is more favorable than it really is, and thereby increase the chances for approval.

Bypassing the Negotiator. Another common position when a negotiator lacks authority is that compromise on an issue is impossible as a matter of policy. Information gathering then is used to determine who established the policy, who has the power to change it or make an exception to it, and the feasibility of obtaining an exception to the policy. Attempts to obtain an exception can occur directly within the negotiation or by approaching the person with actual decision-making authority. The action of appealing directly to the decision maker rather than the negotiator is referred to as **bypassing.** If exceptions are sought by bypassing the other negotiator, the issue becomes whether to proceed secretly or with the knowledge of the other negotiator. Two criteria should be considered in deciding:

1. The reaction of the other negotiator and other persons.
2. The importance of the other negotiator's goodwill.

Anticipate the reaction of the other negotiator, as well as of anyone else who needs to be considered. If there is a significant possibility that these others will try to prevent the desired decision if disclosure is made, then secrecy may be in order. The need for secrecy, however, must be balanced against the need to maintain goodwill with the negotiator and other relevant participants.

In considering the need to maintain goodwill, gauge whether the other negotiator's goodwill is of value. A secret approach to obtaining a policy change or exception without the other negotiator's knowledge may cause embarrassment or resentment. If the effort to alter or obtain an exception to the policy is successful, the other negotiator certainly will learn of it. Even if it is unsuccessful, the other negotiator may well discover the attempt.

Situational Tactic 28:
The Use of Surprise

Key Concept 84

If appropriate, use surprise by unveiling startling new, apparently attractive terms during the negotiation to catch the other side off guard or prevent a thorough analysis.

The tactic of surprise consists of unveiling startling new terms during a negotiation. The terms are structured to be, at least superficially, much more attractive to the other side than they had anticipated. They are presented to catch the other side off guard. The negotiator who introduces the surprise offer then presses for an immediate agreement. That negotiator points out, through a spontaneous and innocent-sounding but well-planned presentation, the ways in which the new proposal meets the other side's prior objections or problems, and how it fulfills the other party's needs, interests, and goals. Demands, issues, and events can be similarly presented for persuasive impact.

The tactic of surprise should be used only if:

1. It is likely to move the other party in the desired direction, or the party introducing the surprise is desperate.

2. Apart from anything else, the surprise will not provide the basis for a claim of fraudulent misrepresentation.

The reason for exercising a degree of caution before engaging in a tactical surprise is that it can backfire. Instead of persuading, the surprise and the attempt to force a quick decision can cause the other party or its negotiator to become distrustful or fearful, or to lose face. Any one of those effects may lead that party or its negotiator to harden its position instead of being moved toward the desired agreement. When another negotiator springs such a surprise, it should be countermeasured, unless it clearly offers a net advantage for your side.

Countering Tips for the Surprise Tactic

The best counter to the tactic of surprise is patience. Slow the process down. You can ask questions and insist on further explanations and elaborations. It is appropriate to acknowledge a need for time to study the new proposal or the new information. It also is fitting to firmly resist any pressure and, if necessary, to demand an adjournment to allow adequate time to consider the matter. This resistance to pressure and insistence on adequate time to respond applies regardless of whether the negotiation is being conducted in person, by telephone, or through written communications.

Such countermeasures are equally necessary (even if they seem more difficult to maintain) when surprise is skillfully used in conjunction with a deadline. On the other hand, this is by no means to suggest that it is always advantageous to combine the tactics of surprise and deadline. Indeed, there are undoubtedly times when such a combination will either engender a reaction of resistance or make the surprise seem more suspicious, and therefore make it more likely to produce adverse effects.

Situational Tactic 29: Appealing to the Personal Interests of the Negotiator or Decision Maker

Key Concept 85

Appeal to the personal interests of the other negotiator or nonparty decision maker when that will cause disregard for the other party's interests.

Personal interests refer to that which is of personal importance to a particular negotiator, decision maker, or party. Assuming that a party is not negotiating for himself or herself, all negotiators still have their own business, professional, social, psychological, and economic interests. Likewise, when the real decision maker is not personally the party, that decision maker also brings a similar set of personal interests to the process. These personal interests are different from, and may conflict with, those of the party being represented. During such a negotiation, one must be aware of and exploit all legitimate opportunities to influence the other negotiator or the other party's real decision maker through appeals to their personal interests.

Case in Point 7-6

The strike of the professional football players in 1987 may have been caused by an appeal to a negotiator's personal interests in a negotiation 10 years earlier. Arguably, the 1977 negotiation resulted in a collective bargaining agreement that traded away the players' free agency rights for mandatory union dues and a closed shop. In 1977, the union was financially weak. One commentator attributes the trade-off to an appeal by management to the personal aspirations of the then head of the union to strengthen the union's treasury.

Using Threats

Appeals to personal interests may be particularly useful where the other negotiator is a government official or a member of another bureaucracy that may not wish to risk personal embarrassment. One negotiator tries to convince another that it is in their personal interest to avoid embarrassing disclosures. Any threat must gauge the other negotiator's personality and likely reaction, as well as one's power to fulfill the threat. This analysis also applies to threats of negative personal consequences to other types of negotiators.

Case in Point 7-7

A general contractor is negotiating with a labor department official because its subcontractor has failed to pay some workers on a construction project. The general contractor says:

"Look, we are negotiating with you because technically a general contractor has legal responsibility for a subcontractor's violation of Davis-Bacon requirements for these workers. The violations were not our fault. In fact, as you have seen, we were defrauded by the subcontractor also. We are attempting to work this out with you in good faith. You are here under federal law as the United States government. The question has come up regarding whether we should withhold from the wages due and remit the withholding directly to the I.R.S. You take the position that we should just pay it to the workers and deal with the I.R.S. later if we are challenged, and that you will not help to clarify this with the I.R.S. Now, I recognize that there are different agencies, but this still is one country. There is only one federal government. You can't tell me one position as one agency, and then subject me to a possible contrary position by another agency when your only authority comes from the federal government. We'll go to our congressman and the media. One career bureaucrat is forcing citizens to violate the law as interpreted by another agency. Doesn't it make more sense to you to work together to clarify this with the I.R.S.?"

Of course, the appeal must be legitimate rather than illegal. Bribery, fraud, and other illegal conduct are excluded.

Combinations of Tactics

Even more than strategies, situational tactics are used in combination with each other. As described earlier, informational tactics are an integral part of every negotiation, regardless of the goal, strategy, or other tactics involved. Situational tactics can also be employed in any combination, as long as they do not conflict or undermine one's position. Generally, negotiators using multiple tactics should also avoid creating an undesired impression of inconsistency. There are times, however, when a negotiator actually seeks to convey an impression of inconsistency. By doing so, a negotiator might succeed in keeping the other negotiator off balance.

Comprehension Checkup

The answers to these questions appear on page 332.

1. At the outset of the negotiation, the negotiators review the issues to be discussed. After those issues have been agreed on, the other negotiator injects a new issue which changes the overall picture from your perspective. You should _____.
   a. reopen all issues
   b. make people the problem
   c. create movement
   d. terminate

2. You believe that the other side will capitulate under pressure. A good tactic is
_____.
   a. insert a new issue
   b. create movement
   c. deadlock
   d. appeal to the other negotiator's personal interests

3. Both parties have preconditions causing a deadlock. The tactic to use is
_____.
   a. terminate the negotiation   c. deadlock
   b. focus on the process   d. linkage

4. A primary countermeasure to a deadline is _____.
   a. patience   c. tone
   b. adjournment   d. fact creation

5. If the other negotiator lacks authority, you can counter and _____.
   a. bypass the negotiator   c. deadlock
   b. adjourn   d. make a surprise proposal

6. If the other side uses the tactic of surprise by making an apparently attractive, but startling new proposal, the countermeasure is _____.
   a. insert a new issue   c. focus and downplay
   b. focus on the process d. patience

7. The party which has created an impasse is the one that is responsible for breaking the impasse.   T   F

8. Adjournment should not be used at all if it allows the other party to reconsider.   T   F

9. Threatening to terminate the negotiation is a countermeasure to deadlock and a tactic of last resort.   T   F

10. You should seek information about the negotiator's personal interests, needs, and goals when the negotiator represents a party.   T   F

8
Tactics Involving More Than Two Negotiators

Key Concepts

86. Direct participation of the client or ultimate decision maker in the negotiation requires a careful risk-benefit analysis.

87. Negotiating in teams is acceptable if it is cost-effective, internal conflict is not a serious issue, and effectiveness is enhanced.

88. The outcome of a negotiation can be favorably influenced by enlisting the help of allies.

89. Media or community pressure can force parties into public positions that are difficult to change without losing face.

90. Multiple-party negotiations require more elaborate planning and analysis, but involve the same types of negotiation goals, strategies, and tactics as negotiations between two parties.

91. Gift-giving and entertaining are sometimes expected, but can also be illegal or in violation of company prohibitions.

The Language of Negotiating

To make full use of the key concepts, you must understand the following key terms:

197

Team negotiating   Media or community pressure
Mutt and Jeff (Good Cop–Bad Cop)   Multiple-party negotiations
Allies

Introduction

In some negotiations, tactics are directed toward individuals other than
just the negotiators. This happens when the negotiator chooses to use
active client or decision-maker participation, negotiating teams, media
or community pressure, allies, or alternative dispute resolution. In order to effectively negotiate in these circumstances, the negotiator must
understand and account for the roles played by these additional participants and their effect on the process.

Situational Tactic 30: Active Client or Decision-Maker Participation

---

Key Concept 86

*Direct participation of the client or ultimate decision maker in the
negotiation requires a careful risk-benefit analysis.*

At times negotiators are outside professionals who represent a client.
At other times, they represent a client and also are members of the client organization, but are not themselves the ultimate decision makers.
The tactic of active client or decision-maker participation can be used in
either situation. Obviously, it is unavailable to the negotiator who is negotiating on his or her own behalf, or who is the ultimate decision
maker.

Deciding Whether to Involve the Client or Decision Maker

During the course of a negotiation, the client or decision maker always
is involved as the one who ultimately decides on whether to agree to
terms. In some negotiations, however, that person plays a more active

role by directly participating in negotiation sessions. The decision on whether to actively involve the client or decision maker *does not* depend on the chosen goal or strategy. The tactic of active participation can be implemented with *any* goal or strategy. Instead, the decision to use or not to use this tactic is based on pragmatic criteria. The factors that determine whether the tactic should be chosen are described in the following sections.

The first factor concerns negotiations conducted directly by the client or ultimate decision maker before the negotiator became involved. Sometimes a client or ultimate decision maker actually agreed on basic concepts or terms before the negotiator began. The second factor is whether the client or decision maker has good negotiating skills, a knowledge of the market values and practices, and an ability to work as a part of a negotiating team. In addition, to be effective, that person cannot be emotionally caught up in the issues or with persons on the other side.

Disadvantages of Decision-Maker Participation

The analysis for deciding whether to actively include the client or decision maker begins by examining the advantages of having the negotiator go it alone. The involvement of other persons from the negotiator's side should only be considered if there is a definite advantage in doing so. At times, the client or decision maker lacks the skill to effectively negotiate, or is too emotionally involved.

Negotiating alone can prevent errors that arise out of a lack of negotiating skill or emotional instability. At times, the negotiator serves as a buffer to prevent heated exchanges between the party and the other side that can poison the atmosphere and destroy an opportunity for a good agreement.

Another possible disadvantage arises when another person discloses information which should either not be disclosed at all, or at least not at that time. Unwanted disclosures may come from statements of fact or opinion; questions which inadvertently reveal information; visible reactions to the other negotiator's offers or positions; or other forms of direct or indirect communication. It is often difficult or impossible for many persons to play the proper role on a negotiation team. At times, this role includes being silent and impassive, except for certain controlled reactions that are designed to further the negotiation plan. Some people inadvertently reveal eagerness or anxiety that indicates a weakness or a willingness to accept the other party's position without obtaining further concessions. The professional negotiator is sufficiently skilled to control disclosures of verbal or nonverbal information. His or her efforts might be undermined by the slips of a less skilled client or decision maker. In addition, information inadvertently revealed by a client or decision maker may be mistaken for an acceptance of the other party's offer, while the negotiator is still seeking to improve the offer through further negotiations.

The additional presence also may cause the negotiator to err. A negotiator who perceives that a client or decision maker expects to hear certain things said may make the mistake of posturing just to satisfy those perceived expectations. That posturing, though, may be wasteful and even counterproductive to the progress of the negotiation.

Similarly, where personal rapport or ill will is a problem, the added presence usually prevents the type of candid exchange that two skilled, professional negotiators engage in when they work alone. Candor is not necessarily a violation of anyone's interests. Instead, it often furthers those interests by searching for a middle ground on which to base an agreement. The candid exchange of selective information is crucial for a negotiator, and should not be interfered with by the presence of outsiders.

Advantages of Decision-Maker Participation

The presence of the client or decision maker at some negotiations may be beneficial in a variety of ways, including:

1. The improvement of relationships.

2. Expediency.

3. Unity of purpose.

4. Communication.

The Improvement of Relationships.   The presence of additional persons at the negotiation may benefit the relationship between the parties. This is especially important when the goal of the negotiation is for the parties to form a long-term working relationship. In these situations, the presence of those who will be working together should an agreement be made, allows them to begin developing a relationship. It also provides the opportunity to form a common and clear understanding of the terms and spirit of the agreement. They may be able to experiment with developing a methodology for working together, perhaps by using problem solving to resolve initial disputes and disagreements. Their experience in the negotiation gives them an opportunity to decide whether they are sufficiently compatible for the projected working relationship. (Not every negotiation for a working relationship requires the active participation of the persons who will work together if an agreement is reached. In some instances, they will already know each other or will have established a relationship from some other interaction. That interaction may be sufficient for them to determine whether they can have a good, future working relationship.)

Expediency. In some instances, direct participation should be limited to certain portions of the negotiation. Doing this can help one avoid many of the difficulties described earlier, while still providing an opportunity to experiment to determine compatibility. Even law firms, as clients, can benefit from this tactic when the reestablishment of a working relationship is sought, as Case in Point 8-1 shows.

Case in Point 8-1_____

Two law firms had a working relationship with each other before one instituted litigation against the other concerning a contingent sublease of space. With authorization from the respective law firm clients, counsel for the parties had worked out an agreement which basically resolved the matter. The agreement included one firm's subleasing certain space to the other. The nature of the sublease required some future interaction between the parties. However, because of the litigation, the parties had stopped speaking to each other. A few minor details remained to be resolved. Both negotiators agreed to have client representatives present to discuss and settle those details. The client representatives were both partners from the law firms. When the two negotiators observed their respective client representatives interacting productively, they left the room, ostensibly to discuss the form of the documentation that was needed. The negotiators deliberately left the client representatives together so that they would have an opportunity to reestablish a working relationship. When the two negotiators returned, the minor details had been settled and the client representatives were talking in a relaxed manner.

Unity of Purpose. A negotiator's position can be strengthened by the presence of a client or decision maker who can effectively communicate his or her accordance with it. Of course, the negotiator must be confident that the client or decision maker possesses the necessary negotiating skills to make the agreement clear. The impression of unity can be jeopardized if the client or decision maker makes undesirable disclosures or inadvertently reveals a willingness to agree to terms that the negotiator could otherwise have improved upon.

Communication.   If the other negotiator appears to be blocking a settlement or misinterpreting the situation, a session with the clients or ultimate decision makers present can be useful to improve communication. One then can make statements which are heard directly by the other party. This may either deter the behavior that is blocking progress, or eliminate the misunderstanding. To avoid potential errors by your own client or decision maker, you may try to arrange for only the other party to be present.

Situational Tactic 31:
Negotiating in Teams

Negotiators occasionally have to decide whether to work alone or to work in a team. **Team negotiating** has distinct advantages in the right situation; it can be ineffective, however, under the wrong circumstances. Negotiators need to weigh the advantages and disadvantages of working alone or as part of a team.

Key Concept 87

Negotiating in teams is acceptable if it is cost-effective, internal conflict is not a serious issue, and effectiveness is enhanced.

Disadvantages of Team Negotiations

In general, single negotiators are more common than those who work in teams. There are three basic reasons to consider working alone:

1. The cost factor.
2. Consistency of style.
3. The avoidance of internal conflicts.

The Cost Factor.   It often is not cost-effective to have more than one negotiator. Frequently, additional negotiators will not add anything of sufficient significance to justify their involvement. Depending on circumstances, the presence of additional negotiators might involve additional monetary costs. Furthermore, if some members are less-skilled negotiators, they may appear weak or commit other errors.

Maintaining Consistency of Style. Working as part of a negotiating team may conflict with the style of the person handling the negotiation. Multiple negotiators may act inconsistently with each other. Such inconsistency weakens their party's position, unless it is done as a deliberate role-playing maneuver (as discussed later in this section). Although one negotiator will be designated as the leader, the other(s) may make disclosures or otherwise react in ways that are counterproductive to the approaches being taken by the leader. Even when the other team members are not supposed to make statements, their nonverbal reactions can disclose information that was not intended to be disclosed. One side generally should communicate with a single and unequivocal message.

Avoiding Internal Conflict and Errors. Negotiating teams also have the potential for internal conflict. It often is extremely difficult for team members to be present without becoming more actively involved than was planned. Very often this additional activity leads to intragroup conflict. With or without justification, the other team members may strongly believe that they have something to add which the team leader has missed. A confrontation among team members might ensue, which could result in the negotiation's failure.

Advantages of Team Negotiations

There are five potential benefits in using a negotiating team instead of a single negotiator. These potential benefits must be compared to the factors that favor a single negotiator in order to determine the efficiency of using the team approach. They are:

1. Active client or ultimate decision-maker participation.
2. Specialized knowledge.
3. Collective judgment.
4. Notes and observation.
5. Role playing.

Decision-Maker Participation. The first potential benefit is that of active client or ultimate decision-maker participation. Advantages for deciding whether to include the client or decision maker are presented in Chapters 2, 11, and 12.

Specialized Knowledge. The team approach should be used when there is a need for specialized knowledge that none of the negotiators possesses. Examples of specialized knowledge include the law, engineering, personnel rules, medical information, or any other area involved in the substantive issues under consideration.

Collective Judgment.   The third potential advantage for team negotiating is illustrated by the old adage, "Two heads are better than one." The nature of the negotiation may be such that the collective wisdom and judgment of more than one negotiator is necessary to successfully conclude the negotiating process. Most often, this occurs when a creative, new approach appears to be necessary.

Notes and Observation.   It may be that the negotiation is sufficiently complex that it is necessary for an additional person to keep notes. Notes can be helpful for a periodic review of the progress of the negotiation. Moreover, the otherwise uninvolved team member may be in a better position than the leader to observe the negotiation. The notes and observations of the less-involved team member can be analyzed by the leader during the negotiation process, during breaks, or between sessions.

Role Playing.   Another potential benefit to negotiating in teams is to create the possibility of role playing. In one type of scenario, a team member is designated as the information-gathering player, while another observes the proceedings.

The best-known team role playing is referred to as either **"Mutt and Jeff"** or **"Good Cop–Bad Cop."** In these roles, one negotiator is hard and difficult—a "tough guy," while the other is nice, reasonable, and more accommodating. Together, they seek to manipulate the other party's negotiator. After the tough guy has alienated the other negotiator, the nice guy enters the scene with a conciliatory appearance. By offering a kind of relief to a tense situation, the nice guy may be able to seduce the other negotiator into making concessions or agreements. This approach is so well known, however, that it is generally no longer effective. In fact, when multiple negotiators on the same team spontaneously and genuinely disagree so that a Mutt-and-Jeff situation actually *does* exist, the other party's negotiator may refuse to believe that their actions are honest. Since the Mutt-and-Jeff game is so well known, to be effective the team must utilize a creative, dynamic version to disguise it. The roles may be used only at certain points. Team members also can switch roles at various points. Any other version that disguises the true nature of the tactic can be used as well.

Countering Tips for the "Tough-Guy" Approach.   The following countermeasures can be used against the tough-guy member of a Mutt-and-
Jeff team:

1. Exhaust the tough guy by not responding or by ignoring him or her.
2. Assume a tough-guy role yourself.
3. Publicly blame the tough guy for sidetracking the negotiation.
4. Terminate the negotiation, either temporarily or indefinitely, with
    the express explanation that it is due to the tough guy's conduct.
5. Expose that the tough-guy tactic is being used so that the other side
    becomes reluctant to engage in it further. Be careful, however; ex-
    posure could cause a defensive denial in order to avoid loss of face.

Some of these countermeasures involve predicting, describing, or
identifying what the other negotiators are doing. These countermeasures can cause embarrassment or anger at having been discovered. If,
however, this causes the other negotiators to lose emotional equilib-
rium, the time may be ripe to push for a concession or movement, as the
following model statement reveals.

> "...So now, if you're ready to stop playing good guy–bad guy, or any
> other games, perhaps we can make some progress. Now there is re-
> ally no valid reason why we should not agree to..."

How to Use Team Negotiating

Especially careful planning is essential whenever team negotiations are
used. Responsibilities must be established for gathering data and information beforehand, as well as for handling logistics. The functions of
each member of the team must be defined for both the planning stage
and the negotiating sessions themselves. Team members all must clearly
understand their duties and responsibilities. All must be aware of the
limits on information disclosure, concession patterns, and positions.

A leader is essential. The designated leader must have firm control
over the other members. Quiet directives and adjournments should be
employed freely by the leader to maintain control. During the negotiation, the leader should be physically located so as to direct the actions of
his or her team throughout the negotiation. At the same time, however,
the leaders of each team normally should sit across from, or next to,
each other. The purpose of this copositioning is to:

1. Facilitate communications.
2. Allow a clear view of nonverbal communication.
3. Demonstrate the leader's power within the team.

Labor-management negotiations often involve teams. A negotiating team for a labor union may be structured in the following way:

1. A leader and main spokesperson.
2. A note taker.
3. A financial expert.
4. A production expert.
5. An attorney who, unlike the union members themselves, does not have an ongoing working relationship with management.

By not having an ongoing working relationship with management, the lawyer (or any other outside negotiator) is freer to:

1. Criticize management.
2. Raise difficult points.
3. Be a target for management's criticisms.

This point regarding the attorney's role on a negotiating team is not just limited to labor-management negotiations. It may apply whenever the other party's team has members with whom the client needs to maintain good and close working relations. Likewise, if the other side is employing a similarly structured negotiating team, it may be preferable to focus on the other party's lawyer or other outside negotiator when making criticisms or focusing on difficult points. The appropriateness of these general criteria to a particular negotiation depends on the specific individuals who make up the rest of the team and how they will behave if the outsider is the focus of the attention.

When faced with a negotiating team, it must be decided which members are going to be the focus of communications. In addition to the considerations concerning outsiders, this assessment may vary during the negotiation depending on the issues and on spontaneous developments. The person or persons to be focused on should be either:

1. Those who are more receptive and are capable of convincing other members of their team; or
2. The difficult member(s) who must be neutralized, either by showing that they are not intimidating, or by overwhelming them.

When Does Safety in Numbers Become Overkill?

The number of negotiators can be important. Some people tend to be intimidated or overwhelmed when they are outnumbered. Others don't care. Still others react defensively and become hardened. If the latter reaction is a significant possibility, the negotiator should take steps to indicate the size of the negotiating team to his or her counterpart so that the other side does not feel a sense of unfair surprise when it arrives to negotiate. Finally, being outnumbered can be stressful and cause fatigue for some negotiators.

Countering Tips for Being Outnumbered. The following precautions should be utilized if a negotiator fears being outnumbered:

1. An agreement should be sought in advance regarding the size of the negotiating team.
2. A team should be assembled that avoids the possibility of being seriously outnumbered.

The last option should not be chosen, however, when it will result in outnumbering the other side and causing it to react defensively. At the same time, unwieldy numbers of team members must be avoided. Beyond a certain size, the danger of internal conflicts and a loss of coordination outweighs the benefits of adding members to the negotiating team. The appropriate, maximum number for a given negotiation will depend on the nature of the negotiation, as well as on the potential team members' specialized talents and personalities.

Situational Tactic 32: Forming Alliances

Key Concept 88

The outcome of a negotiation can be favorably influenced by enlisting the help of allies.

Allies are those individuals or entities who can favorably influence the other party and its position in the negotiation. The tactic of using allies is appropriate with any strategy and with any client goal. Its only limitations are:

1. Whether allies exist.
2. The cost of using allies.
3. Whether using allies will backfire.

Do Allies Exist? A negotiator must determine whether any persons or entities who might be potentially effective as allies can be brought into the particular situation. Often, it is hard to find someone with the requisite degree of influence or expertise. Also, for political interests of their own, some potential allies may be unwilling to assume your position in the negotiation.

What Costs Are Involved? The next issue is cost. An ally's assistance may not be free. It can involve either an economic cost, a noneconomic cost, or both. The ally's assistance itself may be the subject of an entire separate negotiation. The potential cost of the ally's assistance must be weighed against the potential benefits of using him or her in the negotiation.

Can It Backfire? The last issue to evaluate is whether there is any chance that the attempt to involve the potential ally will backfire, and, most dangerously, that the potential ally will instead lend support to the other side. This can occur from belief, principle, self-interest, or a refusal to pay the costs demanded by the potential ally.

The ally can have its own agenda or priorities. For example, a sister union's participation in a negotiation can shift the focus to items that are not of real interest or significant value to the local union.

Recruiting Allies

Three sources should be considered when recruiting allies:

1. Internal allies.
2. Parties already involved.
3. External, but influential, parties.

Internal Allies. Internal allies are sympathetic persons who are members of the other party. Any effective appeal to such potential allies cannot compromise their relationship with their own side. Whether such allies are willing to act will depend on their own self-interest, relationship with each party and negotiator, position within their entity's hierarchy, and the difficulty of accomplishing the request.

Parties Already Involved. In both transactional matters and disputes, allies may be found among the involved parties. For transactional matters, such other parties may be directly concerned, or they may be indirectly affected by the results of the negotiation. In disputes, there may be more than two parties already involved, as well as potential additional parties.

External, But Influential, Parties. External allies include such people as family, friends, business associates, and government officials; in short, anyone who is not presently involved or directly affected, but who has influence over the other party.

Case in Point 8-2_____

During the negotiations between the United States and Panama regarding a new Panama Canal treaty, American officials were sometimes in conflict among themselves. Pentagon officials leaked the conflict to the press, which stimulated increased congressional opposition to a new treaty. For the Pentagon officials who opposed the proposed treaty, various members of Congress were allies or potential allies.

Case in Point 8-3_____

When the professional football players struck in 1987 and the owners decided to continue to play games with substitute players, a critical economic factor was how the television networks and their advertisers would react to the substitute games. For both sides, the networks and their advertisers were crucial potential allies. One of the key reasons that the strike failed was that the networks and most of the advertisers supported the substitute games.

Establishing the Proper Point of Contact

To the extent that a choice exists, one decision that needs to be made is who should contact the potential ally. Factors to be taken into account in making this decision include:

1. Personal influence, friendship, or the potential ally's feeling of indebtedness to the contact.
2. A status of at least equal seniority between the contact and the potential ally based on their positions of leadership, seniority, or other professional or social standing.

Controlling the Relationship With an Ally

For ongoing relationships, the repeated use of an ally can lead to an overdependence on that ally. The ally then is positioned as the pivotal force in the negotiation. This gives the ally the ability to wield power and influence. It also allows it to initiate or increase demands for benefits in return for its continuing support. Moreover, the parties may become so dependent on the ally's intervention that they lose their capacity to negotiate alone with each other. If the ally then disappears or refuses to intervene, the parties must relearn how to interact and negotiate productively without the ally.

> **Case in Point 8-4**_____
>
> In 1987, the Chicago school teachers union engaged in a strike. During past strikes, the union and the school board depended on the mayor of Chicago, the governor of Illinois, and the state legislature to intervene by providing additional funds for wage increases. The historical role of these mutual allies created a dependence on outside intervention for a financial bailout on the monetary issues. This time, however, the outside officials refused to become involved. The parties appeared rather lost as they attempted to negotiate without their former allies.

The dangers of becoming overly dependent must be considered against the short-run benefits provided by the ally, as well as the party's ability to maintain the alliance. Also, since certain allies can be extremely beneficial, it may, at times, be necessary to review your relationship. A continuing alliance should itself be viewed as a separate, long-run negotiation.

Using Allies to Remove a Difficult Negotiator

In some negotiations, deadlocks or difficulties can arise when you confuse the unreasonable, aggressive, or uncompromising attitude of the other negotiator with the other party's instructions, interests, needs, or goals. If, however, the other negotiator is indeed hostile, a tactical assessment must be made about whether the other negotiator should be removed from the negotiation. Once the decision to remove the hostile negotiator is made, allies (either internal or external) are called upon to help. The allies might try discrediting the hostile negotiator or may move to bypass him or her. Care should be taken in trying to remove a difficult negotiator. If you fail, you run the risk of strengthening the relationship between your opponent and his or her party, who will think that the hostility or unreasonableness just proves that their negotiator is doing a good, tough job.

Situational Tactic 33: Media and Community Pressure

Key Concept 89

Media or community pressure can force parties into public positions that are difficult to change without losing face.

Some negotiations directly involve or affect the public interest. Often in such negotiations, the parties and their negotiators are sensitive to media accounts and to the community's response to them. The sensitivity to media accounts and community reaction is called **media or community pressure**, which can be generated so that it takes advantage of this sensitivity and influences the outcome of the negotiation. Negotiations using media and community reaction can include interactions involving only private parties. This occurs when the public is judging the parties and is in a position to affect at least one of them. For example, the public's role as consumers may be used if the quality of a party's product or service is an issue.

In these types of situations, the negotiator tries to communicate messages to the media and to the public that will either create pressure on the other party, or lessen pressure on one's own side. Positions must be tailored for their persuasive impact on the media and the public. The rhetoric may well include appeals to decency, fairness, and public interest. The use of public statements, press conferences, news releases, and the like, can be evaluated and used as appropriate.

Case in Point 8-5

In strikes of government employees that disrupt or curtail public services, one side usually makes an effort to pressure the other through the media and community support. In the 1987 Chicago teachers strike, not only did each side attempt to direct media and community pressure against the other, but they also tried to use this pressure to influence the mayor, the governor, and the state legislature.

Situational Tactic 34: Multiple-Party Negotiations

Key Concept 90

Multiple-party negotiations require more elaborate planning and analysis, but involve the same types of goals, strategies, and tactics as negotiations between two parties.

Multiple-party negotiations involve more than two negotiators. Having more than two parties involved in a negotiation tends to substantially increase the number and complexity of the issues and their possible alternatives. However, the same strategies, tactics, planning procedures, and communications techniques are used as with a two-party negotiation.

Situational Tactic 35: Keeping Your Perspective on Gifts and Entertainment

Key Concept 91

Gift-giving and entertaining are sometimes expected, but can also be illegal or in violation of company prohibitions.

In business deals, parties sometimes give gifts or entertain the other party. These practices should be strictly distinguished from bribes or other improprieties. Sometimes, though, business gifts and entertainment can be useful and proper. They can even be expected. Accordingly, they should be considered when appropriate in a business context.

Comprehension Checkup

The answers to these questions appear on page 332.

1. Company A and Company B are involved in a heated dispute. There will be no further dealings between the companies once this dispute is resolved. You are the negotiator for Company A, and were not involved in the dispute. At the negotiating session, you should use a negotiating team made up of yourself and some Company A employees who were directly involved in the dispute.   T   F

2. Assume the facts given in Problem 1, except that A and B want to resolve the dispute through problem solving and resume their relationship, provided that two key employees of A and one key employee of B can really put aside their animosity. These new facts weigh in favor of including Company A's employees in the negotiating session.   T   F

3. Company A and Company B are about to engage in a joint venture which will necessitate that employees of each company work together closely. As the negotiator for A, these facts alone weigh in favor of using your company's employees as part of the negotiating team.   T   F

4. A negotiating team need not have a clear leader.   T   F

5. Becoming dependent on an ally is not a serious concern.   T   F

6. Attempting to bypass the other side's negotiator can inadvertently strengthen that person's position within that side.   T   F

7. When facing Mutt-and-Jeff tactics, you can _____.
   a. confront the tough guy   *d.* all of the above
   b. ignore the tough guy   *e.* none of the above
   c. openly identify the tactic

9
Legal Considerations When Negotiating

Key Concepts

92. Attorneys should be used when their legal knowledge, business judgment, or negotiating skills are useful.

93. Formal written agreements are preferable in most negotiating situations, unless custom or practicality dictate oral agreements.

94. Any evidence of agreement must be written carefully so that it later will not be misconstrued.

95. Alternative dispute resolution can provide a binding or nonbinding means of using an outsider, other than a court, to decide a dispute.

96. Litigation involves parties locked together in a legal contest. Owing to the finality of judicial decision making, litigation may be the only feasible means of resolving especially contentious disputes.

The Language of Negotiating

To make full use of the key concepts, you must understand the following key terms:

Risk-benefit analysis	One-text mediation
Formal written agreements	Arbitration
Oral agreements	Nonbinding and binding arbitration
Written offers	Final-offer arbitration
Oral acceptance statements	Prearbitration bargaining
Letters of intent	Summary jury trials
Confirming letters	Minitrials
Alternative dispute resolution	Litigation
Mediation	

Introduction

The legal system has a pervasive impact on many kinds of negotiations. Statutes, ordinances, regulations, judicial decisions, and court or alternative dispute resolution processes all regularly impact negotiations. On one basic level, negotiated agreements are contracts which the parties expect to be able to enforce. Many business professionals learn many aspects of the substantive and procedural law while engaging in their negotiations.

This chapter provides insights into the use of lawyers, different types of agreements, litigation, and alternative dispute resolution. It is important for business professionals to know how to most effectively use their own lawyer, as well as to understand some vital legal considerations for negotiations.

Dealing With One's Own Attorney

Key Concept 92

Attorneys should be used when their legal knowledge, business judgment, or negotiating skills are useful.

An attorney should be used in negotiations whenever the particular attorney has one or more of the following skills, which would be useful to you in your negotiation:

1. Negotiating skills which are needed.
2. Legal knowledge.
3. Business acumen to provide business advice.

If an attorney will be involved, the nature of the lawyer's function must be decided. The attorney can be:

1. The negotiator, without the client present.
2. The lead negotiator, with the client present (see page 200 regarding active client participation).
3. A member of the negotiating team, but not its leader (see page 202 concerning negotiation teams).

In order to avoid confusion, the lawyer's role should be decided before the negotiation begins. If a portion of the negotiation occurs before the lawyer's role is determined, positions may have been taken which cannot be reversed, at least without terminating the negotiation. This situation can create grave difficulties that might have been avoided if the lawyer's negotiating skill, legal knowledge, and business advice had been available from the start.

Lawyer and client need to work together to decide their proper roles. While the client must make the ultimate decisions as well as decide on the roles to be played, the rest of the process depends on the lawyer, the client, and the nature of the matter. The wide variations among lawyers, clients, and types of matters precludes set formulas. However, for any type of serious agreement, except when a simple form can be used (an issue which requires legal advice), legal counseling should be a part of the process from the outset. For example, between business partners, a buy-sell arrangement should not be a "handshake" agreement. Furthermore, without experience in such arrangements, certain issues may not be anticipated; these include:

1. Long-term disability.
2. Funding for the buy-out, so that the company is sufficiently liquid, possibly including life or disability insurance.
3. A valuation method that creates a mathematical or arbitration model, in order to avoid costly and time-consuming litigation.

Risk-Benefit Analysis

In receiving legal advice, clients are entitled to clear counseling that allows them to make informed decisions. This means that the advice should address:

1. Potential risks.
2. Estimated chances that risks will occur.
3. Potential benefits.
4. Estimated chances of achieving benefits.

As a client, you have a right to demand that your attorney provide a risk-benefit analysis, and not just talk about legalistic conclusions. A **risk-benefit analysis** is a thorough examination of the chances of success or failure in reaching a negotiation goal, along with an estimate of the relative cost of achieving the goal or any part of it. The risk-benefit analysis should include the factors of time and cost. Although neither can be predicted absolutely, some probable ranges can be estimated.

Choosing to Negotiate Directly While Using a Lawyer

There are times when clients should negotiate directly. At least in part, this may be without counsel, or with only a minimal presence of counsel. This is sometimes helpful in continuing or reestablishing a working relationship between the parties. This gesture is not in any way an unethical attempt by a lawyer to communicate directly with a party who is represented by counsel. Its purpose is to allow limited, direct interaction between the clients on issues that are best left to them. Several examples will illustrate this point. One of the ways in which this can occur is when there has been prior client-to-client negotiating in the same transaction.

Case in Point 9-1

The seller and the purchaser of an industrial building negotiated the price before either engaged an attorney. An inspection of the premises revealed a previously unnoticed defect in the roof, the cost of which to repair was relatively small in comparison to the purchase price. Nevertheless, the cost of repair was still a significant sum. Both clients desired to meet at the site, view the roof, and determine an appropriate price adjustment. They continued to work together without legal advice. Their desire to do so was based on a wish to avoid legal fees, to resolve the matter on the spot, and to work comfortably together to negotiate a fair price. They, in fact, quickly succeeded in negotiating a fair compromise of the issue.

Lawyers' schedules can create time pressures. On rare occasions and under extreme circumstances, the unavailability of an attorney may necessitate direct negotiation between the parties. This decision should be strictly limited to such rare and extreme occasions. Otherwise, it would be an unethical attempt by one lawyer to circumvent the other party's lawyer. Extremely careful planning with lawyer and client almost invariably is essential for such a direct client negotiation.

Case in Point 9-2_____

The seller of a medical practice needed a quick decision by a potential purchaser. The seller's attorney's repeated attempts to contact the buyer's lawyer were unsuccessful. The seller, therefore, was forced to contact the potential buyer directly, in order to receive the necessary quick response.

Formal Written Agreements

Key Concept 93

Formal written agreements are preferable in most negotiating situations, unless custom or practicality dictate oral agreements.

Formal written agreements consist of contracts drawn with detail and specificity. They explain all the terms of the settlement or transaction and reflect the full and complete agreement of the parties. The document may be labeled as an agreement, or it may be in the form of a letter. The essential quality of the document is that, properly drawn, it clearly expresses the parties' intentions, rights and obligations, and the consideration provided. If correctly drafted, both the parties and third parties will be able to read the document and understand its points.

For the most part, agreements of any real significance should be in writing and should be signed by the parties, even if that is not required by law. This helps to prevent misunderstandings about rights and obligations. Moreover, this aids immeasurably whenever a party must enforce the terms of the agreement. Once there is testimony in dispute about the terms or even the existence of an oral agreement, proof can be difficult or impossible to obtain. In any event, doing so certainly will be far more difficult than if there is a properly written agreement. Furthermore, credibility issues can lead a judge, jury, or arbitrator to a determination which, unknown to it, actually is contrary to the truth.

Using Oral Agreements

Oral agreements are spoken offers or acceptances of an agreement itself and the terms and conditions that define it. Oral agreements can be used in certain specific situations; these include:

1. When the parties have a trusting relationship.
2. When the negotiation is simple.
3. When the stakes are low.
4. When local customs or practices dictate using an oral agreement.

In more unusual situations, a party may be so offended by the suggestion that a "handshake" deal is insufficient that it refuses to proceed. However, in matters requiring counsel, written agreements should be the norm because the matters usually will be complex and significant.

Other Types of Agreement Documents

Key Concept 94

Any evidence of agreement must be written carefully so that it later will not be misconstrued.

Business professionals must be aware that, at times, their own writings can be used as the equivalent of a formal agreement. Therefore, great care must be taken in writing letters, memos, notes, and so forth, so that their apparent meaning clearly supports and certainly does not contradict your understanding of an agreement. In addition, although the best method to document an agreement usually is a formal written agreement executed by the parties, several alternative methods exist. If custom or cost efficiencies militate against the use of a formal written agreement, one need not rely on oral agreements alone.

Written Offers

A **written offer** is a written statement of the terms which one party is willing to agree to, and that is presented to the other party for acceptance. Acceptance means that the other party agrees to accept those terms as the agreement. Written offers (with other evidence) can establish the terms of agreements. Acceptance of a written offer may be shown in several ways. These include oral statements, the other parties' conduct, and written acceptances. **Oral acceptance statements** are naturally the most difficult to prove if they are disputed later. Therefore, it is best to require written acceptance that must be received by a certain date in order to avoid the problem of letters that have allegedly been mailed but never received. Conduct, as evidence of an acceptance of a particular agreement, also may be difficult to later prove. The problem of proof is demonstrating not only that the conduct shows acceptance of an agreement, but also that it shows acceptance of that particular form of the agreement rather than some other version of an agreement. Written acceptances are best from the standpoint of later enforcement. These may come close to or may, in fact, constitute a formal written agreement.

Written offers normally should contain an expiration date. Otherwise, they may be "accepted" much later, after a party no longer desires the transaction or settlement. A court then may be faced with adjudicating the validity of the alleged acceptance based on a standard of reasonableness, that is, legally treating the offer as having been extended for whatever is decided to have been a reasonable time.

Letters of Intent

Letters of intent state that a party seeks, or is willing to enter into, an agreement by outlining certain major terms, with the remaining provisions to be worked out later. The major terms typically include the identity of the specific item to be purchased (such as particular land, services, goods, and so on) and the total price.

Often, letters of intent specify that they are subject to the resolution of all remaining terms in a formal written agreement executed by the parties. This caveat is inserted to avoid having courts rule that an agreement had been reached on the major terms, that the minor terms can be implied by reasonableness and custom, and therefore, that a complete and binding agreement exists. As with offers, letters of intent usually should contain expiration dates.

Confirming Letters

A **confirming letter** is a letter directed to the other party or its counsel to endorse the details and terms of an agreement. Since it is signed by only one party, it is less effective as proof of an agreement than a formal agreement. Furthermore, it is essential that delivery be through a means that can be proven in court later.

In the absence of any evidence that denies or contradicts, a confirming letter provides powerful evidence of an agreement in the event of a subsequent dispute. Therefore, it is imperative to respond to confirming letters even though they do not in fact reflect an actual agreement between the parties. A confirming letter may be quite lengthy, so that a detailed response would be time-consuming. When this happens, a short response may be preferable, as the following model statements indicate.

"Your July 18, 1987 letter is completely in error. There is not now and there never has been an agreement on the terms of the sale of the medical practice."

"Contrary to your August 5, 1987 letter, we never have agreed to deviate from the terms of our August 1, 1987 letter. If you wish to accept those terms, notify us in a writing delivered within 5 days from the date of this letter."

Notes and Memorandums

The terms of an agreement may be recorded in the internal notes or memorandums of a party. Since the other party does not generally respond to one's notes (and sometimes memorandums), their value in the event of a dispute is less than that of confirming letters that are transmitted contemporaneously. Even when the notes or internal memorandums are perceived to reflect one party's understanding, the documents may not reflect the contemporaneous understanding of the other party, unless they provide a specific account of the narrative interaction between them. If the documents record the words of each party, or at least the substance of their remarks within the context of the overall conversation and surrounding events, the documents can be used to derive the parties' understanding and intentions. Therefore, to the extent possible, notes or memorandums regarding an oral agreement should contain the comments of each person at the meeting, speakers in a telephone conversation, and so forth.

Of course, one party's notes may be disputed by the other party. But assuming the notes are made in the ordinary course of business, and not under suspicious circumstances, notes can provide some evidence in addition to oral testimony in the event of a dispute.

Alternative Dispute Resolution

Key Concept 95

Alternative dispute resolution can provide a binding or nonbinding means of using an outsider, other than a court, to decide a dispute.

Due to rising costs and frequent delays, **alternative dispute resolution** has become an increasingly popular means of resolving disputes outside of a traditional judicial environment. In addition, it can encourage and allow the parties to structure the settlement process to fit their own needs. Even when the process can theoretically be tailored to meet these needs within the judicial system, such efforts often fail. These failures tend to stem from a combination of custom and a mental attitude of the parties, as well as their negotiator-litigators, which often is more attuned to doing battle than to creatively structuring a settlement process using the range of alternatives discussed below for alternative dispute resolution.

The structure of the alternative dispute resolution is the first item for discussion in determining whether to use it. The only exception is when the litigation or dispute arises from the breach of an agreement that specifies a particular form of alternative dispute resolution. Alternative dispute resolution also can alter the process often created by conventional litigation if it provides:

1. A more efficient and economical means of obtaining information from the other party than the normal judicial process provides.

2. Incentives for each party to investigate and realistically evaluate its own situation.

3. A means of establishing a dialogue between the parties.

4. Feedback from a respected, neutral source regarding the realities of the parties' positions which may motivate them to make difficult decisions instead of procrastinating.

5. A neutral mediator who can propose solutions which the parties either are unaware of, or are afraid to suggest.

Tailoring the alternative dispute resolution may be either substantive or procedural, as the following negotiating scenario demonstrates.

Negotiating Scenario_____

When the partnership was formed, no provisions were drafted into the agreement regarding dissolution if the partners later disagreed on basic business decisions. The statutory remedy provided only for a sale of the assets and payment of the liabilities. Due to the nature of the business, the sale of the assets, including goodwill, would not be very profitable compared to the ongoing operations. The operations were capable of being divided. This more profitable solution for both parties was agreed on as part of the initial negotiation regarding the form, procedures, and issues for alternative dispute resolution. The specific division of the business operations was later resolved through arbitration.

Alternative dispute resolution can be used regardless of the negotiation goal or the strategy being employed. Its usefulness depends on its form, the quality of the personnel involved, the costs, its length, and the expected results. All these factors must be compared with the same factors applied to a resolution through the judicial system.

Some major recent criticisms of alternative dispute resolution as compared with the judicial system include the following:

1. Loss of the right to a jury trial.
2. Sometimes, more limited opportunity to force discovery of needed information from the other side.
3. Limited judicial review.
4. Lack of general procedural fairness and public scrutiny in the selection and evaluation of prospective arbitrator-judges.
5. Lack of judicial independence for arbitrator-judges.
6. No general code of judicial-arbitrator ethics.
7. Inferior qualifications and professionalism.
8. Loss of public access to trials-arbitrations.

For those considering alternative dispute resolution, the last of these criticisms raises a public policy and political issue for the general community. Should the press and the public have access to proceedings concerning health and safety hazards, public figures, and so forth? These are political and policy issues.

The other criticisms must be viewed against the specific judicial and alternative dispute resolution systems which could be utilized in a particular matter.

The Nonbinding Nature of
Alternative Dispute Resolution

Much of alternative dispute resolution, such as mediation, nonbinding arbitration, summary jury trials, and minitrials, is not binding on the parties. Nonbinding alternative dispute resolution can be disadvantageous to a party that is less able or less willing to bear the expenses of proceeding through both nonbinding and binding phases. Almost certainly, there will be more expenses if one must first proceed with a minitrial before reaching a real trial. This can cause significant, unfair pressure on that party to acquiesce rather than face the additional expense. The attorney should consult with the client before agreeing to engage in a nonbinding alternative dispute resolution procedure whenever the added costs may lead to an undesirable settlement if the nonbinding phase fails.

Future-Use and Present-Use
Mechanisms

Alternative dispute resolution can be applied to either future use or present use. For future use, the involved parties may want to provide a mechanism with which they can resolve any future disputes. As they draft agreements that require an ongoing relationship and future interaction between the parties (other than just a mechanical periodic payment of a specific sum) they can establish an alternative dispute resolution mechanism that is tailormade to the specific types of problems they are likely to encounter. For example, in the settlement of a class action against a mortgage company for improperly delaying credits when mortgages were paid off, class members had to submit claim forms to receive payment of lost interest. Class counsel and the mortgage company agreed that, if the mortgage company disputed any claim forms, the class member's claim would be arbitrated. The arbitration procedure was to have the arbitration conducted in the city where the attorneys and the court case were located, but class members across the country could present their positions at the arbitration by telephone.

In contrast, the present use of alternative dispute resolution arises where the parties either already are engaged in or soon expect litigation. Regardless of its use, cost-benefit analyses are required.

Mediation and Arbitration

There are various types of alternative dispute resolution mechanisms. Mediation and arbitration are the two most popular forms. Mediation is nonbinding and tends to be preferable under the following two conditions:

1. A neutral party has a reasonable likelihood of facilitating voluntary agreement by the disputing parties.
2. The disputing parties need to work together in a continuing relationship after the matter in issue is resolved.

By contrast, arbitration tends to be more useful than mediation under the following conditions:

1. A settlement is unlikely without a neutral decision.
2. The disputing parties' relationship will end once the issue is resolved.

To choose either mediation or arbitration, one must balance the likelihood of success of each against costs and time factors. Arbitration also can be used after a failed mediation, regardless of whether the parties' relationship will continue after the current conflict is concluded.

A key issue today is which alternative dispute resolution method should be chosen for any particular controversy. Hybrid methods include neutral fact finding, or the use of an ombudsman to address complaints against institutions made by constituents, clients, or employees. The latter method is informal and nonbinding.

Mediation

Mediation is the exploration by a neutral party (the mediator) of the views and the positions of disputing parties to discover any possible zones of agreement. If so, the mediator either encourages the parties to make concessions, or clarifies a misunderstanding that has prevented an agreement. The mediator does not express his or her own views on the merits of each side's positions, but rather is a facilitator of understanding and negotiating movement.

With mediation, the mediator tends to be passive at first while learning the parties' true positions and priorities. Then, the mediator becomes more active. In the active stage, the mediator will facilitate or press for concessions without a loss of face, or create alternative proposals for the parties to consider.

Timing is essential since mediation cannot succeed unless the parties are ready to compromise. Mediation is most effective when either the parties are inexperienced negotiators, or they have become overly committed to their positions. It is less effective under the following conditions:

1. A party is stymied by internal disagreement.
2. There are major differences in the parties' expectations or in economic positions.
3. The conflict between the parties is intense, complex, or strongly divided on priorities.

Mediation often is appropriate for parties that have an ongoing relationship and therefore are motivated to settle in order to protect it. A successful mediation process usually consists of nine distinct stages:

1. Initial contact with the mediator.
2. Preparation by the parties.
3. The establishment of procedures to follow.
4. The mediator establishes credibility and control of the process.
5. The parties state the problems and the issues.
6. Clarification of the problems and the issues.
7. The creation and analysis of new solutions.
8. The selection of a solution.
9. Before drafting a written agreement for the parties to sign, the basic terms of the agreement are summarized and, if necessary, clarified.

Some of the benefits which mediation can achieve include the following:

1. The proposal of realistic expectations.
2. The bringing together of parties to communicate.
3. The dispassionate moderation of the parties' problems within a productive atmosphere.
4. The opportunity to obtain confidential information from the respective parties to determine if a zone of agreement exists, and to provide appropriate feedback if it does.
5. The search for joint gains and the encouragement of inventive thinking.
6. The suggestion of compromises that the parties would be unwilling to propose themselves.
7. The deflation of unreasonable claims and commitments to certain positions.
8. The persuasion of parties to accept new ideas that they would be

more hesitant to accept if they had been suggested by the other side.

9. The chance to help the parties to clarify their values and their bottom lines by considering the implications of not reaching an agreement.

10. The discovery of ways for a party to save face while changing positions.

11. The articulation of rationales for an agreement in order to promote acceptance of the proposal.

The mediator's role can vary depending on her or his leadership ability, both while establishing procedures and during the actual bargaining sessions.

Mediation has become increasingly popular. In some jurisdictions, an attempt to mediate is required by the court. This, however, has both positive and negative aspects. Among the positive features are:

1. The reduction of court backlogs and the time before the matter is considered.

2. Lower legal costs.

3. A sometimes superior means of resolving highly emotional battles.

4. A tendency to produce agreements which the parties abide by longer than decrees imposed by a judge.

On the other hand, mediation can have its drawbacks. These include:

1. An unfairness and useless delay if the mediators are ineffective.

2. The pressuring of a weaker party into an unfair agreement.

Case in Point 9-3

A developer sued a bank for fraud. The lawyer-negotiators for the developer and the bank each were overly impressed with their own legal arguments, which led to a deadlocked negotiation. In addition, the bank was unwilling to disclose to the developer that it needed an otherwise unreasonable structure for the settlement in order to have a government agency pay a substantial portion of the settlement. After they agreed to try mediation, the mediator was able to help each side see the realistic strengths and weaknesses of the legal arguments. She also convinced the bank to be candid about the reason for structuring the argument as it proposed so that the developer could appreciate the bank's needs.

Through the resultant bargaining that ensued with continued assistance from the mediator, the parties reached agreement.

One-Text Mediation. One kind of mediation is called **one-text mediation** in which the mediator obtains information about the issues and then circulates draft proposals or ideas to get feedback from the parties. The mediator then submits a final proposal with a recommendation that both sides accept it. Each party must then either accept or reject the suggested agreement.

Arbitration

Arbitration is a decision-making format in which private outside individuals, rather than judges or the parties themselves, decide the merits of each side's position. There are two types of arbitration: nonbinding and binding.

Nonbinding Arbitration. **Nonbinding arbitration** is advisory; that is, the judgment offered by the arbitrator need not be accepted by the disputing parties. Unlike mediation, which is nonbinding as well, nonbinding arbitration involves having a neutral party render a decision. Mediators do not offer decisions, but rather guidance, with the process. In nonbinding arbitration, the process goes one step further: the advisory decision is offered as a suggested final settlement.

In nonbinding arbitration, the arbitrator's decision is only as effective as the decision maker's ability to influence the parties' settlement positions. This depends on the parties' personalities, predisposition to respect the advisory opinion, respect for the arbitrator, analysis of why the arbitrator reached his or her decision, and the alternatives to accepting the nonbinding decision. Nonbinding arbitration is more effective than one might suspect. If unsuccessful, though, it adds an additional layer of expenses to the total cost of obtaining a resolution of the dispute.

Binding Arbitration. **Binding arbitration** results in a decision offered by the arbitrator that the disputing parties *must* accept. The results of binding arbitration are enforceable in court. Binding arbitration involves relinquishing control over the outcome to a decision maker who may be an unknown quantity. However, the parties can structure the process so that they have a right to choose the arbitrator. This helps create a greater likelihood that the parties will perceive the procedure as fair throughout.

A particular form of binding arbitration is **final-offer arbitration** wherein each party simultaneously submits a final offer from which the arbitrator selects the final decision. The arbitrator cannot choose any other outcome. This mechanism is therefore strictly a win-lose form of arbitration. As such, it often carries with it significant risk and uncertainty. Accordingly, it can provide an effective incentive to settle before the arbitrator's decision.

The decision makers may be specialists in the particular field in which the issue arises, such as real estate, securities practices, insurance, and so forth. Normally, there is either one arbitrator or three arbitrators. If there is one arbitrator, either the parties agree on a particular arbitrator, or the parties agree to use an arbitrator from a particular organization. If there are three arbitrators, each party normally appoints an arbitrator, and those two arbitrators then jointly choose a third arbitrator to prevent the possibility of deadlock.

Arbitration may prove to be advantageous or detrimental, depending on the particular case. Some of the key advantages of arbitration are:

1. A fresh view with both creative and face-saving solutions.

2. Lower costs than a prolonged dispute that could result in litigation, deadlock, or strike.

3. At times, a faster resolution than litigation.

The possible negative consequences include:

1. Decreasing the negotiator's efforts due to a reliance on the arbitration.

2. Chilling the parties' willingness to compromise because the arbitrator may split the difference.

3. Less of a commitment on the part of the parties to carry out the arbitrator's decision than if they had voluntarily reached an agreement (which is important if good faith efforts by a party are needed to implement the decision).

4. Expenses which may equal those for litigation, depending on the procedure.

5. The narrow grounds for appealing a bad arbitration decision (for example, when the decision exceeds the arbitrator's authority, or is manifestly unjust).

The outcome of arbitration may not be optimal when all the needs of both parties have not been sufficiently explored. However, it still may be preferable to a continued impasse. In addition, unawareness of the facts or of the applicable legal principles will impair the arbitrator's determination. Therefore, as in a trial, the parties, usually through counsel, must strive to persuade the arbitrator by presenting all the important information.

The arbitration process establishes its own standards and guidelines to identify the issues, make discoveries of information, present evidence, and so forth. Each arbitration also establishes the rules and criteria by which the decision maker makes a decision. At times, the rules are similar to those used by the judicial system; in fact, the arbitration process often resembles a lawsuit. It generally consists of five stages:

1. The initiation of arbitration.
2. Preparation by the parties.
3. One or more prehearing conferences.
4. The hearing itself.
5. The arbitrator's decision.

An important concern in deciding whether to arbitrate is whether the arbitrator may be less careful than a judge because of the extremely limited scope of judicial review of arbitrations. Since the courts give far more leeway on appeal to an arbitrator than to a judge, some believe that certain arbitrators become less careful in hearing evidence and making decisions.

When considering arbitration rather than litigation, the following factors also must be considered:

1. Increased privacy (confidentiality).
2. Generally much more relaxed rules for the admissibility of evidence.
3. Far more limited discovery of information from the other side.

Although court cases can be subject to long delay before trial, some arbitrations also encounter problems of delay. Once a multiple-day trial starts, it often is held on consecutive days. Arbitration hearings can have time periods between hearing days. The schedules of the arbitrator, parties, lawyers, and witnesses can cause significant delays in commencing or completing a hearing. Using three arbitrators may increase the scheduling problem. Even so, the arbitration process generally is more expedient because of the advantages listed on page 229.

Emerging Issues With Arbitration. One emerging issue is whether some neutral parties really are neutral. Where a company or association builds a binding arbitration provision into its agreements, it also may force the use of arbitrators from a group with which it has other business relationships. Sometimes the arbitrators are actually dependent on the company or association for repeated income from arbitrations. The neutral then has a conflict of interest that can cause bias.

There has also been criticism of systematic industrywide arbitration whereby the industry forces consumers into arbitration proceedings where the arbitrators are part of that industry. Most dramatically, small investors have testified before congressional committees that standard form contracts unfairly maneuver them into arbitrating disputes with commercial stockbrokers where the arbitrator is part of the securities industry, and therefore is inherently biased. Opponents of the present system advocate more consumer rights in choosing arbitrators. Possible bias must be considered when entering into contracts that require arbitration.

Prearbitration Bargaining.   **Prearbitration bargaining** refers to the attempt made by one party to generate a favorable position by bargaining the other party down *before* arbitration. If successful, this creates a bargaining range with figures that are relatively advantageous for the first party. The theory is that the arbitrator will learn of the parties' prearbitration range and be influenced by it. Some arbitrators' analyses are affected by the parties' last offers. In those instances, the last offers establish the outer perimeters for the arbitrator's decision. This is a prearbitration tactic to be used when possible, and to be guarded against if the other negotiator attempts to use it.

Countering Tips for Prearbitration Bargaining.   The countermeasure is to maintain a relatively high (or low, as the case may be) bargaining position. By doing so, you maintain a very favorable position going into the arbitration because you have made no or few concessions. Then, if the arbitrator does learn your negotiating position, it will support rather than undermine you.

The countermeasure should be employed if both of the following conditions apply:

1. There is a likelihood of arbitration because the negotiation will become deadlocked.

2. The other party offers smaller concessions than those it demands, thereby creating a danger that an unfavorable prearbitration bargaining range will be revealed to the arbitrator.

The tactic also lessens the chances to resolve the matter before the arbitration or mediation. The parties focus on setting the stage for a mediation or arbitration rather than on reaching agreement early enough to avoid them.

Summary Jury Trials

A recent development in alternative dispute resolution is the summary jury trial. A **summary jury trial** is actually a specialized form of nonbinding arbitration which is conducted by a real judge and jurors in which the parties present their evidence and arguments in an abbreviated form and receive an advisory decision. Typically the procedure is completed within one day with the attorneys telling the "trier of fact" (the jury) what their witnesses would testify to, rather than actually having the witnesses speak. That which the attorneys represent regarding the testimony must be done in good faith, based on depositions, interviews, records, and so forth. Any exhibits that could be used at trial can also be used in this process. If a party is an individual, the party should be present for the summary jury trial, or if the party is an entity, a representative with settlement authority should be present. However, if a government entity is a party, it may be impossible to have a representative who has settlement authority present due to the legal requirements for settlement authorization. The presence of the client or the client's representative means that the summary jury trial entails active client participation with the relevant tactical considerations involved in client participation in the negotiating process.

Minitrials

A **minitrial** is similar to a summary jury trial, but instead of using real judges and jurors, it uses designated persons to play those roles. More typically, a minitrial is conducted as if it were a bench trial. After the cases have been presented, the "judge" acts as a mediator. If a settlement is not reached through mediation, the parties are informed of the "judge's" decision.

Using Alternative Dispute Resolution as a Ploy

Alternative dispute resolution may be used as a ploy. If it is not binding, it can be part of strategies that do not seek agreement, such as those of delay or discovery. The strategy of negotiating not to seek an agreement, but instead to influence third parties, can be the reason for a publicized call for alternative dispute resolution. Even if seeking an agreement is desired, such a publicized call for alternative dispute resolution may well be a tactical ploy involving allies, media pressure, or community pressure.

> **Case in Point 9-4**
>
> During the 1987 professional football players strike, the union appeared to be in an ever weakening position. Late in the strike, the union publicly called for a return to work coupled with the use of alternative dispute resolution procedures. The union's public proposal was for a resumption of games combined with immediate mediation, followed, if necessary, by binding arbitration. To some experts, the union's public offer to submit all the issues to alternative dispute resolution was a ploy to win fan and media support by appearing to be reasonable and fair. Additionally, since the union suspected that the owners would reject their proposal, it hoped to enhance its credibility by appearing more cooperative.

The countermeasure to such a ploy is to publicly unmask it, thereby making the other side appear Machiavellian and disingenuous.

Relating Alternative Dispute Resolution to Other Types of Negotiation

Alternative dispute resolution does not replace negotiation. The parties and their negotiators should employ the same types of negotiation goal analysis, planning, strategy, tactics, and communication techniques that are used in any other form of negotiation. These must be channeled and adapted, however, to fit the particular format of the alternative dispute resolution method that is being used.

Litigation

> ## Key Concept 96
>
> *Litigation involves parties locked together in a legal contest. Owing to the finality of judicial decision making, litigation may be the only feasible means of resolving especially contentious disputes.*

Litigation is a legal contest that occurs within a judicial environment. It is a negotiation tactic since most cases settle. The litigation creates the negotiating reality that either the parties will resolve their differences through negotiation, or a judge or jury will resolve the matter. It also creates costs and a time frame for the case that previously did not exist. Through depositions and other discovery, parties get access to otherwise unavailable information.

In analyzing litigation, one must consider the conditions under which the negotiation commences. For transactional or other deal-making negotiations, the parties normally interact voluntarily because they are motivated by the potential of mutual gain. The litigation context is quite different. The parties are generally involuntarily locked in a negotiation by necessity. In this context, seeking to avoid loss is as common a motivation as the possibility of unilateral gain. Unlike deal making, the avoidance of loss and achievement of unilateral gain are far more prevalent motivations than mutual gains. At times, litigation may be the only feasible method for resolving a dispute. This includes establishing a precedent for protecting the client's rights now and in the future.

Several other conditions also tend to differentiate litigation negotiations from transactional matters:

1. *Uncertainty.* In litigation, the parties feel an uncertainty or ambivalence about negotiating; for them it would be clearer to fight than to engage in bilateral negotiations. This is in contrast to the more positive atmosphere of a transaction, where the entire purpose of interacting is to try to reach agreement.

2. *Rigidity.* Often due to ambivalence, frustration, fear, or anger, the parties are more rigid and less apt to compromise. Usually, they have attempted previously to resolve the matter with each other, but have failed.

3. *Suspicion.* The parties feel that they cannot trust each other.

The situation may include a loss for both parties, instead of an economic gain for either. Nevertheless, avoiding further loss may not be the motivating force for a party. For instance, even when fees and costs exceed the value of the concessions demanded by each party, they may remain unwilling to agree to the compromises necessary to reach an agreement. This resistance may arise from one or both parties' perception that the potential compromise is unfair or from some emotional or psychological need. Thus, a conflict may continue in spite of clear motivations of material gain.

Exploiting the Threat of Litigation

For our purposes here, litigation includes the *threat* of litigation, as well as actual litigation. If taken seriously, the threat of litigation can have the same negotiating impact as filing suit. Used as a threat which can be avoided if the other party will only act "reasonably," it may force it to settle in order to save the cost of retaining litigation counsel. Generally, litigation increases the costs for parties who fail to agree through other means. This factor is not applicable for parties who have their regular counsel handle the matter, or who already have engaged counsel to evaluate the case or to demonstrate their willingness to litigate.

The appearance of litigation counsel in response to the threat of litigation usually effects the negotiation process in one of two ways. First, it may lower client expectations, due to an assessment of the litigation that is less favorable than expected. This can result in an increased flexibility of the positions taken in the negotiation. Second, there may be an increased intransigence. This results from the client's readiness to use its fresh "hired gun" to fight, or from favorable assessment of the possible litigation.

Where the parties have an ongoing working relationship, the potential impact of actual or threatened litigation on that relationship must be evaluated before deciding to bring suit. Litigation can cause a relationship to deteriorate or remain intransigent. Similarly, charges and countercharges should be anticipated and evaluated in terms of the potential effects on third parties, including customers, business associates, and others whose attitudes are of concern. Further, if a lawsuit is likely to receive publicity, negotiators should consider what effects the publicity might have on the proceedings. Will the publicity cause the other party to weaken or harden its position? Even if the suit will not receive publicity, a complaint that a defendant perceives as inflammatory may be taken as a personal attack so that the dispute becomes a matter of principle, and settlement becomes more difficult.

Timing and the Decision to Settle

The vast majority of cases are settled before moving to formal litigation. In fact, they are more likely to settle when the timing of the settlement provides an extra incentive to do so. Once a suit has been filed, however, a settlement can still be reached at any time. In the main, settlements tend to occur when:

1. One or both parties will save a relatively significant amount in litigation expenses.

2. One or both parties' counsel will avoid a significant amount of pretrial preparation.

3. There is relatively little, or no time, left to settle before the trial will commence.

Expense. Just as it is easier to settle cases when the timing of the settlement negotiations creates an economic incentive to do so, the opposite is also true. If realistic settlement negotiations do not take place soon enough, it is possible that the litigation costs that have been incurred will make it more difficult to settle the case. This is because the expenditures may lower the amount that the defendant is willing to pay in settlement. A plaintiff's expenditures can cause him or her to demand a higher settlement, possibly higher than the defendant is willing to pay. The passage of a long period of time also may cause the plaintiff to raise its bottom line.

Emotions. In certain cases, emotions affect negotiation timing. This can occur in any type of case, but more often occurs in emotional contexts such as when business partners break up a partnership. Such partners may have strong emotional feelings and needs that affect their settlement positions, especially in the early stages of the case. They may feel guilt or fear public disclosure of their problems and secrets. The strong emotions and the reasons for them can be quite diverse. If strong emotions are present, it is especially important to wait to negotiate until the client is ready to be realistic, unless one wants to capitalize on one's opponent's confusion. If the other party's emotions have rendered his or her settlement objectives unreasonably low, the opportunity exists to present a favorable offer that may only be accepted before the other party can clearly focus on his or her goal.

Be very cautious if you as the client, or the decision maker with whom you work, are emotionally charged up at the outset of litigation. In emotionally charged cases, litigation can be a draining experience as the underlying facts are recounted each time the case is brought up. In addition, a "spare-no-expense" instruction to counsel (or authorizations of great expense) can, in hindsight, appear to have been a sad mistake. While good lawyers counsel clients to objectively consider these aspects, self-awareness is important so that the advice, if given, is really heard.

Finally, it is sometimes said that "a bad settlement is better than a good lawsuit." That is absolutely wrong. Whether to settle or to litigate, and then whether to settle or proceed to trial, depends on the specific matter. Lawsuits can result in better outcomes depending on the case, just as alternative dispute resolution and other methods can at other times. Judgment is the critical factor, in order to decide on the most advantageous way to proceed.

The only clear rule is that, for any serious matter, having an excellent trial lawyer is critical. Many attorneys understand the process, and are "litigators." Far fewer also are top-notch trial lawyers. In arbitrations as well as trials, the attorney must be skilled both at presenting evidence and in the art of persuasion.

Strategies Compatible With Litigation

Litigation is especially useful for a no-concessions or for a no-further-concessions strategy. It also can usefully support all other strategies, except that of conceding first. Depending on circumstances, litigation may be appropriate for any type of negotiation goal, except certain cooperative or defensive goals.

Comprehension Checkup

The answers to these questions appear on page 332.

1. The lawyer should always lead the negotiating team.   T   F

2. It is up to the attorney to identify the areas for risk-benefit analysis, but the attorney's client should try to add to areas identified by the attorney.   T   F

3. Alternative dispute resolution can be binding or nonbinding.   T   F

4. Mediation always should be the first step to avoid arbitration or litigation.   T   F

5. Company A and Company B are involved in a heated dispute. There will be no further dealings between the companies once this dispute is resolved. You are the negotiator for Company A, and were not involved in the dispute. At the negotiating session, you should use a negotiating team which includes those directly involved in the dispute.   T   F

6. Positions taken before an arbitration or mediation can affect the outcome of the arbitration or mediation.   T   F

7. Alternative dispute resolution should always be used rather than litigation.   T   F

8. If the direct participation tactic is used while working with an attorney in a negotiation, the other tactic that also must be used is_____.
   a. litigation   d. power
   b. team negotiation   e. other
   c. focus on process

9. An attorney's advice should at least include a(n)_____analysis.
   a. risk-benefit   d. rigid
   b. upbeat   e. aggressive
   c. litigation

10. Confirming letters, notes, and memorandums must be carefully drafted as potential _____.
    a. tax records
    b. recollections
    c. writings
    d. evidence
    e. none of these

11. If the disputing parties are unlikely to voluntarily follow a recommendation of an outsider, they should use _____.
    a. mediation
    b. minitrials
    c. arbitration
    d. summary jury trial
    e. other

12. Jones and Rogers are your subordinates. They each run a department. They now are in a dispute over which department should handle certain functions. From your standpoint, the departments need to work smoothly together. You do not care which department handles the functions. You should play the role of _____.
    a. mediator
    b. arbitrator
    c. ally
    d. gift giver
    e. other

13. Assume all the conditions of Problem 12, except that now you firmly believe that the functions should be performed by Rogers' department. You should play the role of _____.
    a. mediator
    b. arbitrator
    c. ally
    d. gift giver
    e. other

10

Communication Skills for Negotiating Effectively

Key Concepts

97. Negotiation is a process of exchanging information in which deliberate disclosures can enhance a negotiator's control, whereas accidental disclosures can weaken it.

98. Polite communications facilitate positive information disclosure and careful listening; they also help minimize conflict.

99. *Avoid* a power struggle unless it effects control of the outcome or future negotiations.

100. Make only deliberate and selective verbal and nonverbal information disclosures to advance the negotiation.

101. State rationales for positions to be persuasive. Communicators subconsciously process or "mentally filter" messages. Therefore, persuasiveness is enhanced when signals are clear and free of internal inconsistencies or multiple meanings.

102. To ensure the clear and direct transmission of a message to a decision maker, it is sometimes necessary to go around, or bypass, the opposing negotiator.

103. In negotiating, receiving information effectively is as important as sending it.

104. Nonverbal cues can augment one's knowledge of a negotiation by either confirming or contradicting verbal information.

105. Meetings, formal or informal, make the exchanges personal, which can create a greater commitment to negotiate. If necessary, use private channels for more candid exchanges.

106. Telephone calls can be used to obtain specific information or for efficiency, but use adjournment rather than be caught off guard.

107. Communicating in writing avoids unwanted interruptions, helps prevent misunderstandings, and adds a degree of significance to the position or other information.

The Language of Negotiating

To make full use of the key concepts, you must understand the following key terms:

Polite communications	Careful listening
Power struggle	Cues
Bargaining against oneself	Nonverbal cues
Selective information disclosure	Formal and informal meetings
Rationale	Private channel
Mixed messages	Home-field site

Introduction

Key Concept 97

Negotiation is a process of exchanging information in which deliberate disclosures can enhance a negotiator's control, whereas accidental disclosures can weaken it.

Negotiation is a process which consists of exchanging information. Information exchange may be by design or by accident. Since outcomes can be affected by imperfect exchanges of information, each negotiator seeks to manipulate the opposing participants by attempting to control the processes of communication.

Some studies suggest that negotiations that result in agreement often proceed through three distinct communication stages:

1. The early articulation of statements, positions, and defenses of positions to build strong and persuasive arguments and to demonstrate some form of power.

2. The search for solutions using the factors and limitations established during the first stage.

3. The mutual striving among participants to find terms of agreement which satisfy all sides.

Effective communication skills are essential for a negotiator. The communication process is an integral part of negotiations and forms the medium through which the negotiators decide whether to agree. The skills used encompass both the sending and receiving of information. The information that is sent must be persuasive. Methods to send information persuasively are covered beginning on page 245. Conversely, in order to receive information properly, the recipient should recognize and analyze all clues, both verbal and nonverbal. Techniques for correctly receiving information are covered beginning on page 255. Finally, different modes of communication are presented on page 261. These communication principles and techniques apply to all negotiations, regardless of their particular goals, strategies, or tactics.

Polite Communications Versus Power Struggles

Key Concept 98

Polite communications facilitate positive information disclosure and careful listening; they also help minimize conflict.

A Gentle Art

Most of the time, the communication process should be a polite one. In **polite communications** negotiators do not try to intimidate each other;

they listen carefully to what is being said, being alert for both clues and positions; and each will give the other an opportunity to speak. At times, they will encourage the other to speak in order to gain additional information. The degree of friendliness and assertiveness may vary, and the words may be spoken forcefully and even a bit roughly. Polite communications need not be docile; however, the process should be basically cordial. A polite communications process has at least three major benefits for the negotiators:

1. It facilitates the disclosure of information.
2. It facilitates careful listening.
3. It avoids unnecessary power struggles.

Facilitates the Disclosure of Information. A polite communications process provides the negotiators with an opportunity to disclose information. By facilitating disclosures, the maximum desired flow and exchange of information can occur. This flow is limited only by the negotiators' respective judgments about whether to disclose information. Politeness helps avoid cutting off valuable information which a negotiator is willing to disclose. The more useful information that is disclosed to a negotiator, the more that negotiator enjoys an increased basis for knowing which strategy, tactics, and positions to choose.

Facilitates Careful Listening. Polite communication also aids the negotiator's ability to carefully listen. By taking turns communicating, each negotiator can concentrate on listening to the other, rather than on interrupting or fighting to speak. Careful listening is extraordinarily important so that the negotiator really consciously hears and recognizes all the information being disclosed.

Avoids Unnecessary Power Struggles. Finally, polite communication helps negotiators to avoid unnecessary conflict in the form of power struggles. Power struggles can waste time, create counterproductive hostility, and even lead to a breakdown in the negotiation process. Polite communication serves to avoid such undesired effects.

Power Struggles

Key Concept 99

Avoid *a power struggle unless it effects control of the outcome or future negotiations.*

In **power struggles** each side fights to dominate the negotiation process. The domination can consist of long speeches, interruptions, or other acts to overpower the other negotiator. Quite often, the struggle for power becomes an end in itself so that the negotiation becomes secondary. For this reason, power struggles should generally be avoided. There are, however, four exceptions to the general rule that polite communications are preferable to power struggles. Power struggles may be appropriate when:

1. It is feasible to control the outcome of the negotiation by dominating the communications process.

2. One must be dominating to avoid being dominated.

3. The other negotiator insists on engaging in undue repetition to the point that any benefits from appeasing the other's ego are outweighed by the waste of time.

4. One allows domination in a power struggle so that the other negotiator can be made to *feel* that he or she has won, in exchange for which the negotiator secures important concessions. In this case, the other party unintentionally discloses information or makes concessions for the sake of ego gratification.

Dominating the Process to Control the Outcome.   If one can dominate the communication process and thereby dominate the substantive outcome of the negotiation, then one should consider doing so. If, however, domination of the communication process will lead the other negotiator to refuse to participate, it will be counterproductive. It can also be counterproductive if it causes the other negotiator to harden his or her positions because of anger or frustration at being unable to otherwise communicate.

As with the use of power as a tactic, long- and short-run effects must be taken into account. One must first analyze whether it is possible to dominate the communications process and second, whether such dominance will have a positive or negative effect on the ultimate outcome of the negotiation. The other negotiator's personality must be given special consideration along with the vital interests and personality of the other party. Certain competitive personalities may cause the other party or its negotiator to take offense at attempts to dominate the communications.

Controlling Communications to Avoid Being Dominated.   With certain exceptions (discussed below), a negotiator should avoid being dominated. It normally will be necessary to assert oneself if the other negotiator seeks to dominate the communications process. Initially, as in preventing undue repetition, the summarization and focus-on-the-process tactics can be used. However, if those tactics fail, the negotiator may have to use interruptions, loudness or some other harsh tone, or blunt phrasing.

Negotiating Scenario

After being harangued for a half hour, and after being unable to either summarize what Negotiator A has said, or to focus on the process because Negotiator A has just refused to stop talking, Negotiator B suddenly shouts, "Wait!" Negotiator A pauses, uncertain of whether this is a sign of capitulation. Speaking both forcefully and more loudly than normal, Negotiator B states:

"Negotiation is impossible without give and take, and without both sides being able to listen to each other. Apparently you intend only to speak, and not to listen, or even to give me the courtesy of being able to speak. That being the case, I am going to leave now. If I am mistaken and you are willing to stop talking and to listen to my position, say so now!"

Avoid Situations in Which the Other Negotiator Repeats Unacceptable Positions. No one should have to listen passively to the same points being made over and over again. This is especially true if the points are lengthy ones. Unless appeasing the other participant's ego will yield substantive results, undue repetition need not be tolerated. In this situation, however, breaking out of the polite communications mode is not normally one's first choice. Instead, one can first attempt to summarize what has been said. Alternatively, one can use the focus-on-the-process tactic.

Negotiating Scenario

In a contract negotiation between two businesses, the other negotiator has been engaging in undue repetition. You can employ summarization in order to maintain a polite communications mode.

"Now, because you're repeating the cost points that you told me earlier, let me say that I understand your position on costs. You've told me that your costs without any profit margin are $2.48 per unit. I understand that."

Capitalizing on Another's Garrulousness. If the other negotiator seeks to dominate the communications process, one should consider allowing this desire, at least for a while. At times the need of the other negotiator to dominate the communications process can be manipulated in order to achieve a more positive outcome. This type of "mental judo" can occur when the other negotiator displays the following behaviors:

1. *A need to dominate the communication process.* In seeking to dominate the communication process, the other negotiator may talk and talk to the point where information is being disclosed regardless of whether it was wise to have done so. This talkativeness results from a variety of egocentric needs including: a desire to teach others about how much they know; sexual attraction; defending against feelings of inferiority; compensating for a fear of silence; and so forth.

2. *Bargaining against himself or herself.* **Bargaining against oneself** means that while seeking to control the communications the other negotiator fails to demand feedback because he or she is talking too much; instead, the other negotiator takes a position, talks, does not receive a clear rejection or counteroffer, and then takes another position by making a concession, while continuing to talk and to "dominate" the communications process.

3. *Engaging in ego gratification.* The other negotiator may be so intent on the ego gratification of apparent dominance that substantive points are relinquished. This does not occur through a lack of feedback, but rather because the negotiator loses sight of the pattern being created by concessions and trade-offs.

Sending Information

Key Concept 100

Make only deliberate and selective verbal and nonverbal information disclosures to advance the negotiation.

The exchange of information requires that messages be sent clearly to avoid misunderstanding or confusion. While this requirement does not further necessitate the complete disclosure of all the information that a negotiator possesses, it does mandate that the messages the negotiator decides to disclose be transmitted with the intention of being completely understood.

Keeping Disclosures Selective and Deliberate

Certain information must be disclosed to successfully negotiate. At the very least, positions must be disclosed. Often, facts, needs, and vital interests should be disclosed so that the other party knows the points to be met if an agreement is to be reached. **Selective information disclosure** refers to the transmission of the information that is *necessary* for the negotiation to proceed favorably. Sometimes a fine line must be drawn between trusting the other side to disclose enough information to reach an agreement and distrusting the other side because it appears to have withheld information in order to dominate the bargaining.

The key in disclosing information is to consider the effect of the disclosure. How will disclosure advance the negotiation from the perspective of the party and its negotiator? If it will not advance the negotiation, then disclosure should not be made. The benefits of persuasion must be weighed against the countervailing risks of creating problems or exposing weaknesses.

Negotiating Scenario

In an effort to create enthusiasm for the proposed project, one negotiator goes too far in talking about how interested the firm is in working with the other party. Doing so raises suspicions that that side is likely to have some serious problems if the deal falls through. As a result, the other negotiator is able to insist on more concessions than either side planned.

Being selective in the disclosure of information can be very difficult; often, it is even more difficult when nonverbal disclosures are involved. It is always important to control nonverbal disclosures since unconscious reactions or behaviors can reveal clues to an individual's secret thoughts or positions. Deliberate disclosure requires a high degree of conscious control over one's verbal and nonverbal information disclosures. Nonverbal communications are analyzed more thoroughly on page 260.

Keeping Expectations at a Minimum.   It is an error to unnecessarily or erroneously raise the other side's expectations. Assuming that one does not want to create the impression that a concession is available, consider the following model statement:

"That's certainly something we can talk about."

A statement like that can create or reinforce an expectation by the other side that a concession is available. Even if the concession could be made, inadvertently disclosing the possibility demonstrates poor technique and could lead to a less favorable agreement. Even worse, if a concession really is not possible, then the raised expectations cannot be met which, in turn, causes feelings of bad faith, a hardening of other demands, or a breakdown of the negotiation.

Timing Disclosures for Optimal Effect.   The timing of information disclosures is critical. Time disclosures to create movement toward an optimal agreement. Properly timed disclosures concerning needs, goals, priorities, and values allow parties to find a zone of agreement. The parties then understand how to structure trade-offs.

Being Persuasive

There are many ways to persuade another party to accept your positions, ideas, terms, and so forth. While there are exceptions, persuasiveness is enhanced by leading the other side to trust your honesty and sincerity. Generally, a negotiator should keep in mind the other side's viewpoint on issues and goals. In this way, the negotiator demonstrates her or his commitment to reaching mutually acceptable conclusions. The following sections present methods to help make one's transmitted communications more persuasive.

Using Rationales.   Communicating persuasively is essential, since the communication is wasted unless it is believed. One way to communicate persuasively is to provide rationales. A **rationale** is a reason given for a position. The rationale makes the other party feel that the position is fair, reasonable, or at least a real position and not a bluff. The aim is to establish a believable, reasonable position which the other party will either accept or, depending on the strategy or tactic chosen, make a concession in order to have the position altered. People are more willing to accept positions that are fair and reasonable than those that are unfair and unreasonable. While a rationale can be used to disguise a party's real reason when it is advantageous to do so, material misrepresentations should be avoided.

There are three exceptions to the general principle that giving the rationale will enhance believability:

1. *When the rationale is inherently clear in the negotiation context.*   In the context of a given negotiation, the rationale for some positions

will be inherently clear; thus, no explicit statement of the rationale will be needed.

2. *When no plausible rationale exists which should be disclosed.* Sometimes the real reason must be kept secret. An example would be if the real reason was developed based on information received from a source that demands anonymity. Then one should search for a plausible rationale to justify the position. At other rare times, there simply is no believable rationale. A position based on instinct is a case in point.

3. *When the only plausible, disclosable rationale involves a material misrepresentation.* A material, that is, significant, misrepresentation can constitute fraud. In addition to being unethical or illegal, engaging in fraud runs the risk of destroying the negotiation if it is discovered by the other party.

Showing How the Position Meets the Other Side's Needs and Interests. Persuasion is achieved by appealing to the other side's needs and interests. Therefore, arguments and other forms of information disclosure are often persuasive if presented from the other side's point of view rather than strictly from one's own. After all, the other side is already motivated to meet its own needs. One needs only reinforce a motivation that is already present, as the following model statement demonstrates.

> "Your own research has demonstrated that our product clearly is superior for meeting your needs than is SimCo's. Given our attractive cost structure, you cannot do better than agree to go with us."

The presentation to the other party may also seek to point out how the alternative to a proposed agreement would be less attractive than acceptance. These alternatives include:

1. A lost opportunity.
2. Litigation.
3. Increased costs.
4. Unfavorable publicity.

Some authorities on negotiating believe that the presentation should always include alternatives even when giving an ultimatum. Including a choice of alternatives makes the ultimatum seem less aggressive or antagonistic.

Building Rapport. Establishing a rapport early on between the negotiators can enhance one's persuasive powers. One method is to concentrate on those points on which the negotiators concur, thereby building momentum toward reaching an agreement. A related technique is to respond first to the portion of a statement with which there is general agreement before rejecting the remainder of the statement. Additionally, it is more persuasive to explain one's statements rather than to simply assert them. In this way, the listener need not choose between blind trust or the immediate rejection of the idea. Sometimes, insinuations rather than direct proposals are better at leading the listener to arrive at the desired conclusions. Very often, conclusions should be left unstated so that the listener will arrive at them himself. A person is often more likely to hold a position when they believe it resulted from their own thinking than when it is offered by someone else. Themes, analogies, and storytelling can be effectively used for this purpose.

Keeping the Listener's Perspective in Mind When Stating Conclusions. Related to showing how a position meets the other side's needs is the notion of momentarily assuming their perspective on the negotiation to determine how the other side understands and values it. By adopting the other side's view, a negotiator may be able to anticipate problems and issues that the other party will likely raise and develop appropriate responses to them. By *stating* your attempt to see the situation in their terms, other parties may form a favorable impression that could enhance one's persuasiveness. This is particularly useful in cooperative negotiations.

Expressing Messages With Conviction. Convey a sense of conviction when expressing a position and its rationale. A confident manner and a professional level of enthusiasm can add a convincing tone. One can speak loudly or softly. The tone of voice can be forceful or matter-of-fact. The important point is that the speaker appears sincere. If the speaker does not seem committed to his or her own words, the listener surely will not be persuaded.

Employing Unusual or Unexpected Means to Reinforce Messages. In general, a negotiator's statements will be more effective if they are conveyed with greater volume or intensity than usual. Visual components (graphs, diagrams, videotapes, and so forth) that dramatically convey or reinforce messages may prove useful. A startling suggestion or proposal might gain the other side's attention. The order in which messages are transmitted is also important. Messages presented first have the advantages of freshness and originality. Those that are presented last often convey seriousness by appearing as though they were the "logical" result to what came before. Finally, messages can be repeated in order to ensure that the other side received them. One should, however, refrain from repetitious presentations which might either bore or offend listeners. The only exception is if you want to wear down the other negotiator so that she or he will yield instead of fighting back.

Building in Concessions. Another technique for persuasion in negotiations is to build in concessions. Some negotiators find it difficult or impossible to believe that the initial position does not have some built-in concessions. These negotiators *expect* concessions and will not feel satisfied until they get some. They are more easily persuaded to settle if they believe that they have "earned it" by first extracting one or more concessions.

Asking the Other Negotiator Questions. In addition to obtaining information, questions can be utilized to give information or stimulate thought. Asking the other negotiator questions may force that person to face the weaknesses of his or her case. Antagonistic questions should usually be avoided. In some rare cases, though, harsh questioning can be useful. These include the following situations:

1. When antagonizing the other party will provoke an emotional, less controlled reaction which a negotiator can exploit.

2. When a negotiator wants to intimidate the other party or negotiator.

3. To counter hostile attacks made by the other negotiator.

4. To persuade by embarrassing the other party or negotiator. (This may be quite difficult to accomplish and runs a substantial risk of offending the other negotiator into retaliation.)

Not Sounding Judgmental About the Other Negotiator. Speak in terms of one's own thinking and feelings rather than those of the other negotiator. By not being judgmental, a negotiator can minimize or avoid defensive responses. An exception is if a negative judgment will convince the other negotiator that his or her actions have been unfair or misguided. Any negative judgment must be limited to a specific behavior, and not aimed at the negotiator as a person.

Defining the Problem That Needs to Be Solved. Stating the problem that needs to be solved before proposing a position may induce the other negotiator to listen more closely to what is being said. This is effective only if the definition is agreeable to the other side, or unless it inspires a useful response.

Timing. Persuasion also involves timing. Some types of proposals, particularly if they are unusual or innovative, are not likely to be accepted immediately. However, they may become acceptable if there is sufficient time for the other side to consider and gain familiarity with them. Accordingly, these types of proposals should be introduced into the negotiation well in advance of either party's deadline for reaching an agreement.

References and Precedents. A negotiator's reputation can be bolstered by references who are known to the other side, or by previous experiences that are credible or verifiable. References and precedents can confirm power, capability, and veracity. Mentioning similar prior situations casually, anecdotally, or even cryptically, can convey a threat without provoking a counterproductive reaction.

Using Statistics and Other Objective Criteria. Whenever possible, objective criteria, such as appraisals, statistics, test results, and so forth, should be cited to reinforce one's persuasiveness. Some negotiators are taught that the negotiation result should be based strictly on objective criteria. Therefore, for persuasive purposes and to satisfy—as well as manipulate—the expectations of objectively based negotiators, objective criteria should be built into rationales as much as possible.

One important countermeasure is to use different objective criteria that favor your position. Other countermeasures include scrutinizing or questioning so-called objective criteria for bias and flawed methodology, challenging its general relevance, and resisting agreement based on a subjective lack of importance for one's own needs, interests, or goals.

Sending Clear Signals

Key Concept 101

State rationales for positions to be persuasive. Communicators subconsciously process or "mentally filter" messages. Therefore, persuasiveness is enhanced when signals are clear and free of internal inconsistencies or multiple meanings.

Thus far, the focus for the sender of communications has been on deliberate disclosures and on persuasion. Both points are aimed at having the listener believe the message as intended. However, the most deliberately chosen and persuasively stated message will be lost or confused if it is unclear. There is a need for clear, precise signals. **Mixed messages** are messages which seem internally inconsistent or contradictory. They should be avoided. Similarly, messages with potential multiple meanings (that is, messages that can legitimately be interpreted in several ways) are also to be avoided. With multiple meanings, the speaker cannot control which meaning will be chosen by the listener.

In seeking to transmit messages clearly, a negotiator must try to recognize the psychological needs of the other negotiator and the other party. These needs may not be articulated or even understood by the other person, but they can affect the way the other person receives the message. Since such psychological conditions can be too sensitive and too deeply rooted to be confronted directly, a negotiator may be forced to silently acknowledge them and work around the limits they seem to establish in the negotiation. Psychological limitations leading to misunderstanding can take the following forms:

1. Stereotyping based on demographic and social data.

2. Generalizing from one attribute to other attributes.

3. Not accepting information that contradicts a preexisting belief.

4. Projecting one's own feelings or characteristics on to another person.

5. Screening out information which contradicts one's self-image or image of another.

These types of distortions impede and sometimes block communication, and can cause negotiators to act contrary to their best interests.

Recognizing psychological and perceptual limitations allows messages to be structured so that they are more likely to be received and understood as intended. Conversely, a negotiator must be alert to her or his own psychologically motivated misperceptions.

Reaching the Other Party

Key Concept 102

To ensure the clear and direct transmission of a message to a decision maker, it is sometimes necessary to go around, or bypass, the opposing negotiator.

In some negotiations, you may sense that the other negotiator is withholding or distorting the information being communicated to the other party, or decision maker. This problem may be intentional or inadvertent, and usually stems from one of the following reasons:

1. Personal interest.
2. Fear.
3. Incompetence.
4. Reporting to an intermediary.

The other negotiator's personal interests may interfere with fair and accurate reporting to the other party. In addition, certain information may reflect unfavorably on the other negotiator. Similarly, if the other negotiator fears the other party's reaction to certain information, it may be communicated inaccurately to the other party. Simple incompetence may be another explanation. The other negotiator's lack of competence in communicating may keep the necessary information from reaching the other party. Finally, the cause of the problem may be in a requirement that the other negotiator report to the decision maker through an intermediate chain of command. The intermediaries may be distorting information about the negotiation in their reports to the decision maker for the same types of reasons that a negotiator might do so: personal interests, fear, or incompetence.

Whenever you believe that the other negotiator or some intermediary is blocking or failing to accurately convey information to the decision maker, corrective action should usually be taken. Two exceptions exist: (1) when the information is aimed at the other negotiator and is never intended to reach the other party, and (2) when progress in the negotiation is satisfactory, so that there is no reason to disturb whatever is occurring by seeking to ensure that additional information reaches the real decision maker.

The decision about the sufficiency of the negotiation's progress, and whether it is likely to improve through communicating certain information to the real decision maker, requires a judgment based on the following factors:

1. The history of this or prior negotiations, including any applicable precedents.
2. The other party's vital interests and any situational pressure or constraints.
3. The personality of the decision maker.

If the exceptions do not apply, and you decide to communicate directly with the decision maker, you can try any of the following means to get through:

1. Make an appropriate inquiry.
2. Make an appropriate request.
3. Demand the client's or decision maker's presence.
4. Use written communications.
5. Call upon allies to bypass the other negotiator.

Make an Appropriate Inquiry.   Inquiry in this situation entails asking questions of the other negotiator designed to first determine whether the information reached the real decision maker. If not, the next questions should lead into a discussion of when (not whether) the decision maker will be informed, so that the negotiations can continue. An inquiry patterned after the following model statements can be used.

"How did he react to those facts?"

"Does she understand that there is a substantial risk unless she authorizes a compromise on these issues?"

In deciding whether this method will be useful, you must gauge the honesty of the other negotiator and the reliability of his or her answers.

Make an Appropriate Request.   An appropriate request consists of asking that the information be transmitted to the decision maker, and that the decision maker's reaction be reported back. Here again, you must assess the honesty of the other negotiator. In addition, you should consider whether the other negotiator will refuse to comply with the request because it is perceived as a breach of negotiation protocol. An explanation may alleviate the other negotiator's concerns, or correct any misperception of the reason for and nature of the request, as the following model statements demonstrate.

"Since this is a basic issue that affects the entire negotiation, I don't feel that I can proceed further until I have a response from your client. I must be sure that I understand his views on this point."

"My client does not feel that your client appreciates how critical this issue is from our point of view. Therefore, we are asking that you inform your client of exactly what I have explained regarding my client's needs, and let us know of your client's response."

Demand the Client's or Decision Maker's Presence. If neither an inquiry nor a request to the other negotiator works, one can instead request or, if necessary, insist that the decision makers be present at the next negotiating session. Before doing so, you should consider the potential impact, both positive and negative, that the presence of one or both decision makers may produce, as discussed in the section concerning the presence of clients.

Use Written Communications. Another option is the use of written communications. A letter or proposed agreement can be designed to include all the information desired to reach the real decision maker. With a written communication, the only issue is whether the other negotiator actually will show it to the decision maker. That issue can be dealt with in either of two ways. First, in certain contexts one can seek the other negotiator's permission to send a copy of the written communication to the other decision maker. And second, one can include in the written communication a request that the communication itself be delivered to the decision maker. This approach places enormous pressure on the other negotiator to properly transmit the communication, particularly if the communication is a settlement offer or draft agreement.

Call Upon Allies to Bypass the Other Negotiator. Finally, allies may be used to bypass the other negotiator and convey information to the other side's decision maker.

Receiving Information

Key Concept 103

In negotiating, receiving information effectively is as important as sending it.

During a negotiation, one may need to obtain information from the other party which was not available from other sources, or which needs to be confirmed. This section will focus on receiving information effectively, so that its meaning can be accurately recognized and properly used in the negotiator's analysis.

Before it can be received, information first may have to be elicited. Freely flowing disclosure can be encouraged by appearing to listen attentively, and by not interrupting, arguing, or attacking. By not indicating that the information being disclosed is important, one also can encourage further disclosures. On the other hand, a perceived lack of interest may cause the speaker to stop communicating. In addition, reticence can be countered by questions, discussion (including challenging the other negotiator to defend a point), and informational bargaining.

The receiving of information during a negotiation is a process consisting of two broad phases: careful listening and analysis.

Careful Listening

Listening is a key negotiating skill. Many consider listening to be an easy task which they do well. In fact, it is *not* easy, and often it is not done well. Listening carefully requires energy, concentration, and, for a good number of us, work and practice. **Careful listening** consists of consciously and accurately understanding everything that is being communicated without the interference of gaps (missed portions), mistakes, or unconscious assumptions.

The first step for careful listening is to be open to receiving new information. This means avoiding the pitfalls that distort accurate perceptions, along with maintaining sharp focus on the disclosures. The other negotiator must be given the opportunity to speak. At times a negotiator will need to encourage (subtly or obviously) the other negotiator to continue speaking, as the following model statements illustrate.

> "So that I can understand your concerns, have you ever had a bad experience with this type of arrangement?"

> "How will you judge the success of this deal?"

> "What are your needs, concerns, and goals?"

> "What is it that makes you reluctant to agree to this proposal?"

Accurate listening requires concentration on both verbal and nonverbal messages. It also requires giving verbal and nonverbal feedback to show understanding and consideration of the situation from the other person's perspective. The negotiator must focus on the present, not on what occurred before or what should or will happen next. Concentration must prevail over fatigue, negative feelings from other events, the present interaction itself, other tasks or obligations, or time pressures. The discussion should be adjourned if a negotiator begins to lose focus and cannot maintain concentration. Strange or dramatic nonverbal communication may be a ploy to surprise, intimidate, or disorient the listener. If faced with such behavior, one either should not react at all, or respond with firmness, at least until it can be determined whether the conduct is genuine or merely a tactic. Calmness is essential.

A negotiator must avoid distorting messages unconsciously due to an emotional reaction to the other party, its negotiator, or their strategy or tactics. Without conscious awareness, the negotiator may act unwisely. The two most common emotional problems for negotiators are undue anxiety and anger. Since anyone can be subject to these emotions, a negotiator must be mentally prepared for them. With mental preparation, the energy created by these emotions can often be usefully channeled toward productive concentration. Deep breathing and the tensing and relaxing of muscles may dissipate their ill effects. At times, it may become necessary to take a break in the negotiating session.

Testing Your Listening Assumptions. We all must be alert for information that contradicts our assumptions, preconceptions, or understandings. Otherwise, important information may be missed. Hearing what we expect to hear is a very human failing. As a learning experience, read the following example and write down the scene it suggests and activities that you can visualize occurring. Imagine that someone told you the following:

"Fred drove from Boston to New York on the turnpike with Caroline."

Look at your written description of the event. You may have made certain common assumptions:

1. That the travel was by car.

2. That Fred was driving.

3. That Caroline was in the same car as Fred.

Yet none of those assumptions need be true. Fred could have traveled by bus, truck, motorcycle, or even a covered wagon! If a car was used, Fred need not have been the driver. Caroline could have been following or leading Fred in a separate vehicle.

At times, it is safe and appropriate to rely on listening assumptions. It is neither necessary nor practical to always check every detail. Yet, careful listening distinguishes between (1) the words said and any inferences drawn, so that inferences are consciously separated into assumptions to be evaluated, and (2) those listening assumptions that are safe to rely on, and those that may be dangerous to rely on without verification. In negotiations, one must be especially careful not to mistake his or her own assumptions for material facts or aspects of proposals or positions.

Restatements and recapitulations can be used to verify that your understanding is correct. The following model statement can be used to verify the validity of your assumptions.

> "Let me make sure that I have the structure of your proposal correctly in mind. You propose that.... Now, have I misstated or omitted anything?"

Tips for Dealing With Technical Information. Especially with technical information, negotiators may need to slow the pace of the discussion and confirm their understanding of the data. Follow-up questions can be used to explore or clarify information. The following model statements are examples of suitable follow-up questions.

> "What is the additional cost if we also want ___?"

> "Are discounts available for other items or certain levels of volume?"

> "Can the manufacturing process meet these specifications, and if so, within what budgetary constraints?"

Listeners can confirm their understanding by restating or summarizing what has been said. At times, this can even clarify the speaker's own understanding of the true meaning of what has been said.

> "Let me say this in my own words to make certain that we understand each other."

The techniques of restatement and summarization also help build rapport. Responding to the other's expressions in this way tends to be perceived as a demonstration of sensitivity to the other side's positions, needs, and interests.

Use Care When Receiving Numbers or Statistics. Special care should be taken with numbers. Calculations should be rechecked to avoid errors. Formulas for monetary issues should be translated into their real total dollar impact, as the following model statement illustrates.

> "Let's see. The $5 concession per unit means $300,000."

Case in Point 10-1_____

An offer to pay for certain property rights has been made in the amount of $10 million, to be spread unevenly over the course of 10 years. On closer examination of the proposed payment schedule, it becomes apparent, given the extent of the deferrals and the discount rate, that the present value of the offer is only $3,200,000.

Distinguishing What the Speaker Knows From Interpretation or Hearsay. A negotiator must separate out the facts that are really known by the speaker from the speaker's interpretations, assumptions, and hearsay. The following model statement shows how this may be done.

> "We have the financing. I don't know why you thought we didn't. Just because we had a slight delay, you shouldn't have assumed we failed to get the loan. Please call your client to say that the deal should continue as planned."

Thus, the listener must distinguish between assumptions, opinions, and hearsay and hard data. To do so may require questioning and probing. Otherwise, an unwitting listener may rely on information that is inadvertently inaccurate.

Guarding Against Memory Lapse. When negotiations are spread out over time, care must be taken to accurately restate positions, offers, and demands. Careful listening can be ruined if you can't subsequently remember enough to catch contradictions or other changes. While deliberate misrepresentation may or may not be the case, depending on the ethics of the other negotiator, good faith misstatements can also ruin a negotiation unless they are promptly corrected. Particularly with numbers, notes should be routinely checked unless one's memory is absolutely fresh and clear, a desirable but rare talent among busy people. The same precaution is true when reviewing settlement documents drafted by the other side, or when doing the drafting oneself.

Analyzing Cues

In most negotiations, there is at least some uncertainty about the interests and the values of the other party and of its negotiator, as well as informational uncertainty and inequality. Cues must be utilized to provide missing information. **Cues** are indicators of the other party's or negotiator's true motives, interests, values, strategies, and tactics. The negotiator must distinguish between the intended and the real meaning of the other side's communications. Cues can help a negotiator decipher truths from falsehoods or inaccuracies.

Comparing Articulated Positions With the Bottom Line. Part of assessing cues is to differentiate between the other party's articulated positions and its bottom line. For instance, the other side's first offers or initial positions may be interpreted as reflecting high aspirations. The evaluation of the other party's bottom line considers that party's known or suspected needs, interests, and goals.

Recognizing Concession Patterns. Any evident concession patterns can reveal how the other party really values items or links issues. Additionally, negotiators commonly tend to decrease the size of concessions as they approach the limits of their authority. Thus, a pattern of smaller and smaller concessions can cue a negotiator that the negotiation is nearing the other party's bottom line. Be wary, however, because the other negotiator may be transmitting false cues to deliberately create a false impression.

Key Concept 104

Nonverbal cues can augment one's knowledge of a negotiation by either confirming or contradicting verbal information.

Nonverbal Cues. A great deal of information comes from nonverbal sources. Beyond what one actually says or writes about a position or negotiating goal, one transmits, often unwittingly, one's true opinions or feelings through nonverbal means. **Nonverbal cues** are signs telegraphed without words (or intended words) that either confirm, reject, or contradict verbal communications.

Many negotiators are unaware of other people's nonverbal cues, or even of the ones which they themselves transmit. The major reasons for the former are distractions, a lack of subtle awareness, and too much concentration (or faith) in the verbal communication. Reasons for the latter include a lack of self-awareness, unconscious slips of the tongue (sometimes referred to as "Freudian slips"), and overwhelming emotions. The following model statements exemplify two types of nonverbal cues.

"My final offer is $85,000,...I mean $80,000."

"When Smith gave me his final bid, his body was actually trembling. I wonder whether he can come up with the financing to back it up?"

Of course, not every physical movement should be interpreted as an important nonverbal cue. The blinking of an eye may simply be due to a speck of dust or a new contact lens rather than a response to statements being made. In contrast, the negotiator who lights up like a Fourth of July fireworks display upon hearing an offer is probably conveying an important cue about his or her reaction to the offer. A close observer will likely pick up clear nonverbal cues that convey messages.

Taking notes can be a problem when trying to read nonverbal signals. Many negotiators often look away from the other person to make notes during portions of the negotiations. By taking frequent notes, the negotiator spends more time looking down at the paper than at the other negotiator or party. While some notes may be helpful or essential, habitual and extensive note taking is usually not necessary. It is more harmful than beneficial to take many notes because it causes the negotiator to miss important nonverbal cues. Looking away while listening or speaking also can stem from habit, or from discomfort at watching others closely. Whatever the reason, it will lead to the same unfortunate results: many nonverbal cues will not be observed.

Looking away not only loses the opportunity for observing the other negotiator, but in itself can convey an unwanted message. A lack of eye contact might be perceived as indicative of weakness, uncertainty, guilt, or deception. In contrast, good eye contact can be perceived as intimidating, honest, open, challenging, or help to maintain the other's attention.

Anxiety regarding what to do next in the negotiation also causes many nonverbal cues to be missed. Too many negotiators jump ahead mentally and focus on their future moves, or on what they are going to say next, while failing to concentrate sufficiently on the interaction occurring presently within the negotiation. This focus on the future, rather than the present, leads to a failure to see or to recognize some nonverbal cues. For the same reasons, it also can cause one to miss even verbal cues.

Modes of Communication

Information, offers, and rationales can be conducted through various modes of communication. At times, the choice of communication mode (meetings, telephone calls, or letters or other writings) will be merely a matter of chance. Two parties or negotiators may happen to meet, leading to a negotiation of a pending matter between them. More often, however, the choice among the modes of communication will be a conscious one, based on the advantages and disadvantages of each type of communication to the particular negotiation.

The Impact of Meetings on the Negotiating Process

> ## Key Concept 105
>
> *Meetings, formal or informal, make the exchanges personal, which can create a greater commitment to negotiate. If necessary, use private channels for more candid exchanges.*

Formal meetings are gatherings of negotiators and related others that are held at a scheduled time and place. Negotiators are serious about the activities at formal meetings, otherwise, they have wasted time and energy preparing for and attending the negotiation. Thus, it may be useful to have a preliminary discussion, prior to a formal meeting, to determine whether a meeting has a sufficient probability of being productive to warrant scheduling it. Accordingly, a negotiator can lose credibility by failing to make reasonable proposals and engage in reasonable discussions after scheduling a meeting to negotiate.

In a face-to-face setting, there is an opportunity for give and take, extensive discussion, and visual observation of the participants. The contact is more personal, which may be either advantageous or disadvantageous. Some types of negotiations involve formal meetings, the proceedings of which are likely to be reported publicly. This can be detrimental to the negotiation process. For example, negotiations in the 1962 New York City newspaper strike were criticized for the lack of dependable channels for the confidential exchange of bargaining positions.

Informal meetings are gatherings of negotiators that occur in a more relaxed atmosphere than formal meetings; they can be productive by allowing the negotiators to dispense with rhetoric, be candid with their views, and seek accommodation without a loss of face. Informality also can aid the process by decreasing tension. For this to work, the atmosphere must be one of trust that casual or off-the-record statements will not be publicized or used for tactical advantage. The ability to make off-the-record statements may be either tacitly understood or the subject of explicit negotiation and arrangement. Despite any accord on the use of informal statements or an informal setting, the negotiator still must be adequately prepared and alert to the other side's moves, since the entire negotiation process can be significantly influenced by occurrences in such limited meetings.

Private channels, or behind-the-scenes negotiating encounters, can be a critical alternative to publicly reported negotiations, where either media or constituent groups (unions, associations, and so on) make the negotiation a matter of public interest and possible public pressure. Similarly, the presence of a client or decision maker may inhibit candor and cause counterproductive rhetoric solely to please one's own side. Private channels of communication may be crucial in such situations because important information can still be directly conveyed.

Using Site Selection to Advantage

Many commentators believe that the site of the meeting has an important impact on negotiations. Some think that a **home-field site,** one's own familiar surroundings, such as one's own office, provides a distinct advantage. One thought is that making one's own office the site demonstrates one's power. Getting the other negotiator to travel a significant distance also may generate a psychological commitment to reaching an agreement due to the investment of time, energy, and expense. Another consideration for the choice of site is how it will affect the available resources, including the availability of information. It can be advantageous to meet at the other negotiator's office provided that:

1. The other negotiator will not develop an undue sense of power by succeeding in imposing a choice of site.

2. Any essential information is already present (unless the unavailability of information is to be used tactically to deflect inquiries or require adjournment).

3. The presence of a negotiating team can be assured.

Travel to the other side's office may be necessary. However, with the proper attitude and care, there still should not be a home-field advantage for the other negotiator. In this situation, one must be careful not to allow his or her performance to be adversely affected by:

1. Fatigue.

2. The physical setting, including any impressive aspects of the site.

3. Being outnumbered in the other side's office.

If the choice of site is a critical factor because it affects perceptions of power, possible compromises include choosing a neutral site, or planning more than one session, with the location of the meetings to alternate.

Another consideration in choosing the site is the extent to which it will create a particular atmosphere and tone. The physical layout of the site can also affect the negotiating atmosphere. The setting of the room can create a tone of formality or informality. For example, a cooperative attitude may be fostered by having a living-room-style arrangement without the barriers of large tables or desks.

Tips When Negotiating by Telephone

Key Concept 106

Telephone calls can be used to obtain specific information or for efficiency, but use adjournment rather than be caught off guard.

A telephone call can be a good tool for gathering information before a meeting. It also may be substituted for a meeting for a number of reasons. A telephone call may be preferred due to scheduling difficulties, its cost-effectiveness, or because the negotiation is expected to be relatively brief and simple.

Telephone calls permit discussion with some give and take, although usually less than at a meeting, because telephone negotiations tend to be shorter than those conducted at meetings. There is less of a commitment to negotiate since it is much easier to converse by telephone than to schedule a meeting. Telephone calls can be useful to initially define issues, establish rapport, and obtain background information without becoming as deeply immersed in substantive issues as in a meeting.

Of course, when the telephone is used, direct personal contact is decreased and nonverbal visual communication is nonexistent. The lack of visual cues can cause misunderstandings. While tone of voice and verbal pace might reveal important cues about the other negotiator's thinking, the lack of face-to-face contact can lessen the chances of reaching an agreement without a meeting.

Since one does not usually know in advance that the other negotiator is going to call to initiate or to continue the negotiations, care must be taken to decide whether you are sufficiently prepared at the time of the call to proceed. If not, it is important to defer the negotiation until there has been time to review the matter, and then to return the call to the other negotiator. This is a form of adjournment.

**Letters and Other Written
Communications**

Key Concept 107

*Communicating in writing avoids unwanted interruptions, helps
prevent misunderstandings, and adds a degree of significance to the
position or other information.*

Written communications are useful to transmit detailed and exact information The information can be presented without interruption.
Letters, memorandums, telexes, and so forth, can eliminate the confusion that sometimes occurs at meetings regarding what was said by providing a permanent record, as long as the writings themselves are clear.
Since written documentation of an agreement normally is required,
some written communication usually occurs during the course of a negotiation.

Written communications may slow the pace of the negotiation. This
can be advantageous, disadvantageous, or neither, depending on the
timing needs and interests of the parties. One major disadvantage of a
written communication is that it is not flexible. The negotiator, for instance, cannot engage in information gathering and then take a position. Instead, positions must be taken, unless a letter is limited to invit-
ing the other party to make an offer, requesting the disclosure of
information, or is only transmitting factual information to the other negotiator.

An exception to the usual lack of flexibility of a written communication is a draft of an agreement that already has been reached either
orally or in a summary written form. Such a draft is circulated for discussion and revision. Using written draft is necessary to allow the negotiators and the parties to focus on the precise details and terms of the
tentative agreement. This process may involve meetings or telephone
calls to discuss the draft and alternative versions.

Written materials may be necessary or useful at meetings to clarify,
illustrate, or provide a more concrete form for the information which
will be part of the basis for a negotiation. Construction drawings, charts,
graphs, overlays, computer runs, and other written forms of data all can
help to facilitate a meeting without destroying its flexibility. These can
be supplemented or replaced by other visual forms of presentation, including videos, movies, slides, photographs, and models.

A second major disadvantage of a writing is that it can be a permanent record of a statement or a position. A party may not object to having a permanent record of an offer if it is accepted. However, the party may not want to have such a record if the other party rejects the offer and instead shows it to other parties. In addition, the party or the negotiator may want or need to make certain statements without fear that a written record will be disclosed. For this reason, an agreement that such communications will be treated confidentially sometimes is essential. Even so, it may be best to refrain from making written comments about certain subjects or persons, and limit oneself to oral communications. On the other hand, there should be no hesitancy about having any significant representations or warranties in writing.

At times, a tentative offer should be in writing even though a proposal is not fully developed and only the approval of a basic concept or of a broad outline is sought. However, if not fully developed, there must be an explicit statement that it alone cannot be the basis for an agreement, and that all necessary terms must be agreed on in writing.

In certain instances, a precondition may be that a proposal is to be kept secret, at least unless it is accepted. However, avoiding any written document can help prevent inadvertent disclosures, and make it possible to deny a position in the event that a disclosure is made contrary to an agreement for secrecy. If these are serious concerns, an effort should be made to refrain from using a written proposal.

This reservation is not to discount the importance of written material. Seeing a proposal or a plan in a carefully written form can be far more persuasive than a brief spoken description. Matters that are reduced to writing can appear to be more significant, and can appear to reflect a greater commitment on the part of the writer. A high degree of organization, planning, and knowledge also can be demonstrated through writing. A written offer may be more easily scrutinized, discussed, and studied than the same material that is presented orally, since the latter is dependent on the memory or notes of the listener. All of this may increase the likelihood of reaching an agreement. Furthermore, one may find it advantageous to have a record which is or can be made public. The written communication then can be used to influence allies, the media, the public, or others.

Fax

The facsimile machine, or fax, provides an important mode of communication. Attempts to duck unwanted telephone calls are useless since the message is immediately conveyed anyway. Time pressure can be maintained. Instantly, the message can be delivered regardless of the geographic distance separating people. Furthermore, drafts and other documents can be circulated back and forth without a need for meetings and without delay.

However, with the proliferation of fax communications, at times there may be a backlog to transmit, receive, or move a fax to or from the machine to the intended recipient. For these reasons, overnight mail and messenger services still have a place in the market, even when the intended recipient has a fax machine.

Comprehension Checkup

The answers to these questions appear on page 332.

1. At the outset, the other negotiator demands to set the agenda and engages in lengthy advocacy of that side's point of view. Your initial interaction makes it clear that resistance will lead to a real struggle for control. However, it does appear, at this very early point that the other negotiator is not focused on the exact outcome on some issues that your side considers important. You should _____.
   a. resist the agenda but permit the advocacy
   b. permit the agenda but resist the advocacy
   c. permit the agenda and the advocacy
   d. resist the agenda and the advocacy
   e. inject a new issue

2. The other party has a reputation for initial high pressure to gain control of the agenda, and using that to set a tone and dominate negotiation of the substantive issues. You should _____.
   a. resist the agenda but permit the tone
   b. permit the agenda but resist the tone
   c. permit the agenda and the tone
   d. resist the agenda and the tone
   e. use problem solving

3. After a series of offers and counteroffers, you would state your proposal most effectively as _____.
   a. "$1,500,000 is our price."
   b. "This site is ideal for you because it needs no changes to the structure for your operation, and $1,500,000 is the same price as you'd pay for a site requiring substantial modifications."
   c. "We need $1,500,000 for our cashflow."
   d. "$1,500,000 is the fair market value."
   e. "I'm sure we can find another buyer for $1,500,000."

4. The other negotiator has been engaging in loud high-pressure tactics and simply repeats his initial demand, as if trying to overwhelm you. You decide to resist by confronting these behaviors. The most effective statement is _____.

a. "Stop it now."
b. "You're rude and obnoxious, and I'm not going to put up with it."
c. "Your actions make it impossible to negotiate in a meaningful way. Do you really want to discuss this or should we just stop here?"
d. "Please stop repeating that demand and tone down your voice."
e. "Look, I just can't deal with this."

5. The other side made a proposal which is unacceptable, but you do not want to cut off further negotiation. Your most effective response is_____.
   a. "At this point, let's keep talking."
   b. "No."
   c. "We're looking for something more in the range of...."
   d. "Let me suggest an alternative."
   e. "That's not acceptable because....Let me suggest an alternative."

6. You believe that the other negotiator is not accurately informing that side's decision maker of your good faith attempts to meet their needs. You should *not* _____.
   a. make a significant concession
   b. request a conference call with the decision maker
   c. negotiate to have the decision makers at a session
   d. transmit a written proposal
   e. seek an ally

7. Although being careful to avoid making any explicit or implicit representations, you would prefer not to discuss the details of some of your records. The best approach is _____.
   a. make faster concessions
   b. negotiate at the other side's office without the records
   c. refuse outright
   d. bargain for information
   e. a trial proposal

8. The other negotiator tells you she (1) owns three plants, that (2) manufacture fasteners with (3) rising sales that are (4) expected to double because of a large account which (5) plans to expand rapidly. The following are to be treated as assumptions rather than tentative facts at this point.
   a. 1, 3, 5   d. 4, 5
   b. 1, 2, 3, 4, 5   e. 2, 3
   c. 3, 4, 5

9. Often, negotiations proceed in the following order: demonstrating power or persuasion by advocating positions, searching for solutions, and working together to find satisfactory terms.   T   F

10. Usually, a negotiator should be prepared to make some concessions.   T   F

11. When a negotiator is the only representative of a party at the bargaining table, extensive note taking is critical in order to be able to analyze the process.   T   F

11

Systematic Planning: Prenegotiation Stages

Key Concepts

108. Systematic planning is a critical element for successful negotiation; it helps negotiators to reduce stress, avoid under- or overestimating the other side, and discover potential zones of agreement.

109. Planning time varies with expertise and the relative importance of the matter.

110. Before negotiating, obtain available information about goals, issues, markets, vital interests of the other side and its negotiator, strengths and weaknesses of parties and negotiators, the other side's bottom line, and any influences from economic, social, or political climates. Tentative inferences made now should be reexamined later during the negotiation.

111. Informational gaps lead to informational tactics.

112. Concrete negotiation goals must be determined and prioritized within the categories of *essential* and *desirable*, with a balancing of long-term and short-term goals.

113. Issues for each goal must be identified, as well as possible trade-offs between issues and how the other party may define the issues.

114. Market values, practices, and negotiation customs must be taken into account in prenegotiation planning, as well as the subjective values of the participants.

115. Assess strengths and weaknesses of each side and its negotiator based on vital interests, situational pressures, and constraints. Ask yourself why the other side wants this deal. Plan to eliminate or diminish one's own weaknesses, perhaps through fact creation.

116. Agreements result from each side deciding that it is in its own interest to agree rather than not to have an agreement.

117. Situational pressures and constraints affect negotiations.

118. The other negotiator's personal interests, personality, and negotiating style must be taken into account.

119. Estimate the other side's bottom line based on your "lucky day" fantasy, and then estimate its opening position by analyzing its perceptions and your ability to change them for each issue and goal.

120. Develop any potential win-win outcomes with either gain to one side without real loss to the other side, or with mutual gain.

The Language of Negotiating

To make full use of the key concepts, you must understand the following key terms:

Systematic planning	Jungle fighters
Essential goals	Dictators
Desirable goals	Dream merchants
Long-term goals	Soothers
Short-term goals	Win-win negotiators
Bargaining mix	Fluid dynamics
Situational pressures and constraints	Scripting

Introduction

By this point, the reader has been introduced to the important concepts of negotiation. Ideas such as the optimal approach to negotiating, the importance of defining one's negotiating goals, and the need to control the process of information exchange have been covered. Also, the reader has become familiar with the strategies and tactics that constitute successful negotiations and has gained an understanding of how to employ them. Essential for developing negotiating expertise, however, is the successful adoption of a methodology that can be used to plan an entire negotiation. Chapters 11 and 12 present such a methodology.

Chapter 11 introduces a 14-point structure to be used in planning negotiations. The first 7 points (planning steps) relate to prenegotiation activities. These are covered in Chapter 11. Chapter 12 presents planning steps 8–14 which relate to the negotiation itself. Many of the concepts learned previously will be reinforced as they are reintroduced within the plan. This is an ideal opportunity to learn a vital aspect of negotiation as well as to review important ideas.

Key Concept 108

Systematic planning is a critical element for successful negotiation; it helps negotiators to reduce stress, avoid under- or overestimating the other side, and discover potential zones of agreement.

Most expert commentators on negotiating will acknowledge that effective planning generally is the most important element in successful negotiating. **Systematic planning** is an important means of creating a thorough, well-prepared negotiating plan.

Case in Point 11-1_____

Brown's job is to negotiate the sale of 100,000 pounds of Jeftod, a raw material used in manufacturing. The cost to produce Jeftod is two dollars per pound. A potential purchaser is BARP. Brown enters the office of their vice president, Laurjen, whom he has never met. Initially, they exchange greetings and sit down in large chairs separated by a marble table. After mentioning the weather, Laurjen says, "Let's get right to the point. We need 25,000 pounds and will pay $75,000. Can we make a deal?" How should Brown respond? Obviously, he does not have sufficient information to respond at this point. Should he accept the offer since the profit margin would be 50 percent? Or should he make a counteroffer? If he does make a counteroffer, how much should it be? Brown quickly decides to accept the offer. Upon returning to his office, Brown learns that his boss is quite upset with his decision because she was quite confident that Laurjen would have accepted a counteroffer. Surprised by Laurjen's quick offer, Brown was caught unprepared.

Some people do not plan at all. Others plan for a negotiation by simply thinking about it in a general, unstructured way. By doing so, they cover certain important points, but at the same time, they are unlikely to think of all the important points.

Systematic planning is necessary to anticipate all the potential events and problems of a negotiation. Just as simple checklists can be useful to ensure that nothing is overlooked in other contexts, systematic planning can perform that same function for negotiations. Of course, systematic planning involves far more than a checklist, since each step requires careful analysis of a range of possibilities. Moreover, the uncertain and fluid nature of negotiation can make it a stressful experience. Systematic planning reduces the stress by increasing the negotiator's personal effectiveness and control over the situation.

Key Concept 109

Planning time varies with expertise and the relative importance of the matter.

Through practice and familiarity with the steps, the time expended decreases. Using experience, but being careful not to become sloppy or fall into unthinking patterns, the time can be adjusted for the nature and context of the negotiation. Repetitious negotiations, especially small transactions, can be done more quickly. Thus, with experience in utilizing the planning system and adjustments for the type of negotiation, the steps outlined provide an effective and efficient method to improve a negotiator's performance for any type of negotiation.

Providing cost-efficient negotiations is a vital consideration. Judgment must be exercised so that an appropriate amount of time is devoted, providing quality without creating undue cost. This potential dilemma is no different for planning than for other aspects of business management.

The Negotiating Methodology

Because the information available to a negotiator is never complete and is never without a degree of uncertainty, planning the perfect negotiation is impossible. Nevertheless, effective, systematic planning will greatly reduce negotiating errors and will increase your control of the negotiation. This control, in turn, will significantly increase the number of optimal or nearly optimal deals that are achieved.

The 14 steps for systematic planning are outlined below. The amount of time spent on each step will vary greatly with each negotiation, depending on such factors as experience, whether the negotiation is one of a large number of relatively simple, repetitious negotiations, or whether it is a single, relatively complex and more unique negotiation. The basic 14 steps for systematic planning, however, remain the same. They are:

1. Prenegotiation information gathering
2. Determining goals
3. Identifying issues
4. Analyzing the market
5. Assessing strengths and weaknesses
6. Estimating the other party's bottom line and opening position
7. Considering win-win outcomes
8. Setting the opening position
9. Setting the bottom line
10. Choosing strategies and tactics
11. Considering concessions and trade-offs
12. Determining an agenda
13. Analyzing timing
14. Choosing the modes of communication

Planning Step 1:
Prenegotiation Information
Gathering

Key Concept 110

Before negotiating, obtain available information about goals, issues, markets, vital interests of the other side and its negotiator, strengths and weaknesses of parties and negotiators, the other side's bottom line, and any influences from economic, social, or political climates. Tentative inferences made now should be reexamined later during the negotiation.

The first step in planning is to obtain any information needed and available regarding the following:

Your side's goals.

Issues.

Relevant market data.

Vital interests of each party and of each negotiator.

Strengths and weaknesses of each party and of each negotiator.

The other party's bottom line.

Any effects or influences from the current economic, social, and political climates.

This step in the process occurs as early as possible and precedes any actual negotiating.

Case in Point 11-2

A licensor of technology is gathering facts prior to beginning a negotiation. The information obtained includes the following:

1. The efforts that the potential purchaser has made to develop or to acquire the same or equivalent technology.
2. The benefits, economic and otherwise, that the potential purchaser is likely to obtain from acquiring the technology.
3. The cost and the delay that the potential purchaser will incur in order to implement the technology, if it is procured.

This information will help determine the value of the technology to the impending negotiation.

The methods and sources for obtaining information were presented in Chapter 4. Naturally, the information available is invariably limited and its reliability is often questionable. Therefore, tentative inferences should be made with caution and subjected to reevaluation as additional information becomes known.

Case in Point 11-3

A collective bargaining agreement is to be negotiated. The employer's negotiator is planning for the negotiation, and is engaged in prenegotiation information gathering. This preparation includes the following: ·

1. Updates regarding the law.

2. Reviewing the current contract and related company documents such as employee handbooks, pension or profit-sharing plans, incentive programs, job-evaluation procedures, work rules, posted company policy statements, and so forth.

3. Obtaining data about employees, including seniority information, the history of prior negotiations, information on all grievances and their resolutions since the last collective bargaining negotiation, the mood of the bargaining participants.

4. Facts about the members of the other side's negotiation team, including information concerning their personalities.

The nature of the information needed for planning varies, depending on the factors involved in the specific negotiation. However, the major categories of information that pertain to planning are given in the following sections.

Key Concept 111

Informational gaps lead to informational tactics.

After completing the prenegotiation information gathering, the planner may be struck by gaps or uncertainties in the accessible information. A determination should be made regarding the information which one will seek to learn or to confirm during the course of the negotiation. The results of this determination then are utilized to choose both informational and situational tactics, as well as to help analyze the agenda.

Planning Step 2: Determining Goals

Key Concept 112

Concrete negotiation goals must be determined and prioritized within the categories of essential and desirable, with a balancing of long-term and short-term goals.

During the prenegotiation period, the general goals for the negotiation must be determined. Establishing these goals allows the negotiator to plan more precisely, since each goal requires planning. The nature of the negotiation and the factors involved in the particular negotiation will determine the type of goals that are involved, as well as the specifics of each goal.

Negotiating Scenario_____

A business transaction is being negotiated. The goals include establishing the price, quality of the goods, due dates for delivery, cost and the means of financing, dependability of the other party, length of the contract, and obtaining options to renew.

Negotiating Scenario_____

A dispute between two businesses has resulted in a lawsuit. One of the goals is to get the parties talking again so that they can deal with each other in the future.

Negotiation goals must be sufficiently specific so that they can be used for establishing bottom-line authority for the negotiation. Goals can be clarified by determining the factors which will be used to decide whether a possible deal is the "best deal" and by figuring the minimum amount that is acceptable to one's side. Unless goals are clearly established so that there is a standard with which to evaluate a proposed agreement, the following pitfalls may occur:

1. Negotiators may agree to terms that their clients, parties, or other decision makers reject.
2. Parties may concede too much.
3. Negotiations may fail because parties never realize that they have obtained what they need.
4. Parties may never reach an internal consensus on whether to accept or reject proposals.

Prioritizing Goals

Multiple goals need to be prioritized. This is to ascertain the relative importance of each goal for planning purposes. Next, decisions must be made concerning whether it is essential to achieve all the goals. **Essen-**

tial goals relate to vital interests, whereas **desirable goals** concern nonvital, but important or attractive interests or outcomes. Once essential and desirable goals are determined (a basic prioritization), the goals in each of those categories must be prioritized. Finally, it is important to determine and prioritize both **long-term** and **short-term goals**. Although "long-term" and "short-term" are relative and do not specify *absolute* time periods, short-term normally refers to periods of one year or less, and long-term is usually used for longer periods.

Case in Point 11-4_____

A butcher shop decides that the prices and the quality of the meat are its crucial goals. The store also considers free advertising to be desirable, but nonessential. Depending on its profits, the market, and a variety of other factors, the store either may be willing to sacrifice some degree of quality to obtain meat at a lower price, or it might elect to pay more to receive a higher quality of meat with the expectation that selling better meat will increase its sales. On the other hand, even if the store is willing to sacrifice some degree of quality to cut its costs, the store will not buy rotten meat at any price. Similarly, there will be a cost which the store is unwilling to bear no matter what quality meat can be obtained. Thus, planning is needed to establish a relationship between the vital goals of price and quality. This price-quality relationship not only assigns a priority to one or the other of the two goals, it also creates limits on the trade-offs between them. Furthermore, there may be some trade-off from either or both goals for free advertising. The store must decide on these goals and their priorities.

The identification and prioritization of goals helps determine the issues to be negotiated. In Case in Point 11-4, the potential issues are:

ISSUE ONE: Price alone—Essential goal.

ISSUE TWO: Quality alone—Essential goal.

ISSUE THREE: Price and quality if negotiated jointly—Two essential goals.

ISSUE FOUR: Free advertising—Desirable goal.

ISSUE FIVE: Free advertising with some trade-off of price or quality—One desirable goal and two essential goals.

There are five potential issues, since the butcher shop has to choose whether to negotiate: (1) price, but not quality; (2) quality, but not price; (3) both price and quality; (4) to obtain free advertising; and/or (5) to trade price, quality, or both for free advertising. Even when only money is involved, and not any nonmonetary issues such as quality, the identification and prioritization of the issues is critical. Here, price and quality were essential goals, and were not to be traded off for the merely desirable goal of free advertising. Instead, free advertising was sought without any price or quality concessions.

Some people have a tendency to focus more on the immediate future than on the long-run. Long-term negotiating implications, benefits, and detriments must be carefully compared with those in the short-term. At times, short-term goals may be more important than long-term ones. However, immediacy can lead to pressing too hard and focusing only on the immediate potential deal rather than establishing a more beneficial long-term relationship.

Negotiating Scenario_____

A union and management are engaged in one of a periodic series of negotiations. For management, the potential short-run, favorable benefit of a one-sided agreement may be shortsighted. The potential for alienating the union by pressing too hard for immediate concessions may jeopardize future relations. If there is a reasonable likelihood of causing long-run difficulties, but short-run gains, then the long-term and the short-term goals must be prioritized.

Balancing distant and immediate risks, benefits, and detriments is extremely important for negotiations that involve long-term relationships. As a general rule, an agreement which is not fair to the other side will be honored only reluctantly, if at all, and in the long-run will not benefit either party. The most durable agreements address fairly the needs of both parties. Fairness, though, is a relative term. Since one normally wants the most advantageous deal possible without creating an untenable situation, a negotiator must determine whether an obtainable agreement is so unfair that the other party will not fulfill its obligations. If this is a significant risk, the advantages must be weighed against the consequences of a breach.

Each goal generates its own issue, and has its own priority in relationship to every other goal. When trade-offs between goals are feasible, additional issues will emerge. These new issues consist of a new combination of goals that are subject to trade-offs as a separate new issue. In turn, each issue then becomes the focal point for the subsequent planning steps.

Planning Step 3: Identifying Issues

Key Concept 113

Issues for each goal must be identified, as well as possible trade-offs between issues and how the other party may define the issues.

Once the goals are known, the issues to be negotiated must be identified. Issues arise when the respective parties' goals conflict or when it seems that they might conflict. The areas of conflict are analyzed for the specific points to be negotiated. Analysis can be done on an issue-by-issue basis, as issues with subissues, or both. In addition, the analysis must include whether the issues may be linked, or not. If linkage is possible, the resulting groups of new issues and subissues should be identified.

An issue also can arise when a negotiator creates the issue solely as a trade-off concession that is of greater value to the other party than whatever is being demanded as the trade. Identifying the real issues can help you to recognize when the other negotiator is using this tactic to artificially create an issue.

Some refer to each party's agenda of issues as its **bargaining mix.** The combination of bargaining mixes provides a picture of the issues to be negotiated. The collectivity of issues can be initially categorized into economic or noneconomic groups. Each economic and noneconomic issue then is classified involving advantages for the long-run, short-run, or both.

The process of identifying issues next requires that a negotiator try to determine how the other's side defines the issues. Issues can be modified in light of the views of the other side. Choose to take the initiative in defining the issues when you want to:

1. Create room to negotiate the definitions of the issues.

2. Gain immediate acceptance of a favorable or a fair definition.

If a favorable definition is likely to be accepted by the other party, or rejected without serious negative consequences, it should be attempted.

Before proceeding further, the goals must be reexamined in the context of the issues that have been identified and the information that has been gathered at this point. Clarification may be required. Adjustments should be considered if goals appear to be unrealistic in view of the issues that have emerged thus far. After the issues have been identified and the goals have been reexamined, focus on each issue, and each combination of issues, in terms of the following criteria:

1. Information that has been gathered, and information that still is needed.
2. Specific benefits and detriments following from the issue as they affect each goal.
3. Relevant market factors.
4. Strengths, weaknesses, and interests of each party.
5. The other party's probable opening position and bottom line.
6. Possible win-win outcomes.
7. The actual opening position.
8. The actual bottom line.
9. The strategies and tactics to be chosen.
10. Possible concessions and trade-offs.

Planning Step 4: Analyzing the Market

Key Concept 114

Market values, practices, and negotiation customs must be taken into account in prenegotiation planning, as well as the subjective values of the participants.

Everything that is negotiated has a market. Houses, cars, raw materials, singers, and accountants all have prices based on their value within their market. Even when that which is being negotiated is somewhat unique (such as a beautiful old painting), the market value of the item must be taken into consideration in planning its negotiation. Of course, the subjective attitudes of each party will also influence the opening position and the bottom line. Also, each market has its own characteristics. For instance, in labor negotiations, data must be analyzed regarding compensation rates, both in terms of wages and fringe benefits. Another aspect of market analysis is supply and demand, or the determination of the value of that which is being negotiated in terms of its relative desirability and its availability within the market.

Case in Point 11-5_____

The negotiation is for production of a custom-made item. Fixed costs to begin production are $750,000. The size of the potential sales market will affect the profit margin to be negotiated. Assume that the gross profit margin based only on variable costs is $5 per unit. Using this cost structure, 150,000 units must be sold before the breakeven point is reached. Thus, the extent of the potential market is critical. The uncertainty of the size of the market may lead the manufacturer to demand that the buyer share the initial fixed costs before commencing production.

Types of market practices also may exist. The extension of credit and the nature of the credit terms may be a "given" in the negotiation. Audited financial statements will be expected in certain transactions. The international licensing of technology can necessitate giving the right to manufacture the product in a particular country. Various disclosures of information can be required by law in certain types of transactions.

Information about the market must be evaluated. Market value is a consideration, but it is not the only guide. Long- and short-run factors can affect the price of a given transaction, forcing it either above or below the true market value. The same principle applies to market practices. Some may be too fixed to be modified, but others can be transformed as part of a negotiation, depending on the parties and the context.

In addition to the market value and practices, the market's customs and norms also need to be analyzed regarding negotiation methodology. For example, union officials in traditional labor negotiations might be expected to express their zeal to their constituents by venting various complaints, regardless of whether they involve directly negotiable issues. Some professional athletes may feel free to demand a renegotiation of a multiyear contract after a good season, while it is taboo for management to do so after a bad one. A rug merchant in a Middle Eastern bazaar will be disappointed if the customer walks away after hearing the "price" without haggling for the real price. Negotiators from certain foreign cultures expect a period of formalities and pleasantries before getting down to business. They might reject attempts to negotiate without engaging in these preliminary stages. Thus, unless the market customs and norms are understood, the negotiator may fail, either by not understanding the other negotiator, or, conversely, by not being understood. At the same time, realistic consideration should be given to whether unorthodox approaches will yield better results.

The negotiator must learn as much as possible about market values, practices, customs, and norms in order to assess their potential effect on each aspect of the negotiation. A failure to properly analyze the market can lead to disastrous consequences. At this point, one should estimate the other party's view of the market. In part, this is based on the information known to be possessed by the other party. Although completed for the moment, the market analysis always is subject to change as new information emerges.

After information is gathered and the market is analyzed, the goals and issues should be checked for gaps, inconsistencies, or other errors. Adjustments should be made as needed. It is possible that the reexamination of the earlier planning steps will lead to a recognition of a flaw in the analysis of the current step. This possibility can never be ignored.

Planning Step 5: Assessing Strengths and Weaknesses

Key Concept 115

Assess strengths and weaknesses of each side and its negotiator based on vital interests, situational pressures, and constraints. Ask yourself why the other side wants this deal. Plan to eliminate or diminish one's own weaknesses, perhaps through fact creation.

After establishing the goals and analyzing the market, more information and analysis are required before determining the positions to take. The fifth step in planning the negotiation is to determine one's strengths and weaknesses, and to estimate those of the other side, including each party and each negotiator.

The other side's strengths and weaknesses can only be estimated, since the information available will often be incomplete and factually uncertain. The extent to which this estimate affects one's decisions varies with the degree to which it is considered reliable.

Effective planning can eliminate or diminish potential weaknesses, or points which the other party may perceive as negative. First, the actual or perceived weaknesses must be recognized. Once they are recognized, responses need to be prepared. A useful response may be based on fact creation, which can:

1. Create a strength for one's side.

2. Diminish or eliminate a weakness for one's side.

3. Create a weakness for the other side.

As a general rule, weaknesses and points that the other party is likely to perceive negatively should not be mentioned if the other party is unaware of them; however, there are two exceptions. First, respond in anticipation of a weakness or negative point that the other negotiator or the other party is certain to discover during the course of the negotiation. This will enhance an appearance of strength and confidence. Second, one should respond if disclosure of the weakness or the negative point is required by law.

The nature of the parties' relationship is a critical factor in the assessment of strengths and weaknesses. At least in the setting of a commercial transaction, the parties' relationship can be categorized in one of the following four ways:

1. *Total independence:* Each party has at least one viable other option.

2. *Mutual dependence:* Each is equally without another viable option.

3. *Uneven dependence:* Each lacks a viable alternative, but one needs an agreement more than the other.

4. *One-sided dependence:* Only one of the parties lacks a viable alternative.

To determine or to estimate strengths and weaknesses, three broad factors should be considered:

1. The party's vital interests.

2. The situational pressures and constraints.

3. The other negotiator.

Additionally, it is important to relate these factors to the relationship between your side and the other. For example, what one does with an

assessment of the other party's vital interests will depend on whether
the relationship is one of total independence or mutual dependence.
The following descriptions of the estimating factors will provide
enough information to apply to most relationship possibilities.

Vital Interests

During the negotiation, the parties will articulate positions which may
be real or which may be pretexts. Actual strengths and weaknesses,
however, are best assessed by examining one's own vital interests and
those of the other party. A party which realizes that it can affect another
party's vital interest has identified a strength for itself.

Case in Point 11-6

A prospective applicant for a loan realizes that the bank's vital interests are receiving the repayment of the loan, plus having suitable security if the bank perceives that a realistic danger of non-
payment exists.

To ascertain the other party's vital interests, answer the following
question as completely as possible: Why does the other party want this
deal? The parties' vital interests reveal the needs of each party. Satisfying those needs is what the negotiation is really all about. These needs
also are factors to evaluate in assessing the relative strengths and weaknesses of each party as it approaches the negotiation. If appropriate (for
example, in a mutually dependent relationship), planning should include methods for fulfilling the other party's needs. In addition, understanding and sensitivity toward the needs of the other side can contribute to a good rapport and enhance trust, as expressed, for example, in
the following model statement.

"We appreciate that your client needs improved cashflow. Our proposal meets that need by...."

Meeting the other party's needs creates strength for one's own position by making it attractive to the other side while still achieving one's
own goals. This type of persuasive offer tends to be more effective than
relying on threats.

Types of Vital Interests.   There cannot be an agreement unless all the
parties believe that it is in each of their interests to agree to the same

terms. The interests may be positive or negative; there may also be different interests for each party. The following list provides examples of vital interests:

1. Attaining an outcome that is perceived as fair.
2. Getting as much as possible.
3. Avoiding a loss.

Key Concept 116

Agreements result from each side deciding that it is in its own interest to agree rather than not to have an agreement.

Recognizing Each Party's Interests. It is absolutely critical, in both planning and negotiating, that the negotiator understand that an agreement is never reached unless it is perceived by each party as being in its own best interests because the terms are more advantageous than continuing to not have an agreement.

The value that each party places on the items at issue and the possible negotiating outcomes should be assessed based on their respective interests. For example, in a transactional setting, either the parties must value that which is being negotiated somewhat differently, or the agreement must create more for them to divide than if there were no agreement (that is, the pie must be enlarged). A buyer and seller will not contract to purchase an item if they value it exactly the same, because there would be no gain or profit for either. For instance, an item will not be sold for a dollar unless the seller values a dollar more than the item and the buyer values the item more than the dollar. Agreement occurs when:

1. Each party relinquishes something in return for something else from the other party which it values more.
2. Each party gains something of greater value from a third party than that which it relinquishes (as in a joint venture).
3. A combination of the above.

In these situations, agreement becomes more likely the more that the parties' values differ or the more additional items will become available if an agreement is reached.

Five overlapping issues should be analyzed in order to estimate the other party's vital interests; they are:

1. The other party's genuine needs.
2. The other party's background.
3. The other party's need for an agreement.
4. The personal feelings of the other party and the other negotiator.
5. Other influences on the other party.

Evaluating these overlapping issues entails raising a variety of questions. The answers to these questions will help determine the other party's vital interests and distinguish these from its nonvital interests.

The Other Party's Genuine Needs. The other party's genuine needs often must be distinguished from those it states as genuine (which may be disingenuous or erroneous). A variety of questions can be used to help determine the accuracy of stated positions; these include:

- Why is the other party interested in the possibility of negotiating the matter?
- Are there significant resources that the other party has been willing to commit to the negotiation?
- What does the other party expect to receive?
- Why would what the other party expects to receive be important to the other party?
- What problems does the other party have that a negotiated agreement might alleviate or eliminate?
- What plans or desires does the other party have that a negotiated agreement could facilitate or fulfill?
- How many different interests does the other party have? Are there deeper, more basic needs underlying the apparent needs of the other party?
- Is the party seeking justice or fairness, and if so, is its quest aimed at procedural or substantive matters, or a combination of the two?
- What are the experiences of the other party in similar situations?

Regarding the question of the other party's previous similar situations, one can press for more information by considering two important factors. First, a negotiator should evaluate the other party's strengths or weaknesses based on any changes in its structure or condition since the previous occurrence. And second, the negotiator should judge whether the other party can be expected to repeat its behavior based on the results of the prior negotiation.

The Other Party's Background.　The second factor in ascertaining vital interests is the other party's background. A negotiator should search for clues regarding the issues or the items which the other party has previously deemed to be most important.

Part of the background analysis includes ascertaining the training, occupations, career mobility, and tradition of the person or people involved. Differences in those matters can yield differences in philosophy and values. These differences can provide opportunities for reaching agreements, or conversely, they can impede an agreement. Differences in values may make reaching an agreement easier by allowing more opportunities for the use of win-win solutions and reciprocal concessions that are of a greater value to one side than to the other. On the other hand, differences between participants may lead to misunderstandings and ineffective communication and must be carefully guarded against.

It might help the negotiation if the parties share some mutual background. An initial inquiry should be made to discover any previous negotiation or relationship with the other party. If so, analyze the significance of the common background by considering the following questions:

- Was the parties' previous negotiation or relationship friendly or hostile?
- During the parties' prior negotiation or relationship, did anything happen that might cast light on the other party's current needs, concerns, and priorities?
- Were previous negotiations successful enough for both sides that one could persuasively argue that the present negotiation should turn out as favorably? If not, is it possible to argue that the present negotiation could be a chance to make up for previous difficulties or failures?

The Other Party's Need for an Agreement.　The third crucial factor in trying to determine the other party's vital interests is the nature and the extent of the other party's need for an agreement. Questions that arise regarding the other party's need for an agreement include:

- How much does the other party need to reach an agreement in the negotiation?
- What are the consequences to the other party if the matter is resolved through an agreement?

- What are the consequences to the other party if the matter is not resolved through an agreement?
- What are the alternatives for the other party if the matter is not resolved through an agreement?
- Assuming that the settlement zones of the parties overlap, what is the range of possible outcomes for an agreement to be reached?
- What is the most likely outcome if an agreement is reached?
- What is the range of outcomes if no agreement is reached?
- What is the most likely outcome if no agreement is reached?
- Is the other party willing to take risks?

The Personal Feelings of the Other Party and the Other Negotiator.
Personal feelings are the fourth factor in determining vital interests. The negotiator should consider both the personal feelings of the party and those of the negotiator by considering the following possibilities:

- Whether the personal favoritism or likes of the other party or of the other negotiator are likely to influence that party's goals or priorities.
- Whether any personal dislikes of the other party or the other negotiator are likely to influence that party's goals or priorities.
- Whether such factors as power, prestige, ego acceptance, job security, and personal prejudice will influence the negotiation.

Other Influences on the Other Party.   There are a variety of other possible influences on the other party's vital interests; among them are:

- Psychological effects and conditions.
- Family pressures.
- Social norms, mores, customs, and pressures.
- Business norms, mores, customs, and pressures.
- The long- and short-term political situation.
- The long- and short-term economic situation.

> **Case in Point 11-7**_____
>
> The other party is a businessman who is in serious financial trouble. This businessman owes your firm money. There are no longer any dealings between the businessman and your firm. However, the other party's business continues to operate and to receive credit from its present suppliers. Some of the questions you con-

sider in the planning stage include: Will the other party threaten bankruptcy? If so, how serious is that threat? Will the other party veto the use of a threat of bankruptcy for fear that present suppliers will refuse to continue to extend credit?

Situational Pressures or Constraints

Key Concept 117

Situational pressures and constraints affect negotiations.

In addition to their vital interests, the parties are often influenced by **situational pressures or constraints,** or, those forces or concerns that are outside the direct scope of the negotiation which cause a party either to rule out or avoid potential types of agreements, or, conversely, to achieve them. Although these forces can overlap with vital interests, they arise from specific temporary forces or personal idiosyncracies, rather than intrinsic, general needs. Examples of such situational pressures and constraints include:

- A strong personality on the part of either party which welcomes risk-taking and can withstand uncertainty.

- An argument, term, or agreement which, unless rejected, will become a costly precedent in the future.

- An argument, term, or agreement which, if accepted, will become a useful precedent in the future.

- An excess capacity of a seller, so that additional sales will help to defray the seller's fixed costs.

- High total, fixed, or variable costs of a seller.

- Any special qualities of an item that is offered for sale, or sought for purchase.

- The business, social, political, or personal power possessed by a party.

- Fear of or concern about litigation.

- An actual or potential competitor who may make a deal with one party which would preclude the other party from making its deal.

- Shortages or excesses, which make short- or long-term contracts more or less desirable.

- Expected fluctuations in price or in costs, which make short- or long-term contracts more or less desirable.

■ A negative comment to a third party by one party about the other party that will negatively influence the reputation of the targeted party.

Case in Point 11-8_____

A consultant is in a fee dispute with a former client, who is an influential businesswoman. The consultant decides to compromise the fee rather than risk having the former client criticize the consultant's work to others in the industry.

As Case in Point 11-8 indicates, a sufficiently strong situational pressure or constraint can create a new vital interest.

The Other Negotiator

Key Concept 118

The other negotiator's personal interests, personality, and negotiating style must be taken into account.

The personal interests and personality of the other negotiator must be taken into account. If the other negotiator represents the other party and lacks authority, then the personality and interests of the ultimate decision maker should also be considered. Aspects of personality to consider include:

1. Truthfulness.
2. The need to control.
3. A tendency to either seek or avoid conflict, or, similarly, to compete or cooperate.
4. Any need to project a certain personal image (such as toughness, fairness, arrogance, and so forth).
5. A willingness to subordinate the client's interests to the personal interests of the negotiator and the decision maker.
6. A willingness to take risks, and an ability to tolerate uncertainty.

Case in Point 11-9————————————————————————

A business is negotiating a very large loan with an account representative of a major financial institution. The account representative has a quota of such loans which she is expected to generate. Accordingly, finding and structuring loans which will be approved by the credit department of the financial institution directly reflects her personal interests. Understanding her interests, the business is able to obtain information on the lender's needs and perceptions from the account representative. With this information, the parties can try to structure a mutually acceptable loan.

Discerning Behavioral Patterns Among Negotiating Opponents. Another perspective for assessing the personal factors in a negotiation is to identify the negotiating patterns of the other negotiators, the decision makers, or the parties. Repeated patterns may be considered a negotiation style. One commentator separates styles into "jungle fighters," "dictators," "dream merchants," "soothers," and "win-win."[*]

Jungle fighters see a negotiation as a win-lose war. They can act either charmingly or intimidatingly. Negotiators can counter jungle fighters by not acting emotionally or displaying fear, placing issues in perspective, demonstrating that their aim is not belligerent, pointing out the jungle fighter's lack of actual power, or, if necessary, by overwhelming them.

Dictators are negotiators who try to win by maintaining power and control. The best countermeasures are logical appeals to their self-interest, refusing to react emotionally, allowing them apparent power and control while obtaining crucial substantive gains, or demonstrating the existence of one's own power to destroy them combined with a willingness to use it.

Dream merchants are negotiators who seek to exploit others' "dreams" of success or fears of failure in order to manipulate them. The countermeasures are to refuse to be manipulated, to twist the manipulation to one's own advantage, or to exploit a personal weakness of the other side.

A **soother** is a negotiator who denies the existence of problems or unfavorable facts. The countermeasure is to probe carefully while being secretly distrustful and to use the soother's fear of confrontation and need to be liked and respected.

Win-win negotiators are pragmatists who are committed to achiev-

———————
[*]The following discussion of negotiation styles, here and throughout this chapter, is adapted from Tessa Albert Warschaw, *Winning by Negotiation*, McGraw-Hill, New York, 1980, chap. 2.

ing agreements through appeals to mutual interests. The counter-measures are employing favorable win-win tactics, careful bargaining to take advantage of their willingness to make concessions, and exploiting their willingness to try new approaches and to take calculated risks.

It is impossible to overstate the importance of Planning Step 5, which assesses the strengths and weaknesses of the participants. The vital interests of the participants; the situational pressures and constraints to which they are subject; and the personality traits and interests they reveal all contribute profoundly to a negotiator's ability to successfully conclude a negotiation. These various conditions and needs govern the conduct of every participant during the negotiation and motivate their willingness or unwillingness to agree on particular points. All negotiations extend from the basic premise that each party can influence the outcome for the other. Thus, it behooves a negotiator to account for all the ways that the other party can be influenced.

Planning Step 6: Estimating the Other Party's Bottom Line and Opening Position

Key Concept 119

Estimate the other side's bottom line based on your "lucky day" fantasy, and then estimate its opening position by analyzing its perceptions and your ability to change them for each issue and goal.

Estimating the Other Party's Bottom Line

Based on the information derived from Planning Steps 1, 3, 4, and 5, the next step in prenegotiation planning is to estimate the other party's bottom line. The crucial questions are, first, what is the worst deal you might realistically expect the other party to accept? And second, what is the best deal you could achieve if you had your way? To answer these questions, indulge in the little fantasy that the negotiation will take place on your lucky day. The fantasy should represent the most that you could *reasonably* expect to gain from the negotiation. (Remember, this is a "little" fantasy, not your wildest dream!) In this way, you should be able to avoid either over- or underestimating your situation.

In reality, each party's bottom line will be affected by the value it places on an outcome and the economic and noneconomic costs it attaches to delay, negotiating difficulties, or termination of the negotiation. Each party's bottom line also is affected by its anticipation of the other party's bottom line. Therefore, to estimate the other party's bottom line, you must envision the other side's assessment of your bottom line. Along with estimating the other party's bottom line, negotiators should also try to estimate the other party's likely highest expectation. If the other party is unrealistic, this factor should be taken into account.

Estimating the Other Party's Opening Position

After examining and appraising the other party's likely highest expectation, the negotiator should estimate the other party's opening position. The following questions should be asked to help estimate the other side's opening position:

1. Is the other side likely to open at or above its highest expectation in order to build in trade-offs and concessions or to compensate for underestimating?
2. If the other party is expected to open above its highest expectation, how far above is it likely to be?

Perceptions and Expectations. Perceptions and expectations of the value of items or of the likelihood of gaining them affect each party's positions. The chances of reaching agreement depend on the reality of one's expectations. Conversely, unrealistic demands based on unrealistic expectations will lower the chances of reaching agreement.

Since perceptions affect expectations, you may need to plan to alter the other party's perceptions. Otherwise, the other party's expectations may hinder you in reaching your optimal agreement. Strategy, tactics, reasoned positions, and communications all can be planned to impact and change the other party's perceptions and expectations.

For planning purposes, your estimations of the other party's bottom line and its highest expectations form tentative parameters for the negotiation. In keeping with the system of issue-by-issue analysis, these estimates are made for each issue. Assuming that one's own bottom line overlaps with the estimated bottom line of the other party, this creates tentative zones of agreement. This phase of planning includes anticipating multiple goals and issues, and developing alternative packages of linked items which the other party might seek. Single- or separate-issue planning and linear thinking alone are inadequate if the negotiation is at all sophisticated or complex. Alternative packages of linked items, derived from combinations and permutations of single issues, expand the negotiating opportunities. This increased sophistication will help you face the **fluid dynamics,** that is, the constant changes (both planned and surprising) that occur during most negotiations. (More information regarding fluid dynamics is offered in the section below on "Scripting.")

Anticipating Your Opponent's Opening Moves.   Once one estimates the opening substantive position of the other party, the next step is to consider the manner in which the other party is likely to open the negotiation in terms of timing, agenda, strategy, and tactics. You must decide whether to block, counter, or manipulate the other side's likely opening move. Potential openings of one's own should also be analyzed, including possible "scripts" of actions and responses.

Scripting.   **Scripting** refers to a mental technique for anticipating the course of a negotiation whereby you play out in your mind the series of statements which are likely to be made during a negotiation between yourself and the other participants. This mental process is continued until the projected event is complete. By imagining the negotiation before it occurs, you are actually practicing for it. Imagine possible settings, characters, and dialogues. Feel free to "write" several scripts to try to account for a variety of possibilities. In this way you can avoid being blindsided in the actual negotiation because of tunnel vision in the planning stage. Further, you become practiced at facing the fluid dynamics of an actual situation. Be careful, however, not to assume that in your practicing you have imagined every negotiating possibility. Prepared responses can be quite helpful in keeping control, so long as the negotiator only uses them if they are still truly appropriate given whatever actually occurs.

The earlier steps should now be crosschecked with the estimates of the other party's bottom line and opening position. Any necessary adjustments should be made.

Planning Step 7: Considering Win-Win Outcomes

Key Concept 120

Develop any potential win-win outcomes with either gain to one side without real loss to the other side, or with mutual gain.

Negotiations often involve win-lose issues. What one party gains is necessarily lost by the other party. (As you recall, another name for a win-lose situation is a linear zero-sum game which can refer to either the entire negotiation or to a part of it.) In contrast, other issues involve win-win outcomes in which one party gains without cost to the other party. Win-win outcomes fall into two categories:

1. Gain to one party without a corresponding loss to the other party.

2. Mutual gain.

Gain to One Party Without a Corresponding Loss to the Other Party

The first type of win-win results occur when one party gains, but the other party does not suffer a corresponding loss and wins because an agreement is reached. In other words, the concession costs the party making it either absolutely nothing or so little as to be insignificant. However, the concession is significant to the party receiving it. Thus, both parties win.

Case in Point 11-10

Two parties enter into a risk-free consulting contract. A consulting firm agrees that a fee will not be paid unless the annual savings in costs exceeds the fee. The company hiring the consulting firm gains its services without the risk that the expense of hiring it will exceed the benefits that it will provide. Assuming that the consulting firm is able to determine in advance that the savings in costs to the client are virtually certain to be greater than the fee, the consultant makes the concession of a risk-free contract without incurring any real cost to itself. Thus, a win-win result is achieved.

Case in Point 11-11

A clothing store owner has cashflow problems, and therefore wants 30-day payment terms from the store's suppliers (that is, payment is not due for 30 days after delivery). This will allow the clothing store to sell most of the clothes that it receives before it has to pay for them. The wholesaler agrees, but adds a small interest charge to cover the lost use of the money for 30 days. The store owner solves the store's cashflow problems without having to take out commercial loans, which would be at least as costly as the wholesaler's interest charge. The small interest charge prevents the wholesaler from losing anything by granting the concession of 30-day payment terms. While the wholesaler does not really gain anything, since the small interest charge is simply equal to the lost use of the funds, it can still be considered a winner because its concession helps to maintain a good business relationship with the retailer.

As the preceding cases in point illustrate, gain to one party without a corresponding loss to the other party typically occurs where the parties have different needs. It occurs when the parties are not in a linear zero-sum type of negotiation. Under these circumstances, one party's needs can be satisfied without taking something away from the other party. The party giving the no-cost concession wins rapport and, at times, the ability to later demand reciprocity.

Mutual Gain

As you learned in Chapter 2, negotiation often is conceptualized as a pie with only a set number of pieces available to be divided. However, negotiation for mutual gain alters the size of the pie. It consists of expanding the pie by creatively thinking of new terms. When this can be done and the parties share the benefits, they have achieved a win-win outcome with mutual gain.

Case in Point 11-12

A trucking company is operating with 20 percent unused capacity on a particular route. The company agrees to give an extra discount to a shipper for additional volume above that which is presently shipped on the run. The carrier is thus able to fill its unused capacity, while the shipper saves money through the additional discount. Both parties win without any significant cost to either of them.

Plan for Win-Win Results Whenever Possible

Being able to foresee win-win outcomes often is not easy. In fact, these opportunities probably are missed more often than is commonly realized. Many times the addition of a win-win outcome to a negotiation (or to a part of one) makes the difference between reaching an agreement and not having any agreement at all.

These facts underscore the importance of planning to achieve win-win results whenever it may be possible to do so. In deciding whether win-win results are possible, a negotiator must consider the needs and the objectives of the parties, negotiators, and decision makers. The focus is on whether those needs and objectives are totally compatible, wholly in conflict, or somewhere in between. Thus, in Planning Step 7, the critical question is whether the needs and objectives of both parties can be wholly or partially achieved through a win-win outcome.

After determining the possibility of a win-win outcome, reevaluate the prior planning steps. Make any necessary adjustments to your plan before proceeding to Planning Step 8.

Comprehension Checkup

The answers to these questions appear on page 332.

1. While planning for a negotiation, you discover that there are areas where you lack information and cannot obtain it. You should then plan for____.
   a. win-win
   b. informational tactics
   c. horse trading
   d. work group
   e. zero-sum games

2. There are three issues to be negotiated. These must be prioritized into short- and long-term, and _____ categories.
   a. essential/desirable
   b. strong/weak
   c. subjective/objective
   d. easy/difficult
   e. simple/complex

3. Trade-offs can be _____.
   a. within issues
   b. between issues
   c. *a* and *b*
   d. other

4. You have analyzed the strengths and weaknesses of the other side and its negotiator, including the vital interests and situational pressures or constraints for each of them. After asking yourself why the other side wants a deal, you realize there is a significant weakness for your side. You next consider _____.
   a. accepting it
   b. fact creation

c. objectivity
d. arbitration
e. mediation

5. Your estimate of the other side's bottom line must include _____.
   a. your luckiest day
   b. changing the other side's perceptions
   c. each issue
   d. every goal
   e. all of the above

6. You are negotiating with a party that faces a 20-percent chance of highly adverse consequences from not reaching agreement. The party is reluctant to take risks. You should consider your position to be _____.
   a. very strong
   b. somewhat strong
   c. somewhat weak
   d. weak
   e. unknown

7. Counter jungle fighters by refusing to act emotionally, demonstrating that your objective is not to destroy them, and _____.
   a. displaying admiration
   b. denying problems
   c. indicating a willingness to bargain
   d. showing you have power combined with a willingness to use it
   e. suggesting a minitrial

8. Counter a dictator by refusing to react emotionally and, if power is not available, by _____.
   a. debating
   b. relinquishing apparent control while getting substantive gains
   c. acting as if you like the person
   d. engaging in a bargaining mix
   e. other

9. You should let the other party define the issues.   T   F

10. The market consists of values, practices, and negotiation customs. T   F

11. In planning for a negotiation, there are no opportunities to expand the pie for mutual gain, therefore there is no chance of a win-win outcome.   T   F

12. A buyer and seller have negotiated in the past, with the agreements highly favorable to the seller. For this negotiation, the buyer may be looking to make up for those past results.   T   F

12

Systematic Planning: Negotiation Stages

Key Concepts

121. The opening position for each issue or combination of issues should be set realistically high and above your estimate of the other party's bottom line to allow room for concessions.

122. Set a bottom line below which no agreement at all is better than any offer that the other party could make. Alter the bottom line only if justified by new information or events.

123. Negotiate without authority or with only limited authority to resist pressure, maintain harmony in the session, or engage in information gathering. This choice is a tactical exception to the planning process since no bottom line is planned.

124. Choose alternative strategies and tactics for each negotiation to be used in case first-choice strategies and tactics prove ineffective. Anticipate the other side's strategies and tactics and identify appropriate countermeasures. Be prepared to initiate as well as react.

125. Plan for concessions only when the strategy allows for them. Make concessions real, but relatively small. Provide a rationalization for

each concession and anticipate both concessions from the other party and its reactions to yours.

126. Agendas are set in terms of the order in which actions, issues, or concessions will occur. Fight to control the agenda only if it is essential to establish an order of items or a psychological climate. Be prepared to negotiate the agenda. Even without an agenda, opening moves should be planned with flexibility.

127. Be cautious of creating an unprofitable contract for the other side if it involves an ongoing interaction or relationship.

128. Time the negotiation to occur when it will be most advantageous. By controlling the timing, a negotiator may also be able to control the amount of information known by the other side as well as increase the pressure exerted on it to act.

129. Choose the mode of communication after settling timing issues and analyzing the other parties' reaction to them.

130. Commit yourself mentally to implementing the negotiation plan, and do not be deterred by distractions or fatigue. Continuously analyze the other party's conduct; be mentally ready for the unexpected.

131. Use a prepared but flexible plan with preconceived alternatives. Make adjustments to the plan only after you are absolutely sure that they are necessary. Adjustments may be required to restart stalled negotiations or to redirect negotiations you believe have taken the wrong track. Be goals-rigid and means-flexible.

The Language of Negotiating

To make full use of the key concepts, you must understand the following key terms:

High, realistic expectations	Agenda
Opening position	Symmetrical response
Interim bottom line	Asymmetrical response

Introduction

Having completed the first seven planning steps, the first phase of planning is concluded. That phase was principally concerned with gathering and analyzing information and making judgments and estimates about parties and negotiators. Planning Steps 8 through 14 form the second phase of planning. Using the first phase as a basis, in the second phase, decisions are made by the negotiator regarding *specific* positions to take and the strategies and tactics to employ during the course of the negotiation.

Planning Step 8: Setting the Opening Position

Key Concept 121

The opening position for each issue or combination of issues should be set realistically high and above your estimate of the other party's bottom line to allow room for concessions.

During Planning Step 6, the negotiator estimated the other party's bottom line, expectations, and opening position, and planned opening moves for the negotiation. Step 8 consists of establishing the actual opening position.

The opening position must be established in a reasonable manner. High, realistic expectations are key to achieving a successful negotiation. A **high, realistic expectation** is an anticipated position or goal, the benefits of which are as substantial as possible given the capacities and limits of the negotiation. If expectations are too low, the negotiator may fail to demand as much as could be gained with higher demands. Studies indicate that high opening positions generally lead to more favorable settlements than more modest or low ones. Remember the "lucky day" scenario in which one imagines the best possible settlement with this party, in this situation, at this time.

Although high aspirations lead to better results if an agreement is reached, they can also lead to more deadlocks; and certainly, unrealistically high aspirations can frighten off or offend the other party and drive them away from the negotiation. Therefore, the reasonable opening position is established using realistically high expectations.

Using the information acquired from Planning Steps 1 through 7, a negotiator establishes a high, realistic opening position. The negotiator also makes tentative positions for the rest of the negotiation and for alternative opening positions, including for each issue and combination of issues. Such combinations consist of groups of issues that involve potential trade-offs between the issues.

The result of this analysis is the planned opening position. The **opening position** is one side's initial starting point for the negotiation. It may or may not actually be used depending on whether it still seems appropriate when the time comes for the first offer or counteroffer. That determination is based on the actions taken and the information generated up to that point in the negotiation. The opening position must also be structured as a reasoned posture. This means that a persuasive argument is planned for the opening position, as well as for alternative positions.

Once the other side's opening position and reaction to one's own planned opening position already have been estimated, the negotiator can turn to a review of all the previous steps. One's planned opening position may alter the decisions and analyses made in the earlier phases of planning regarding information gathering, goals, issues, the market, strengths, weaknesses, interests, the other party's anticipated bottom line, and win-win outcomes. This review can also possibly alter one's view of the planned opening position and lead to modifications of it.

Planning Step 9: Setting the Bottom Line

Key Concept 122

Set a bottom line below which no agreement at all is better than any offer that the other party could make. Alter the bottom line only if justified by new information or events.

A crucial part of planning is to set your bottom line. The bottom line is the point beyond which it would be better to reject any offer or demand. At some point, no agreement at all is preferable to the best deal the other party is willing to offer. At that point, no further concessions are to be made, and the negotiation is terminated. This, of course, is a crucial point for the ultimate decision maker, who decides the bottom line. Generally, the decision maker faces the bottom line with the assistance of a negotiator's advice.

Each party's bottom line determines whether any agreement is possible. The substantive differences between the bottom lines constitute the so-called range of agreement. In other words, for an agreement to occur, critical conditions derived from both bottom lines must be met for the parties to successfully conclude the negotiation. Within the range of agreement, there generally must be sufficient opportunity to make concessions, bargain, persuade, or in some way satisfy the critical bottom-line conditions of each party.

Just as in establishing the opening position, all the information generated by the previous steps is used to set the bottom line. Similarly, bottom lines are established for the negotiation as a whole, as well as for each issue in a multi-issue negotiation. If there are potential trade-offs between issues, a bottom line should be established for each relevant combination of issues.

Case in Point 12-1_____

A couple is interested in purchasing a house. Given their goals and interests, the issues for them are the price of the home, its quality, the number of bedrooms, and the number of bathrooms. They decide that their bottom line for each of these issues is as follows:

Price: $300,000

Quality: High

Bedrooms: Four

Bathrooms: Two

They further decide, however, that they are willing to trade off between the price and the number of bedrooms, so that their bottom line for the combination of these two issues is $270,000 and three bedrooms.

Often, it is helpful to begin setting the bottom line with an overview listing all the possible alternatives. In this way, a framework is established to help clarify the decision-making process. The order for examining the alternatives may depend on whether some decisions cannot be made until after other matters are decided. Except for decisions that are necessarily deferred, the alternatives should be considered in order from the most to the least aggressive. More aggressive here does not mean attacking or being quarrelsome. Rather, it refers to alternatives that appear to seek the highest and most favorable outcome, regardless of the odds of success.

Negotiating Scenario_____

In negotiating a particular business lease for raw space, the cost for the improvements desired by the lessee was substantial. The most aggressive alternative for this issue in the negotiation was to have the other party bear those costs.

The effective evaluation of each alternative requires examining the potential benefits and risks associated with that choice and comparing these with the potential benefits and risks of the alternatives. The chances that each benefit and risk will actually occur must also be assessed.

Adjusting the Bottom Line Once It Is Set

Once the bottom line is set, the negotiator should use it to reexamine the prenegotiation steps. If the review reveals a planning flaw it may lead to an adjustment of the planned bottom line. It is important to remember, however, that the bottom line is neither reexamined nor adjusted based on how the other side is expected to react to it. Since the bottom line is based on your alternatives to *not* reaching agreement, the other side's reactions to it are irrelevant. Of some concern to your side, however, are interim bottom lines, which refer to constituent elements of a negotiation, but not to its final outcome. An **interim bottom line** is a limit established for a phase of a negotiation to determine whether it can be achieved. If that phase is completed without achieving it, a different interim bottom line can be implemented. Since the use of interim bottom lines can cause a loss of credibility if it is perceived as a bluff, the negotiator should employ the same measures that are used to manage bluffs (see page 142).

(*Note:* The same defensive measures should be used if new information or some outside event requires the alteration of an already announced bottom line. One must guard against being perceived as untrustworthy.)

If a negotiator does determine that an earlier step needs to be adjusted, the modification is likely to affect the opening position. Further, changes in the opening position may affect the bottom line. If the planned opening position and bottom line do not allow sufficient opportunity to make acceptable concessions, one or the other must be adjusted. The negotiator must take care to hedge against setting both the opening position and the bottom line too low.

Using Unrealistic Bottom Lines

In most cases bottom lines should be based on realistic negotiating assumptions and legitimate needs. There are, however, two exceptions. They are when:

1. The other party has misvalued its position and is not itself realistic.
2. The same benefits can be attained more advantageously elsewhere.

A necessary caution against assuming an unrealistic bottom line is expressed by the principle that "Greed should not be allowed to prevent an agreement."

Negotiating *Without* a Bottom Line

Key Concept 123

Negotiate without authority or with only limited authority to resist pressure, maintain harmony in the session, or engage in information gathering. This choice is a tactical exception to the planning process since no bottom line is planned.

Generally, a negotiator is authorized by a client or decision maker to agree to certain minimum terms. Sometimes, however, a negotiator will elect to negotiate without the authorization to settle and without a specific bottom-line position. The tactic of negotiating with no (or limited) settlement authority provides the following advantages:

1. To resist pressure from the other side for concessions.
2. To maintain harmony at the bargaining table by deflecting any necessary resistance to movement onto an absent decision maker.
3. To gather information that might not otherwise be available in the name of the absent decision maker.

If one is confronted by this tactic, probe to determine whether the limited authority is a tactical ploy, or whether it is part of the other party's basic policy and procedure. The countermeasures are the same as those for dealing with negotiations without authority (see page 188).

Planning Step 10: Choosing Strategies and Tactics

Key Concept 124

Choose alternative strategies and tactics for each negotiation to be used in case first-choice strategies and tactics prove ineffective. Anticipate the other side's strategies and tactics and identify appropriate countermeasures. Be prepared to initiate as well as react.

The list below reviews the strategies and tactics available for use during a negotiation. The choice of strategies and tactics always must be based on the particular negotiation, rather than on the negotiator's personal habits. Even professional diplomats have difficulty following this principle. Their political leaders and culture may create predictable strategies and tactics. When selecting strategies and tactics, make sure they apply to the specific conditions of the matter at hand. Whenever possible, however, try to be unpredictable to minimize the other side's ability to plan. Detailed discussions of these strategies and tactics are provided in Chapters 2 through 8.

Strategies

Strategies can be used either singly or in combination:

Personal credibility	Concede first
No concessions	Problem solving
No further concessions	Purposes other than reaching an agreement
Deadlock-breaking concessions only	Moving for closure
HRESSC	

Tactics

One or more tactics are planned for each strategy chosen:

Disclosing information

Creating facts

Listening for information

Using the funnel approach

Using sources of information

Bargaining for information

Informational discussions

Requiring preconditions

Making or avoiding making the first offer

Demanding responses to offers and to positions

Reciprocity

Win-win proposals

Concessions that are of greater value to one party

Trial proposals

Bargaining

Debate

Conditional proposals

Power

Bluff

Tone

The use of alternative opportunities

Splitting the difference

Focus/downplay

Creating a psychological commitment for agreement

Saving face

Making people the problem

Inserting new issues

Focusing on the process

Creating movement

Deadlock

Adjournment

Patience

Deadlines

Lack of or limited authority

Surprise

Appealing to personal interests

Active client or decision-maker participation

Negotiating teams

Allies

Media or community pressure

Multiple parties

Gifts and entertainment

Alternative dispute resolution

Litigation

The order in which strategies and tactics will be used must be tentatively determined in advance of a negotiation. However, the order is always subject to adjustment as the negotiation unfolds. Basic considerations affecting the choice of strategies and tactics are the expected dynamics of the negotiation, the nature of the negotiation goals, and whether there is more than one issue involved. The selection of strategies and tactics should also include those needed to deal with the following four common negotiating dilemmas:

1. How can a difficult or awkward subject be introduced?
2. What actions can be taken as initiatives to break a deadlock, or to get the negotiating process moving again if it becomes bogged down?
3. What methods will induce the other party or negotiator to become psychologically committed to reaching agreement?
4. What is the most effective way to employ the information-gathering tactics if the analysis of previous planning steps indicates a need for more information?

The means to handle these dilemmas should be considered in the planning stage. The strategic and tactical choices must also be analyzed and refined in view of those the negotiator expects the other side to use. The analysis includes possible reactions of the other side to planned choices in strategy and tactics. Likely countermeasures must be evaluated. This is absolutely critical. For example, problem solving will not work if the other side does not participate in good faith or is engaged in a different strategy.

Initiating Actions and Reactions

One major caveat to selecting strategies and tactics applies to anticipating the other side's conduct in planning its strategy and tactics. The negotiator must focus on initiating actions, as well as on reacting to the other side's anticipated conduct. A negotiation planner must not, however, become controlled or paralyzed by expectations concerning the other side's moves. Although anticipation is critical, it can be overemphasized. Many negotiators spend too much time and effort trying to anticipate the other side's every move. Besides making them feel threatened and defensive, it makes them less flexible and creative.

Using Strategies and Tactics *Before* Negotiations Commence

During the planning stage, the negotiator may be able to affect the subsequent negotiation by using some strategies or tactics. For example, one can engage in information-gathering tactics before the negotiation starts in order to learn more about the market, the other party, the other negotiator, or the situation that is to be negotiated. It also may be possible to create new facts or new issues before the negotiation. The new facts may influence the other party's positions. The new issues also may affect the bargaining process by creating potential trade-offs or concessions.

Planning Step 11: Considering
Concessions and Trade-Offs

Key Concept 125

Plan for concessions only when the strategy allows for them. Make concessions real, but relatively small. Provide a rationalization for each concession and anticipate both concessions from the other party and its reactions to yours.

Along with strategies and tactics, concessions and trade-offs also should be planned to maximize gain. The use of concessions and trade-offs is inappropriate when the chosen strategy does not permit them under any circumstances. Normally, however, concessions are expected. In part, parties tend to expect concessions because they believe that they will be able to shape the other party's actions during the negotiation.

The different value that each party places on a negotiated item creates the opportunity for trade-offs. In short, trade-offs derive from the parties' different economic and noneconomic views of benefits and detriments. For example, parties may place different values on future versus present benefits or costs. One may place great value on security or peace of mind, which can be satisfied at little or no cost to the other. A trade-off should be viewed as a process of sorting, judging, and deciding the option which will work most effectively for you and the other side.

Concessions and trade-offs can be structured either directly or indirectly. For example, "nonspecific compensation" is an indirect concession which is totally unrelated to what is demanded in return, except in terms of its value. Such trade-offs need not even be logically related, as long as their values correlate. This is possible since an item often has a different value to each party.

Planning Concessions and
Trade-Offs

Concessions and trade-offs are made within the parties' anticipated zone of agreement. Figure 12-1 illustrates a case in which there is one issue and three anticipated potential concessions. A rationale is developed for each potential concession so that the position appears rea-

ANTICIPATED ZONE OF AGREEMENT

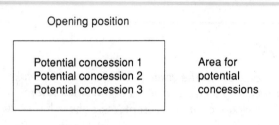

Figure 12-1

sonable and firm. This stability is essential for the negotiator to persuasively present the present position.

The nature and the order of planned concessions must be determined for each issue or combination of issues. The negotiator must also determine whether linkage exists which allows for trade-offs between issues. A multiple-issue negotiation with potential trade-offs between issues could have the anticipated zone of agreement and planned concessions shown in Figure 12-2. The figure illustrates two issues with a separate opening position for each, a potential plan for concessions with

ANTICIPATED ZONE OF AGREEMENT		
Issue one	**Issue two**	**Combination of issues 1 and 2**
Opening position	Opening position	Opening position
Potential concession A	Potential concession C	Trade-off F Trade-off G
Potential concession B	Potential concession D	
	Potential concession E	
Bottom line	Bottom line	Bottom line

Figure 12-2

rationales, and separate bottom-line positions. Also shown is the plan for managing the combination of the issues.

Planning for concessions and for trade-offs accomplishes several important functions:

1. It allows for the creation of apparent concessions which the negotiator does not care about except for their function as trade-offs. For example, a negotiator may bargain over an unimportant issue just to concede it later for a reciprocal concession that is of real value to his or her side.

2. It enables the negotiator to generate several relatively small concessions to grant at critical moments during the negotiation in order to avoid making large concessions.

3. It lets the negotiator conceive persuasive reasons for each potential position. This may not be as easy to do later, during the actual bargaining situation.

4. It allows for the value of potential trade-offs to be established ahead of time. Again, it may be far easier and more practical to make such calculations in advance, rather than during the actual negotiating session. One should know the value of what one is negotiating for before offering any concessions.

Case in Point 12-2

In a negotiation for a lease, the lessee bargained for an early time of possession, just so that the issue of early possession could be conceded in order to arrange for a smaller security deposit.

Case in Point 12-3

A developer is negotiating with a community group concerned with the size and configuration of a planned manufacturing facility. The developer's bottom line will depend, in part, on the following factors:

1. The developer's relative political influence compared with that of the community group.

2. The developer's ability to pass on costs.

3. Any general zoning or permit issues.

4. The availability of alternative sites.

The developer's building plans and specifications allow for a building of six stories. Although the developer would like a building with six stories, it is willing to build one with only four. The two expendable stories function as a potential trade-off for concessions from the community group.

Anticipating the Other Party's Trade-Offs and Concessions

A negotiator must anticipate the other party's likely trade-offs and concessions. This includes anticipating reactions to one's own planned trade-offs and strategy. Adjustments are made to one's own planned trade-offs and concessions based on the expected behavior of the other party.

Planning Step 12: Determining an Agenda

Key Concept 126

Agendas are set in terms of the order in which actions, issues, or concessions will occur. Fight to control the agenda only if it is essential to establish an order of items or a psychological climate. Be prepared to negotiate the agenda. Even without an agenda, opening moves should be planned with flexibility.

The term **agenda** refers to the order in which actions will be taken, issues will be considered, or concessions will be made during the negotiating process. A decision first must be made whether to even set an agenda. At least 12 factors should be considered in reaching this decision. These factors include determining whether:

1. The initial phase of the actual negotiation should be utilized to reduce tension or to build rapport.

2. Information gathering is needed before resolving certain issues so that your position is not undervalued or so that win-win opportunities are not missed.

3. There should be selective information disclosures at an early stage,

because the other party will be more inclined to concede more if it knows the information.

4. Opening positions should be made known at the first session, with an immediate adjournment to evaluate, revise, or formulate it before continuing.

5. It is better to make the first offer or to wait to receive an offer.

6. It is important to get at least tacit agreement on how the issues are defined before proceeding with the rest of the negotiation.

7. A certain issue or issues must be resolved before other issues can be discussed.

8. Relatively easy issues should be negotiated first to create goodwill, rapport, and momentum.

9. It is better to first negotiate the hardest issues to see whether they can be resolved.

10. It is useful to establish an order in which to address all the issues to be negotiated.

11. The other party is unprepared for an extended negotiation.

12. Valuable insights are likely to be gained by allowing the other party to set an agenda, thereby discovering which areas the other party wishes to cover first or to avoid.

If necessary, the agenda itself may be the subject of negotiation. This can include procedures to be followed by the parties during the negotiation, time periods for the sessions, the right to caucus, and the confidentiality of discussions during and after the negotiation. If the agenda is to be negotiated, the planning must include the point during the negotiation at which to do it. In other words, an agenda can include negotiation of the agenda. The same strategies and tactics apply to negotiating the agenda as apply to any other item to be negotiated.

Negotiating Scenario

At the beginning of a controversial negotiation, one negotiator suggests negotiating general provisions first, because these are the easier issues. He argues that by settling easy issues first, a positive and cooperative tone will be established with which to assuage the tensions that surround the more difficult issues.

One theory about setting agendas in negotiations divides the process into two phases. In the first phase, informational tactics are used to discover potential alternatives. In the second phase, other tactics are used in an attempt to isolate and shape an acceptable solution. During either phase, a participant must be aware of being perceived either as the pursuer or the pursued party. The pursuer generally wants to generate interest and avoid complications, whereas the pursued usually wishes to avoid appearing very interested, and to gain information by allowing the pursuer to make the first moves.

A second theory divides the process of setting agendas into three broad phases:

1. An initial informational phase for exchanging information.

2. A competitive phase of offers and counteroffers.

3. A cooperative phase to create mutual gains (if the second phase led to resolved issues).

It has been suggested that those three phases are distinct and sequential. However, an effective negotiator will not be so rigid and will be willing to make (or suggest) adjustments to the sequencing of phases. Modifications can be made by using a variety of tactics. In this way, the desired "phase" can be manipulated by the negotiator at any point during the negotiation.

Additionally, when contemplating an agenda, a decision must be made about whether the negotiation should occur during a single session, or over a number of sessions. The negotiator must consider whether a party will need to consult an expert, a negotiator will need to check with a client, decision maker, or higher authority, or complicated calculations of benefits or costs will need to be made that are likely to delay the proceedings. Delay also can be caused if a group decision is required.

Confidentiality

The confidentiality of disclosures can be a crucial issue on an agenda. Agreement on confidentiality may be necessary before other issues can be addressed.

Case in Point 12-4_____

An inventor is negotiating with a company regarding the manufacturing of one of her inventions. Both parties are concerned about settling on a confidentiality provision in the event that they are unable to agree on the terms of a manufacturing contract. From the company's perspective, it does not want to be bound to silence because it does not want to be restricted from proceeding with its own efforts in that area without having to pay the inventor. For the inventor to further protect her patent rights, a broad provision is desirable to guard against possible future claims by the company that disclosures were not utilized.

Even if one does not have a strong commitment to an agenda, opening moves should be planned and loosely scripted. This prepares the negotiator for the important opening portions of the negotiation, and avoids hesitancy or becoming lost at the start. Even so, flexibility and quick modifications may be appropriate based on the initial dynamics and positions.

Assuming an agenda is planned, the other side's expectations and its reaction to the intended agenda must be envisioned. Potential conflicts or counterproductive differences may require adjustment to the planned agenda.

Avoiding Power Struggles Over Agenda

Even when planning to set the agenda, one should avoid fighting over control of the agenda, unless one of the following conditions applies:

1. You really cannot negotiate unless certain portions of the desired agenda are followed.
2. The power struggle over the agenda is essential to establish the necessary psychological climate for the rest of the negotiation.

In the main, struggles over the agenda are counterproductive. They can even lead to a total breakdown of the entire negotiating process. Thus, battles over an agenda should be avoided unless the exceptions outlined above apply.

Key Concept 127

Be cautious of creating an unprofitable contract for the other side if it involves an ongoing interaction or relationship.

Bargaining too hard may be dangerously counterproductive if it leads the other party to later repudiate the bargain, or if it results in a lack of necessary good faith efforts by the other party in carrying out the agreement. A contract which involves an ongoing relationship, and is or becomes unprofitable for the other party, may cause disastrous consequences, unless compelling reasons exist for compliance with the contractual terms. This danger most often occurs in negotiations for long-term relationships in which it is important that the other party's performance meet a certain level of quality. Of course, any danger must be balanced against the potential profits to be gained.

Planning Step 13: Analyzing Timing

> ### Key Concept 128
>
> *Time the negotiation to occur when it will be most advantageous. By controlling the timing, a negotiator may also be able to control the amount of information known by the other side as well as increase the pressure exerted on it to act.*

A decision must be made regarding the most advantageous time to commence negotiations. Each party's goals, vital interests, situational pressures and constraints, as well as the personal interests and the personality of the negotiator should be taken into account. Both parties must be ready to negotiate to seriously seek an agreement. If early negotiations failed to reach an agreement, the same considerations apply to when to reopen negotiations. The optimal time to negotiate is:

1. When your side is under less pressure to make an agreement than the other side.

2. Before your side's needs become more pressing, creating added pressures.

3. When enough is known about the situation to negotiate intelligently.

As to item 3, in transactional matters the value of the negotiating matter must be ascertained. This includes inspection of buildings or tests of new types of machinery for flaws, as well as information about market price. A need for additional information must be balanced against accepting an early settlement or deal before the other side either discovers an existing weakness or problem for your side or is likely to discover a future weakness or problem. These factors should be evaluated in view of the time-consuming efforts that may be uselessly expended if the other party learns of such weaknesses or problems.

In dispute situations, the parties often initially need to release some of their anger and frustration, or to prove their willingness to be tough. They then must engage in conflict for a period of time before they are ready for a realistic resolution reached by mutual agreement.

In litigation, the deadlines, pressures, and costs strongly affect the planned timing of the negotiations. This is especially true once initial negotiations do not result in a settlement and the pressures have increased.

Deadlines

The time when both parties are ready to negotiate seriously to seek an agreement will be affected by each side's deadline for reaching an agreement. Indeed, frequently, an agreement will not be reached until at least one party's deadline for concluding the negotiation is reached, or even exceeded.

Deadline in this context is used to mean the time by which a party or its negotiator feels that it needs to obtain an agreement. A deadline may be absolute, such as the time by which a particular business deal must be achieved or the opportunity to make the deal will have passed. A deadline may also be apparently absolute for reasons beyond either party's control. Finally, a deadline may be arbitrary, that is, a date chosen by a party in order to help structure the negotiation. Arbitrary dates may be subject to negotiation. In this case, one must consider the likelihood of negotiating a change in the deadline, and the risks and benefits of attempting to proceed past the deadline.

Since a party tends to feel more pressure to compromise as its own internal deadline approaches, it is preferable to be in the following positions:

1. To know the other side's real internal deadline.

2. To not have one's own deadline known by the other side unless one is using the deadline tactic, at least in an adversarial negotiation (it may be necessary to have both sides know each other's deadlines in a transactional, cooperative negotiation.)

3. To have a more flexible, or a later real internal deadline than the other side.

These situations are advantageous because the negotiator is helped by knowing when the other side is under some type of deadline pressure, while avoiding a similar perception by the other side.

Assessing Factors That Affect Timing

The timing of a negotiation may depend on whether long-run contracts are periodically reviewed. A periodic review can reveal whether an agreement still represents a sufficient mutuality of interest. In this manner, the need or the opportunity to renegotiate more favorable terms may be discovered. Timing may also depend on the urgency with which a transitional negotiation is needed to restructure a current agreement.

Case in Point 12-5

A trucking firm leased its trucks under a long-term leasing agreement. Unfortunately for the firm, the market price for such leases had dropped dramatically since it entered into its current lease. This created an overwhelming competitive advantage for the firm's competitors which caused a loss of revenue and placed the firm in a precarious financial position. It became imperative to seek an immediate restructuring of the economic terms of the lease in order to avoid financial ruin for the trucking firm.

Both the other party's timing needs and its reaction to the intended timing must be anticipated. The timing can be modified if the other party's problems or reactions outweigh any benefits to you to stick to the intended timing.

The timing of some negotiations is more structured than that of others. Serious labor negotiations are scheduled, but some litigation negotiations may evolve out of a chance meeting. You should not negotiate terms merely because of a chance encounter if you are unprepared to do so or if the timing is not advantageous. However, even when one is not ready to proceed, the occasion can be used to gather information. This requires active listening, with little or no disclosure of information.

Timing raises the issue of single versus sequential negotiations. If the negotiation consists of multiple sessions, then the timing of each session must be considered. This also applies to structuring successive negotiations that are self-contained but periodic. For example, labor or contractual negotiations can occur yearly or on some other regular basis.

Planning Step 14: Choosing the Modes of Communication

Key Concept 129

Choose the mode of communication after settling timing issues and analyzing the other parties' reaction to them.

After deciding that the time is right to negotiate, the final step is to determine which mode of communication should be utilized. Choices include face-to-face meetings; telephone communications; letters; other written communications; and combinations of modes. (The advantages and disadvantages of these choices are analyzed in Chapter 10.)

The various analyses must include anticipating the other party's reaction to the mode of communication. The negotiator must consider whether a particular mode will be perceived as awkward, inappropriate, offensive, or a pretext for delay. If an adverse response is a significant possibility, the benefits and detriments of using another mode must be considered. The means of communication may have an impact on the timing of the negotiation. Potential delays based on the communication mode must be taken into account. Effects on timing must be weighed against the potential benefits or liabilities from staying with the planned method. If timing will be affected, then the anticipated reaction of the other side regarding altered timing must be considered and any necessary adjustments to the planning steps should be made.

Implementing the 14 Planning Steps

Now that you have learned the 14 planning steps that make up the negotiation process, you must consider how to effectively execute them. This section provides tips on how to manipulate these steps to your advantage. The following section provides a negotiating example in which the steps are applied.

Key Concept 130

Commit yourself mentally to implementing the negotiation plan, and do not be deterred by distractions or fatigue. Continuously analyze the other party's conduct; be mentally ready for the unexpected.

The implementation of the negotiating plan requires a commitment to doing, not merely trying. By *doing*, a negotiator gains confidence. Unless something significant and unforeseen occurs to justify alterations, the opening moves should be performed as planned, even if the plan is thereafter followed imperfectly. One must continually balance the need for flexibility with the need to maintain structure and the impression of knowledgeable confidence it often conveys.

The necessary mental commitment requires energy, focus, and a refusal to allow moments of fatigue or distractions to undermine performance. Mental toughness, the ability to concentrate, and a willingness to accept the challenge are crucial, even in a cooperative or problem-solving negotiation. If necessary, adjournments can be used to deal with fatigue. Be sufficiently rested before beginning a negotiation session. Take special care to rest after long-distance travel, when jet lag might be a problem.

Making the Opening Moves

Opening moves are important, therefore restraint should be exercised at the beginning of the negotiation. The initial stages are used partially to determine the other side's predispositions regarding strategy, tactics, positions, or motives. Identifying predispositions necessarily precedes coming up with the best means to influence them and appraising the ways in which they might affect the other side's reactions.

Constantly Analyze the Negotiation

A negotiator must constantly evaluate the negotiation in order to mark its progress or assess its failures. In complex negotiations note taking can help keep track of positions and points of agreement. These also can be utilized to uncover patterns of behavior and goals as well as detect false cues. Analyses during the negotiation must not ignore the possibility that the other party or its negotiator may be shortsighted, economically irrational, or unpredictable. Information gathering and trial proposals may be used to discern the reasons for such conduct. Similarly, they may be employed to make sense of seemingly unexplainable activities. Negotiators must be mentally ready for the unexpected, since no one can always anticipate or analyze perfectly.

In addition to taking notes, negotiators should use economic or utility models to assess the value of that which is being negotiated. Care should be taken, however, to balance what they indicate against so-called "human imponderables." Feelings and emotions can be potent motivating forces that overwhelm rational evaluations. Unpredictability or irrationality can be advantageous in forcing the other party to adopt a worst-case scenario analysis, thereby increasing its uncertainty and stress. On the other hand, unpredictability or irrationality may make negotiation impracticable. A lack of consistent values during the negotiation and other types of irrational behavior can make it impossible to negotiate effectively. Feelings of frustration or disgust can lead to termination.

Adjusting the Negotiating Plan

Key Concept 131

Use a prepared but flexible plan with preconceived alternatives. Make adjustments to the plan only after you are absolutely sure that they are necessary. Adjustments may be required to restart stalled negotiations or to redirect negotiations you believe have taken the wrong track. Be goals-rigid and means-flexible.

Before making adjustments to the plan, test its usefulness by checking the accuracy of your theories about the other party and its negotiator and by repeating certain of the steps. The planning process may need to be repeated to adjust for problems in timing or to account for new information. Repeat planning steps before changing the plan itself, but make changes once it's clear that the current plan is not going to work.

One may need to alter the negotiating plan if the other party or its negotiator have difficulties with attitude changes, making decisions, short-term learning, cognition, or perception. In this situation, be prepared to take the following steps:

1. Increase the clarity or the simplicity of the messages that are communicated.

2. Alter or modify strategies or tactics.

3. Change the expressed reasons for positions.

4. Change positions.

5. Adjust timing to make proposals earlier or to lengthen deadlines.

Adjustments may involve a split-second mental process or require a more time-consuming effort, perhaps during an adjournment or between sessions. Either way, it should be a conscious process based on the planning framework of 14 steps. This will help to avoid blind reactions which are not well thought through.

Although some degree of action based on intuition is appropriate and inevitable, careful analysis is necessary in order to test intuitive judgments. Thoughts should not be rationalized to artificially place them within definitional categories.

The constant analysis and need for adjustments always return to the most basic and yet profound question: "What's really going on here?" One should continually ask oneself:

1. Is the process moving?

2. If so, in what direction?

3. Is that direction the most advantageous, or even advantageous at all?

By focusing on these questions, the negotiator can decide to either maintain or change the current course of action.

Discovering Symmetrical or Asymmetrical Responses. In deciding whether to remain firm or to be flexible, one factor to consider is whether the other side tends to respond to you symmetrically or asymmetrically. If its behavior is **symmetrical,** then firmness is likely to be met with firmness and flexibility with flexibility. If the other side responds with **asymmetrical** behavior, then your firmness will likely be met with flexibility or, conversely, your flexibility will cause the other side to stand firm.

Working Through a Negotiation

The 14 planning steps apply to all types of negotiation. In this section, an example is given in which they are all applied. Follow along (as a member of the negotiation); remember, constantly analyze the situation and be alert to the changing circumstances of the negotiation. Would you make decisions different from the ones presented?

Negotiating Scenario_____

You are to negotiate an employment agreement for a doctor who has one year's experience beyond her residency. The potential employer is a group of doctors in the same specialty, who are in a partnership.

Planning Step 1. You gather information from the client and from other doctors regarding the market for a doctor in this specialty. You must consider what can be expected for a client with her level of experience. What is an appropriate salary? What are the customary fringe benefits? Is there potential for a future partnership? The client already has been given a proposed contract by the partnership that indicates the partnership's positions on various issues.

Planning Steps 2 and 3. You learn from the client that her goals are to:

1. Obtain a salary and fringe benefits that are reasonable for the employment market she is in (a short-term goal).

2. Obtain reasonable provisions for pregnancy/maternity leave should she have children in the future (a long-term goal).

3. Maintain a good relationship with the other doctors, with a view toward becoming a partner after two years (a long-term goal).

The various potential fringe benefits are considered as separate issues. These include:

1. Malpractice insurance.

2. Major medical insurance with pregnancy coverage.

3. Disability insurance.

4. Paid vacation time.

5. Paid sick leave time.

6. Paid pregnancy and maternity leave time.

7. Paid time for continuing medical education.

8. Expenses for membership in professional societies and associations.

9. Provisions regarding a car phone.

10. Provisions regarding a home computer.

You review all the goals with the client to distinguish essential from desirable goals. The client considers an overall financial package of salary and fringe benefits to be an essential goal. You probe to fine-tune the differences and learn that among the fringe benefits, all of the insurance-related issues are essential. Compensation for educational and professional expenses are desirable, but not essential. The car phone and computer are low priorities.

Additional issues you consider include:

1. The length of the contract.

2. Whether any references to or specific provisions for a future partnership will be included in the contract, and, if so, the terms.

3. Provisions for terminating the contract by either party.

It is determined that the client's goal is for a two-year contract, with a provision that, if both parties wish to enter into a partnership agreement, discussions regarding such an agreement will begin at least six months prior to the expiration of the current contract.

Planning Step 4. The information you have gathered from outside doctors (the market) provides you with what you need to know about the fairness of the proposal. You determine that in the main the terms of the proposal reflect what a doctor with your client's specialty and experience could reasonably expect. You recognize, however, that certain specifics must be negotiated.

Planning Step 5. In considering the strengths and weaknesses of the other side, you note that it is known that the partnership has a vital interest in securing the services of a young, well-qualified specialist with whom they can all get along. It also is known, given their employment offer, that they believe that your client meets their criteria. Apparently, no one else is currently under consideration for the position. On the other hand, it is not vital to the partnership that *your* client be hired; you realize that there are undoubtedly other doctors who also could meet the partnership's needs. If there is no agreement, the partnership will be inconvenienced by a delay, but it can certainly cope with that if necessary. You also discover that your client has a vital interest in obtaining this type of position, and would like it to be with this particular medical group. If there is no agreement, however, the client certainly will be able to find other satisfactory employment opportunities. Thus, the strengths and weaknesses seem roughly equal, with both parties personally anxious for an agreement, but with both parties also able to withstand the possibility of not reaching an agreement.

Planning Step 6. You continue your prenegotiation plan by estimating the other side's opening position and bottom line. The other party's opening position already has been presented in its draft contract. You next estimate the partnership's bottom-line expectations by using its contract proposal as the starting point. The contract proposal is fairly reasonable, although it omits certain desired fringe benefits and any reference to pregnancy or maternity leave. It is believed that the partnership is willing to make some concessions to improve the contract for the client, since it would not be reasonable for the partnership to be using a no-concessions strategy on all the various contractual issues.

Planning Step 7. You next consider the likelihood of win-win outcomes. The partnership's proposal has no reference to a car phone or a home computer, although both of these items would benefit the client's medical practice and, therefore, the partnership. Either a trade-off on salary or a requirement by the employer that the client obtain these items will have favorable tax consequences for the client. Thus, there will be a gain to the client without a corresponding loss to the partnership. The partnership's proposal also does not have provisions for time off for purposes of continuing medical education. A provision for this will be included in the client's counterproposal, and may be viewed as a win-win outcome, since both parties will gain from the client's obtaining a certain amount of continuing medical education.

Planning Steps 8, 9, and 10. Having completed your prenegotiation activities, you next set the opening position, bottom line, strategy, and tactics. You establish a high realistic opening position for each issue, except for some of the fringe benefits for which the original offer already is satisfactory. You also consider an acceptable bottom line for each issue, and for those issues that can be traded off against each other. You and the client consider the idea of demanding increases in all of the offered fringe benefits, even those that are already quite acceptable, in order to create potential concessions that are of greater value to the partnership than to the client. You reject this possibility because in this particular negotiation there is a danger that seeking to increase every aspect of the initial offer would be perceived as unreasonable, thereby adversely affecting the chances of reaching an agreement. You settle on both HRESSC and problem-solving strategies, with informational, win-win, and bargaining tactics.

Planning Step 11. You decide to plan concessions and trade-offs for the salary and fringe benefit issues. You note that there are many potential cross-issue trade-offs among the salary, each potential fringe benefit, the length of the contract, possible future partnership provisions, and termination provisions. In light of the multidimensional nature of this negotiation, it is recognized that this step may very well need to be replanned as the negotiation progresses and the initial plan is implemented and adjusted.

Planning Steps 12, 13, and 14. Finally, you assess the agenda, timing, and modes of communications. The planned agenda is to prepare and submit a written counterproposal on behalf of the client, followed by a discussion between the negotiators. Timing is not an issue because both sides are eager to reach an agreement and are ready to negotiate. Written communications and proposals will be used, as well as face-to-face meetings and telephone calls.

A sound plan for a multidimensional negotiation almost always has alternatives. As each step is completed, earlier steps are reexamined to consider whether any modification is needed. Issue-by-issue planning is required, as is cross-issue planning to the extent that trade-offs between issues are required or desirable.

Final Negotiating Tips

The importance of effective planning cannot be overstated. By following the system for planning presented in this book, the negotiator will be as well prepared as possible. As you know, however, the plan that is formulated is not etched in stone. Rather, it is intended to provide useful but adaptable guidelines. An important secret is to be *goals-rigid and means-flexible*. While not abandoning goals, an effective negotiator must be willing to recognize and to use unanticipated means to achieve those goals. Similarly, it may be necessary to recognize and to discard means that are not working effectively. The negotiators' goals are to obtain or to exceed their side's bottom line. Tough, but flexible implementation of the plan allows the negotiator to exploit opportunities that would otherwise be lost. This approach enhances the chances of achieving a successful result.

A final note of caution is warranted: Never underestimate the other party or its negotiator. Bold acts can be appropriate, if tempered by realism and a touch of humanity. History constantly reminds us that many a grave error can be traced to foolishly underestimating or ignoring the other side's true capabilities.

Comprehension Checkup

The answers to these questions appear on page 332.

1. Your opening position should be _____ your realistic expectations.
   a. higher than
   b. equal to
   c. slightly lower than
   d. unrelated to

2. The bottom line should _____.
   a. stay unchanged
   b. usually allow room for concessions

    c. be much better than any alternative
    d. be used without authority

3. You are negotiating a sale in which another potential buyer has offered $1,400,000. There is no need to sell at this time, and the item is believed to be worth $1,600,000. Your bottom line should be _____.
    a. $1,400,000
    b. $1,425,000
    c. $1,600,000
    d. $1,625,000

4. Alternatives must be analyzed in terms of _____.
    a. risks
    b. benefits
    c. probabilities
    d. all of the above
    e. *a* and *b*

5. The other side is known to be very high pressure. You want your negotiator to resist the pressure, maintain harmony in the initial session, and engage in information gathering. One reasonable choice to consider is _____.
    a. very high opening position
    b. very low bottom line
    c. limited authority
    d. large concessions

6. After considering strategies that allow you to initiate actions as well as to react, your next step should be to _____.
    a. anticipate the other side's strategies
    b. set the bottom line
    c. establish an opening position
    d. prepare trade-offs
    e. set the agenda

7. There are four issues to be negotiated. Concessions are to be considered _____.
    a. within issues
    b. between issues
    c. as countermeasures
    d. *a* and *b*
    e. *b* and *c*

8. The other side seeks to control the agenda because it legitimately needs to have certain issues decided before others. Your needs are not effected, but you prefer control. You should _____.
    a. resist
    b. allow it
    c. move for closure
    d. set preconditions
    e. terminate

9. A very emotional scene occurred on a Thursday morning, with each party wildly claiming the other violated a contract. Both key decision makers tend to be hot-headed. The negotiation can be held that after-

noon or evening, or on the following Monday. The timing of the negotiation should be _____.

a. irrelevant
b. that afternoon
c. that evening
d. adjourned indefinitely
e. Monday

10. You are about to negotiate with Companies A and B to form a joint venture
to manufacture a new product. Company A always pushes for a larger
share of the profits for itself, while Company B pushes for an equal allocation of profits, which is your goal as well. You do significant other business
with Company C, whose CEO is a potential ally to influence Company A.
You should plan to do negotiations with:

a. A
b. B
c. C
d. A and B
e. A, B, and C

11. Your client/boss wants you to take positions without rational reasons. Her
approach is usually to say: "This is what we want. Period." This approach
may lead to _____.

a. values
b. leverage
c. termination of negotiation
d. b and c
e. a, b, and c

12. The other side's concessions have slowed down and become smaller. This
could mean _____.

a. they are approaching their bottom line
b. false clues are being offered
c. it is time to set an agenda
d. a and b
e. a and d

13. Ariel, the other negotiator, initially says: "We will pay $2.65 per unit."
Later in the negotiation, Ariel states: "Would you consider $2.70 or
$2.75 per unit?" At that point, you should proceed as if the other side's
bottom line is _____.

a. more than $2.75
b. $2.75
c. less than $2.75

14. Your negotiation plan has a strategy and tactic that appear ideal. At this
point you should _____.

a. negotiate
b. consider the agenda
c. plan alternatives
d. choose mode of communication
e. evaluate timing

15. You and your staff spent a great deal of time planning for a significant negotiation and have been extraordinarily thorough. As planned, you carefully switch from HRESSC for the first issue to problem solving for the second issue. The other side suddenly demands that you accept an approach that you have not considered, which is virtually the opposite of the ones you and your staff planned. You should _____.
    a. reject it
    b. accept it
    c. use a snow-job
    d. adjourn
    e. set a deadline

16. It is always advisable to drive the hardest bargain you can.   T   F

17. The reactions that you anticipate by the other party to your possible countermeasures and concessions should effect the use of creative ideas.   T   F

Answer Key to Comprehension Checkups

The comprehension checkup questions can be found at the ends of the chapters.

Chapter 1

1. F
2. F
3. T
4. F
5. F

Chapter 2

1. *d*
2. *d*
3. *b*
4. *a*
5. *c*
6. *e*
7. *b*
8. *c*
9. *a*
10. *b*
11. *d*
12. *e*
13. *c*

Chapter 3

1. *b*
2. *c*
3. *a*
4. *b*
5. *d*
6. *b*
7. *c*
8. F
9. F
10. T

Chapter 4

1. *c*
2. *b*
3. *d*
4. *c*
5. *b*
6. *a*
7. *e*
8. F
9. T
10. F
11. T

Chapter 5

1. *c*
2. *a*
3. *a*
4. *d*
5. *b*
6. *a*
7. *c*
8. *d*
9. T
10. F
11. F
12. F

Chapter 6

1. *c*
2. *c*
3. *b*
4. *a*
5. *d*
6. *b*
7. *d*
8. *b*
9. *a*
10. *c*

Chapter 7

1. *a*	6. *d*
2. *c*	7. F
3. *b*	8. F
4. *d*	9. T
5. *a*	10. T

Chapter 8

1. F	5. F
2. T	6. T
3. T	7. *d*
4. F	

Chapter 9

1. F	8. *b*
2. T	9. *a*
3. T	10. *d*
4. F	11. *c*
5. F	12. *a*
6. T	13. *b*
7. F	

Chapter 10

1. *c*	7. *b*
2. *d*	8. *c*
3. *b*	9. T
4. *c*	10. T
5. *e*	11. F
6. *a*	

Chapter 11

1. *b*	7. *d*
2. *a*	8. *b*
3. *c*	9. F
4. *b*	10. T
5. *e*	11. F
6. *e*	12. T

Chapter 12

1. *b*	10. *e*
2. *b*	11. *d*
3. *c*	12. *d*
4. *d*	13. *a*
5. *c*	14. *c*
6. *a*	15. *d*
7. *d*	16. F
8. *b*	17. T
9. *e*	

Index

About the Authors

MARK K. SCHOENFIELD is a partner with Torshen, Schoenfield
& Spreyer, Ltd. in Chicago, where he specializes in civil
litigation and corporate and business law. For more than 16
years he has taught negotiation skills to business
professionals in a broad array of fields throughout the
nation. He is the author of two books and numerous articles
on the subject.

RICK M. SCHOENFIELD is a partner with Ettinger &
Schoenfield, Ltd. in Chicago. He specializes in plaintiff's
personal injury and civil rights litigation, and is an
experienced negotiator in areas ranging from contracts to
juvenile delinquency and criminal law.

Final Examination

The McGraw-Hill 36-Hour Negotiating Course

If you have completed your study of *The McGraw-Hill 36-Hour Negotiating Course*, you should be prepared to take this final examination. It is a comprehensive examination, consisting of 50 questions.

Instructions

1. If you like, you may treat this as an "open-book" exam and consult this textbook while taking it. That approach will help to reinforce your learning and to correct any misconceptions. On the other hand, if you prefer to establish a superior understanding of the subject matter, you may choose to take the examination without reference to the textbook.

2. Answer each of the test questions on the answer sheet provided at the end of the exam. For each question, write the letter of your choice on the answer blank that corresponds to the number of the question you are answering.

3. All questions are multiple-choice, with from two to five alternative answers to choose from. Always select the answer that represents in your mind the *best* among the choices.

4. Each correctly answered question is worth 2 points on a scale of 100 percent. You must answer 35 questions correctly to have a passing grade of 70 percent. A passing grade entitles you to receive a *certificate of achievement*. This handsome certificate, suitable for framing, attests to your proven knowledge of negotiating.

5. Carefully fill in your name and address in the spaces provided at the top of the answer sheet, remove the answer sheet from the book, and send it to:

Alison Spalding
Certification Examiner
36-Hour Negotiating Course
Professional Books Group
McGraw-Hill, Inc.
11 West 19th Street
New York, NY 10011

A. Company A is negotiating to buy goods from Company B.

1. A's first step to plan for the negotiation is to _____.
   a. gather prenegotiation information
   b. identify issues
   c. determine its own goals
   d. analyze the market
   e. assess the other side's weaknesses

2. Goods of equal quality are available from other sources, so that price is the real factor. Other sources' prices appear to range between $250 and $325 per unit. A's goal is _____.
   a. aggressive
   b. competitive
   c. cooperative
   d. self-centered
   e. defensive

3. After A sets its opening position, it should _____.
   a. analyze the market
   b. choose tactics
   c. establish an agenda
   d. set its bottom line
   e. bargain for information

4. A's initial strategy should be _____.
   a. no concessions
   b. deadlock-breaking concessions only
   c. HRESSC
   d. concede first
   e. problem solving

5. When A first tries to get information from B, A should use _____.
   a. the funnel approach
   b. narrow questions

    c. silence

    d. the creation of facts

    e. bargaining for information

6. Based on all of the information given in Questions 1 to 5, A should initially use the tactic of _____.

    a. power

    b. bluff

    c. split the difference

    d. face-saving

    e. alternative opportunities

7. During the negotiation, A finds itself in an unwanted power struggle and deadlock with B. A should use _____.

    a. insert new issues

    b. deadlines

    c. surprise

    d. focus on the process

    e. patience

8. If the deadlock still is not broken, A next should _____.

    a. blame B

    b. attempt creation of movement

    c. terminate

    d. concede and close

    e. supercrunch

B. M seeks to enter into a long-run contract with N to provide services to N, a very new company. M learns that N is undercapitalized, but has great growth potential. M needs this deal.

9. After completing the planning steps through determining goals, M should _____.

    a. estimate N's bottom line

    b. estimate N's opening position

    c. identify issues

    d. consider win-win outcomes

    e. assess strengths

10. Because N is undercapitalized M should consider _____.

    a. aggressive goals

    b. building in enough concessions to make the contract profitable for N

    c. allies

    d. avoiding making the first offer
    e. surprise

11. After setting its bottom line, M should _____.
    a. set its opening position
    b. decide the timing
    c. set an agenda
    d. choose strategies
    e. consider concessions

12. Based on all the information given in the introduction to the M/N negotiation, M should not _____.
    a. disclose all information
    b. selectively disclose information
    c. create facts
    d. use funnel approach
    e. bargain for information

13. M knows the market regarding price and terms; it should _____.
    a. demand reciprocity
    b. engage in debate
    c. require preconditions
    d. make the first offer
    e. avoid making the first offer

14. M must consider _____.
    a. intraorganizational negotiations within N
    b. interorganizational negotiations between M and N
    c. alternative dispute resolutions
    d. *a* and *b*
    e. all of the above

C. W wants to purchase a corporation owned by X and Y.

15. W's goal is _____.
    a. aggressive
    b. competitive
    c. self-centered
    d. cooperative
    e. defensive

16. After W completes the planning steps through identifying issues, it should _____.
    a. consider win-win
    b. analyze the market

    c. determine tactics
    d. decide strategies
    e. estimate X and Y's bottom line

17. X and Y offer to sell their stock at a higher price than the price of the corporation's assets. Both prices are acceptable, since both are below W's bottom line. W should _____.
    a. buy the stock
    b. buy the assets
    c. switch to goals other than to reach agreement
    d. engage in closure
    e. use HRESSC

18. After choosing strategies and tactics, W should _____.
    a. determine an agenda
    b. establish the timing
    c. set a bottom line
    d. consider trade-offs
    e. analyze the market

19. After some brief discussions with X and Y concerning corporate liabilities, W sends a letter of intent, which simply states: "I intend to buy your stock for $3 million and this is a letter of intent confirming that fact." W then goes to a lawyer to have a formal contract drawn. W's performance should be rated _____.
    a. good
    b. bad

20. W can enhance its persuasive force by using _____.
    a. primacy
    b. recency
    c. reasonable repetition
    d. all of the above
    e. none of the above

21. W decides to form a partnership with T and O, in order to have sufficient funds to proceed. The partnership should not provide for ways of splitting up if it does not work out since that would set too negative a tone at the outset.
    a. true
    b. false

D. F had a 5-year contract to supply all the popcorn and soft drinks required for Z's operations. Z claims that F's popcorn is of poor quality, and refuses to accept any more. F denies the claim.

22. After negotiation that completes the negotiation planning steps through analyzing the market, F should _____.
    a. consider win-win outcomes
    b. choose alternative dispute resolutions
    c. assess strengths and weaknesses
    d. estimate its bottom line
    e. estimate Z's opening position

23. After considering concessions and trade-offs, F should _____.
    a. set an opening position
    b. decide about an agenda
    c. do prenegotiation information gathering
    d. seek allies
    e. check for win-win outcomes

24. Danger signals indicating that emotions may be interfering with a negotiator's performance include all but which one of the following? _____.
    a. belief that your side is fair
    b. feeling uncertainty or discomfort
    c. significant misunderstandings
    d. being preoccupied with the negotiation
    e. a trembling hand

25. F does not understand why Z is taking the position that the popcorn is of poor quality. F should use the strategy of _____.
    a. no concessions
    b. problem solving
    c. HRESSC
    d. concede first
    e. purposes other than reaching an agreement

26. Based on information in the F/Z introduction and Question 25, F should use the _____ tactic as its first tactic.
    a. litigation
    b. trial proposal
    c. make-people-the-problem
    d. funnel approach
    e. allies

27. If F believes that there is an impasse because of miscommunication, but that Z would be willing to compromise if the communication problem can be solved, F should suggest _____.
    a. minitrial
    b. arbitration

    c. mediation
    d. litigation
    e. summary jury trial

28. If other measures fail, F should _____:
    a. arbitrate
    b. litigate
    c. mediate
    d. abandon the claim
    e. need more information to decide

29. F confronts a claim by Z's negotiator that its offer to settle is 10 percent more than she is authorized to pay. F should not _____.
    a. make a concession
    b. appeal to her self-interest
    c. negotiate for her recommendations of F's offer
    d. insert new issues
    e. use allies

E. Will wants to sell commercial property which has a building suitable for manufacturing with a warehouse.

30. After Will estimates the other party's bottom line and opening position, he next _____.
    a. determines goals
    b. sets an opening position
    c. analyzes the market
    d. chooses tactics
    e. considers win-win outcomes

31. Will must take into account the vital interests of _____.
    a. each potential buyer
    b. each negotiator
    c. *a* and *b*
    d. none of the above

32. After deciding about an agenda, Will should decide _____.
    a. timing
    b. tactics
    c. strategy
    d. mode of communication
    e. price

33. If Will's real estate broker and the brokers for potential buyers often have transactions together, Will must be aware of _____.

    a. zones of agreement
    b. work group efforts
    c. jungle fighters
    d. linear zero-sum game
    e. horse trading

34. Will is confronted by a jungle fighter. A countermeasure is _____.
    a. refuse to react emotionally
    b. placate
    c. display fear and concede first
    d. bluff
    e. bargain for information

35. A negotiator representing a potential purchaser of the property should engage in prenegotiation information gathering concerning _____.
    a. structural and mechanical conditions
    b. environmental conditions
    c. market values
    d. *a* and *c*
    e. all of the above

F. A seller is selling a house to a buyer, but the deal has not yet closed.

36. The seller learns that the well which supplies all of the water is polluted. The seller should _____ that fact to the buyer.
    a. not disclose
    b. disclose
    c. disclose if asked
    d. refuse to proceed with the sale
    e. close the sale quickly

37. In setting goals and an opening position, the seller should initially _____.
    a. be goals-rigid and means-flexible
    b. set his opening position as on his luckiest day
    c. use a no-concessions strategy
    d. *a* and *b*
    e. *a* and *c*

38. In the sale of the house, the seller will at least use _____.
    a. informational tactics
    b. HRESSC
    c. whipsaw

    d. problem solving
    e. split the difference

G. Fred is negotiating for an increase in his salary.

39. He should _____ an agenda.
    a. plan
    b. not plan

40. Unless there are contraindicating facts, Fred should initially use the strategy of _____.
    a. no further concessions
    b. concede first
    c. HRESSC
    d. closure
    e. propose other than reaching agreement

41. If he plans an agenda, Fred should _____.
    a. insist that both sides use it
    b. disregard it
    c. allow management to set an alternate agenda
    d. use gifts to achieve his raise
    e. cannot determine from information given

42. Fred finds his boss engaged in the tactic of debate. Which of the following is not a countermeasure? _____.
    a. different interpretations and facts
    b. uncover false assumptions
    c. split the difference
    d. replace a point with a stronger point
    e. face-saving

43. Fred has not yet received a response to his opening offer. He should _____.
    a. make a small concession
    b. demand feedback
    c. adjourn
    d. bluff
    e. change the tone

H. Management is locked in a significant dispute with the employees over working conditions. A strike appears to be increasingly likely.

44. A lockout of employees may improve management's control of the timing of any work stoppage. This must be balanced against _____.

    a. aggression
    b. unifying employees
    c. deadlock
    d. power struggles
    e. irrationality

45. The union negotiator states: "I can get my people to settle every-thing for a wage increase of from 5 to 9 percent." Management should consider that the union would accept a wage increase of
_____.

    a. less than 5 percent
    b. 5 percent
    c. 7 percent
    d. 8 percent
    e. 9 percent

46. The best way for management to phrase its response to the union negotiator's statement about an acceptable wage increase is _____.
    a. "Why should we believe you?"
    b. "Because of the company's difficult profitability picture, we can try to meet your needs for increased wages by a 2 percent in-crease."
    c. "How about 2 percent?"
    d. "Do you think 3 or 4 percent would do it?"
    e. "Five percent, but no more, and there will be a lockout in 36 hours unless it's accepted."

47. The union and management should attempt to make concessions which are _____ than those of the other party.
    a. no larger and more predictable
    b. no larger and less predictable
    c. smaller and more predictable
    d. smaller and less predictable
    e. equal to and less predictable

48. Management is more concerned with the cost and precedent of im-proved working conditions than it is with a wage increase of up to 9 percent. Which of the following actions should management take?
_____

    a. announce its true concern (information disclosure)
    b. accept a 9 percent wage increase (surprise tactic)
    c. demonstrate a preference for improving working conditions in-stead of wages (focus/downplay)
    d. split the difference
    e. request an arbitrator or mediator

49. If the other party has a cooperative tone, you must be prepared to
_____.
    a. shift to problem solving
    b. make concessions
    c. be aware of concession patterns
    d. relax
    e. insert a cooperative goal

50. If both sides have taken public positions, it will be _____.
    a. easier to manipulate public opinion
    b. more difficult for either to make concessions
    c. easier for either to make concessions
    d. information bargaining
    e. mutual bluffs

Final Examination
Answer Sheet:
The McGraw-Hill 36-Hour
Negotiating Course

See instructions on page 1 of the Final Examination.

1. _____	11. _____	21. _____	31. _____	41. _____
2. _____	12. _____	22. _____	32. _____	42. _____
3. _____	13. _____	23. _____	33. _____	43. _____
4. _____	14. _____	24. _____	34. _____	44. _____
5. _____	15. _____	25. _____	35. _____	45. _____
6. _____	16. _____	26. _____	36. _____	46. _____
7. _____	17. _____	27. _____	37. _____	47. _____
8. _____	18. _____	28. _____	38. _____	48. _____
9. _____	19. _____	29. _____	39. _____	49. _____
10. _____	20. _____	30. _____	40. _____	50. _____